Capital City

How it all happened
Branch banking
Money market banking
The money and foreign exchange markets
The Stock Exchange
The insurance world
The commodity markets and the Baltic Exchange
The Bank of England
Where the City goes now

by the same authors
in Methuen Paperbacks

THE SECOND GREAT CRASH

Capital City

LONDON AS A FINANCIAL CENTRE

HAMISH McRAE
&
FRANCES CAIRNCROSS

MAGNUM BOOKS
Methuen Paperbacks Ltd

A Magnum Book

CAPITAL CITY
ISBN 0 417 01620 4

First published 1973 by Eyre Methuen Ltd
First paperback (revised) edition 1974 by Eyre Methuen
Magnum edition published 1977

Magnum Books are published by Methuen Paperbacks Ltd
11 New Fetter Lane, London EC4P 4EE

Made and printed in Great Britain
by Richard Clay (The Chaucer Press) Ltd, Bungay, Suffolk

To our parents

Contents

Acknowledgements

The authors and publishers would like to thank the following for permission to reproduce extracts from the books listed below: Dent & Sons Ltd and Little, Brown and Company for *Collected Verse from 1929 On* by Ogden Nash; The Institute of Bankers for *A Day in the Life of a Banker*.

Introduction

When the West German Television Corporation wanted to show what it felt were the most successful and the least successful aspects of British industry. To show the least successful it filmed the archaic techniques of Clyde shipbuilders. To show the most successful it chose the financial services of the City of London.

This is how foreigners see the City – quite simply, as the financial capital of the world. But in Britain the City's reputation is rather different. A lot of people view its activities with suspicion and distaste. They see it not as a peculiarly efficient sector of British industry but primarily as the centre of share dealing, where the fate of companies and their employees is decided by a handful of sharp young market operators. Indeed, to read much of the City press, one might be forgiven for thinking that this was the most important thing that goes on in the Square Mile. This book tries to show that there is a lot more to the City than share dealing.

Surprisingly, there is little post-war literature on the City's financial institutions. Probably the best accounts of how the City works today are to be found not in books but in a growing number of official studies: the Radcliffe report on the Working of the Monetary System of 1959, the Prices and Incomes Board report on bank charges of 1967 and the Select Committee on Nationalized Industries' report on the Bank of England, compiled in 1969–70. The books that do exist tend to deal either with special aspects of the City or individual institutions, or to be largely descriptive. As well as looking at the structure of the City, this book tries both to analyse how the main financial institutions work and to assess how well they do their job.

A word about the balance of the different chapters and the ground they cover. We have not discussed a number of activities which others might consider a part of the City. We have not, for example, talked about property development; we have devoted relatively little space to unit and investment trusts, building societies or trustee savings banks, and hardly any to the 'asset strippers' whose names so regularly fill the headlines of the City pages. Where an institution is relatively well known, as the clearing banks or the Stock Exchange are, we have spent less time describing how it works and more discussing whether it works well. With the more esoteric money markets and commodity markets we have devoted more space to description and less to analysis. We have largely ignored the question of the impact the Common Market will have on the City, partly because the book is essentially a study of the City as it works in 1973/4. But we also suspect that for most City institutions, the direct effect of Common Market membership will remain small.

The two tables which follow, on the invisible earnings of and employment in the various City institutions, are intended to give two measures of size. In terms of invisible earnings, the favourite City measure, insurance is far and away the largest. However, banking, and particularly the Bank of England and the City offices of the clearing banks, employs the largest number of people. The Stock Exchange comes next, while employment in the money, foreign exchange and commodity markets is extremely small.

When, 100 years ago almost to the month, Walter Bagehot first published *Lombard Street*, he explained that he had chosen the title to show that although he was writing about the City's money

Employment in the City 1964–6

Banking:	
Bank of England and clearing banks	30 130
British overseas and commonwealth banks	5 814
American and other foreign banks	3 751
Accepting houses	3 381
Other banks	6 502
Discount houses	427
Total banking	50 005
Insurance:	
Insurance companies	28 228
Insurance brokers	20 382
Underwriters and underwriters' agents (mainly Lloyd's)	1 212
Total insurance	49 822
Stockbrokers and jobbers	15 071
Commodity markets and merchanting	14 031

Source: An Economic Study of the City of London by the Economists Advisory Group (directors, John H. Dunning and E. Victor Morgan) (London, George Allen and Unwin, 1971).

Invisible earnings, 1972

	£ million
Insurance	300
Banking*	77
Merchanting	32
Brokerage etc.	59
Total	468

* Excluding interest received by UK banks and other financial institutions and the profits of their overseas branches, subsidiaries and associates.

Source: UK Balance of Payments 1973.

market, he meant to deal 'with concrete realities'. As he put it then:

> A notion prevails that the Money Market is something so impalpable that it can only be spoken of in very abstract words, and that therefore books on it must always be exceedingly difficult. But I maintain that the Money Market is as concrete and real as anything else; that it can be described in as plain words; that it is the writer's fault if what he says is not clear.

We believe that the same apprehensions about the City of London and its financial institutions persist today, but it is still true that the City is a very concrete and real place.

The City, indeed, is a village. Almost all the firms and the markets described in this book are clustered within a few hundred yards of each other, some down small lanes and alleyways, others in tower blocks along the bigger streets radiating out from the Bank of England. Most of the top people in the City – or at least within the central community of the money markets, banks and stock market – know and usually like each other. They probably meet from time to time over lunch. There is no such thing as a free lunch in the City. It is the occasion when cautious hints are dropped, delicate information traded, lucrative acquaintances sealed.

Like every village, the City is exclusive. It resents outside interference – particularly if it comes from Whitehall – and it takes a long time to accept newcomers, though the new entrant may not be aware of this. Indeed, a few of the City's most successful figures would still be set down as outsiders by many City men.

Finally the City has a certain sense of corporate responsibility: ideally it would rather hound its own rascals than let itself be policed too openly by the Bank of England or (the ultimate indignity) handed over to the Department of Trade and Industry.

With the obvious exception of the first chapter, most of the information in this book has been gathered from interviews and discussions with people in the various City institutions, some in the course of our ordinary work as financial journalists on *The Banker*, *Euromoney* and *The Observer*, some specifically for the book.

One of the least-known qualities of the men who work in the City is their generosity. A great many people have been prepared to give us hours of their time, patiently explaining mechanisms whose workings, to them, were self-evident. We were astonished by the willingness of strangers to help us, and by the hours that our friends were prepared to spend to try to make sure, even when they disagreed with our arguments, that our facts were correct. The mistakes that remain and the views expressed are, of course, our own.

We should like to name everyone who has helped with this book. But since that would include virtually everybody we know in the City it is sadly impossible. We would just like them all to know how grateful we are. A number of people have read specific chapters in the book, some on behalf of official City bodies, and contributed substantially to the final version. They include Patrick Coldstream, James D'Albiac, John Edwards, Colin Fitch, Richard Fry, Sidney Golt, Richard Mansell Jones, Professor Peter Mathias, David McWilliam, Alan Parker, Professor L. S. Pressnell, Professor Graham Rees, Robin Reeves, Timothy Renton, Victor Sandelson, Professor Brian Tew, Sally White and Professor Jack Wiseman; and the staffs of the Bank of England, the Baltic Exchange, the Banking Information Service, the British Insurance Association, the Corporation of Lloyd's, the Stock Exchange Information Office and Williams and Glyn's Bank.

A few others, who helped us as much as any of these, would, we know, prefer not to be named. At our publishers, we are grateful to Barbara Littlewood, who got the project off the ground, to John Naylor, who waited more than a year for it to arrive, and to Helen Fraser, who saw it through the press.

To the three people who read the whole draft of the book, we are especially grateful: Sir Alec Cairncross, Mary Campbell, assistant editor of *The Banker*, and Paddy Barwise, of the London Business School.

The book has been patiently typed and retyped by Mrs Deana Williams, and the index has been prepared by Mrs Margaret Walls.

Writing a book takes longer than one could have believed possible. To our relatives and friends whom we have shunned during the interminable gestation period we would like to say that we are sorry, and that we intend to make up for lost time right away.

HMD McR
FAC

London, 1973

1

How it all happened

On almost any measure you care to take, the City of London is the world's leading international financial centre. More international insurance passes through London than anywhere else. There are more foreign banks in London than in any other city. More foreign securities are quoted on the London Stock Exchange than any other. If anything, in the 1960s London's dominance increased. The City established itself as the centre first of the new eurodollar market; and then of banking's greatest growth area, international medium-term lending.

To try to explain why the City's institutions work as well as they do – and to point out where they are failing – is the main purpose of this book. For part of the explanation one must naturally look at the way the various City institutions and markets operate today. But another part of the answer lies in the City's past: in how, over some three centuries, it evolved first as a centre for international trade and then for international finance.

The common explanation for the City's current international success is that it is an inheritance of the nineteenth century, of the years when sterling was the centre of the world money system, and when Britain was the world's major colonial power and first industrial nation. The City itself tends to believe this. Before the 1967 devaluation of sterling it was widely argued that the prosperity of the City depended on world confidence in the pound. The truth is the reverse: it was the very controls used to prop up sterling that encouraged London banks to nurture the eurodollar market and thus lay the base for the City's post-war revival.

In fact the direction which the City's development was to take was discernible long before sterling was a world currency or Britain built up her Victorian empire. As for the industrial revolution, the City was involved only at one remove; indeed, it took place almost independently of the City. The prime influences on the early City were none of these. They were rather the peculiar economic and geographical position of London itself, and the enormous volume of government borrowing in the eighteenth century to pay for Britain's foreign wars. In the twentieth century the City has seen a return to the conditions of the eighteenth, in the sense that it has once again had to live on its financial skills.

IMPACT OF LONDON'S COMMERCE

The most remarkable thing about London in 1700 was its size. It was already the largest city in the world, with a population of some 600,000 and growing fast. This alone had far-reaching economic effects. Londoners had to buy their food from the rest of the country, thus putting cash into the hands of the farming population and allowing them to build up savings. It also meant that London developed as a market centre. Today Smithfield is still the largest wholesale meat market in the world. But how was it that well over half a million people found their living in London? London was not and never has been important primarily as an industrial centre. The answer lies in the international orientation of the City, and its trade: for an estimated quarter of the capital's working population depended for their livelihood directly on port work.

The port of London dominated the country's foreign trade. At the beginning of the eighteenth century some 80 per cent of England's imports and 70 per cent of her exports passed through London. London's traders needed ancillary financial services – and at the same time generated the capital which financed them.

They required commodity auctions to market their goods, ship auctions to buy and sell vessels. From the quayside and coffee-house auctions of the eighteenth century were to evolve the commodity futures markets and the Baltic Exchange of today. They needed to insure their ships and cargoes. English merchants had been able to insure their ships since Tudor days but there was no formal mechanism for introducing clients to underwriters. By the early eighteenth century a specialized profession of insurance brokers was emerging which collected the signatures of rich merchants prepared to underwrite marine insurance policies. By the middle of the century the brokers were meeting in Edward Lloyd's coffee house; by the end Lloyd's had its own premises and was operating very much as it does now.

Above all, these traders needed to finance their activities – and here is the origin of London's money market. The instrument used to finance both domestic and international trade, the bill of exchange, had been employed by Italian bankers centuries before.* The important development in the City in the eighteenth century was the system of discounting these bills – or exchanging them for cash at a discount – which greatly increased their attraction as a means of providing credit. To start with it was domestic bill finance that grew most quickly. But it in turn provided the mechanism which in the years following the Napoleonic Wars was to make the City the main centre for financing world trade: the international bill on London.

Bill finance developed largely as a result of Britain's peculiar eighteenth-century banking legislation. In 1708 the Bank of England had been granted a monopoly in joint-stock banking, which meant that other banks could only be partnerships. The number of partners in any bank was limited to six. This restriction made branch banking on any scale out of the question and in

* It is still in common use today, as explained in chapter 3, p. 57.

practice split English banks into two groups – a host of 'country banks' in the provinces, and a smaller number of 'private banks' mainly in London. Traces of both survive today: Barclays was formed out of a group of country banks, while Coutts and C. Hoare are directly descended from the London private banks.

The small size of the country banks precluded their granting large-scale loans, for they did not have the deposit base to carry them. But they could make funds available to traders and industrialists by discounting their bills of exchange, for these bills could, if necessary, be rediscounted – or exchanged for cash again – in London. Through the same mechanism country banks in surplus areas could employ their spare funds. Thus rich farmers and wealthy Londoners lent their cash to provide the emerging industrial areas with working capital. After 1800 there grew up a specialist group of 'bill brokers', who put the holders of bills of exchange in touch with people with sufficient cash to discount them. To start with they merely received a commission for this service. But by the mid-1820s some had developed into discount houses, carrying bill portfolios themselves and borrowing short-term funds from the London banks. In the late 1820s the Bank of England was resigning itself to the role of lender of last resort to these discount houses, and the money market structure that exists today was, in its essentials, complete.

By discounting bills of exchange the banks provided industry with working capital. They did not supply long-term funds on any substantial scale. Yet these funds were available. To see who borrowed them one has to look at the second feature that shaped the City in the eighteenth century – the continual calls from the government for money with which to fight Britain's foreign wars.

EFFECTS OF GOVERNMENT DEBT

The sheer weight of the government's borrowing needs ensured that its debt dominated the capital market. By 1721, public debt already stood at over £50 million. From then until 1739 it declined slightly as the country enjoyed the last long period of peace of the century. Between that year and 1815 the country was at war for two out of every three years. By 1816 the debt had risen to £709 million. As Professor Morgan, the most recent historian of the Stock Exchange, points out, 'The debt, in relation to the national income and to the total value of property, must have been as great as that left by either the First or the Second World War.'*

It was the government's need for funds that had led in 1694 to the foundation of the Bank of England, a chartered company, set up by a group of wealthy London merchants and financiers to lend money to the government. It was the country's first joint-stock bank, and thanks to the Act of 1708, the only one for over a century.

The Bank of England went on to become the government's banker. Before the government found its feet in the stock market, the Bank's major business was lending to the government. Later it handled the issue of government stock and subscriptions for Treasury bills. Loans to the government were paid in the form of Bank of England notes which were convertible into cash on demand (except for a period during the Napoleonic Wars) and soon comprised the bulk of London's note circulation.

However, the Bank's main preoccupation throughout the eighteenth century was making profits for its own shareholders. Besides its government business, the Bank of England acted as private banker to some of the larger London trading companies and merchants. True, in the second half of the eighteenth century, the Governors of the Bank first began to appreciate how much influence the Bank's policy could have on the economy. For a while, it began to act in effect as lender of last resort, running down its holdings of cash at times when money was tight. However, when the Bank's notes were temporarily not convertible during the Napoleonic Wars, the Bank found it could relinquish the responsibility for monetary policy which it had reluctantly assumed. It did not take it up again until the 1820s.

As the Stock Exchange developed in the eighteenth century, it

* E. Victor Morgan and W. A. Thomas, *The Stock Exchange* (London, Elek Books, 1962), p. 43.

was dominated by government debt. Even at the end of the Napoleonic Wars, it still dealt in very little else.

Government issues in the eighteenth century were floated by contractors, syndicates of merchants who drew up lists of would-be subscribers. The contractors would then bid competitively for the loan, for which the successful contractor would be liable even if some of the subscribers on his list defaulted. From this primitive form of underwriting developed the technique used in the earlier part of the nineteenth century for foreign loans. Some contractors for government loans such as Sir Francis Baring were merchants who turned later to raising funds for foreign governments.

By 1800 stock-broking had emerged as a specialized profession, the distinction between broker and jobber was recognized, and most present-day dealing techniques were already in use. The Exchange had been formally constituted and had acquired managers and trustees, the Official List and regular settling days. In 1802 it moved to permanent premises on its present site by Chapel Court.

NINETEENTH-CENTURY INTERNATIONAL DOMINANCE

At the end of the eighteenth century it was still Amsterdam and not London which was the world's main financial centre. But London had already developed a number of sophisticated financial institutions – Lloyd's, the Stock Exchange and a money market through which savings and the demand for funds across the country were matched up. Substantial sums could be channelled into government debt. And thanks to the rapid growth of foreign trade passing through the port, London's international orientation had been firmly established.

In the nineteenth century the City was to become more than a purveyor of financial services. It acquired an international money market which attracted short-term funds from all over the world and invested them in finance for trade; and it developed a long-term capital market on which a large part of the funds for the industrialization of the rest of the world were raised. By the eve of the First World War the City had become the focus of the world's international financial system. Sterling, the currency in which both short- and long-term lending was denominated, was deemed as good as gold. And the Bank of England found itself the guardian of a truly international money system, the gold standard.

This was as much a result of the peculiar pattern of British trade and overseas investment as of the City's financial expertise. As Britain emerged as a major international trading power, the City's money market learnt to finance first Britain's own overseas trade, and then a growing volume of trade between third countries, which frequently never touched British shores. Britain's initial industrial leadership meant that the City's capital market found a demand for long-term funds in countries wanting to finance imports of British industrial products and to build up their own export sectors.

The international money market which emerged in the City during the nineteenth century revolved round three institutions: the merchant banks, the discount houses and the Bank of England. The merchant banks' role in providing trade finance grew out of their own early trading activities. The instrument they developed, the 'bill on London', was merely an adaptation of the inland bill of exchange used by the country banks in the previous century. To make the bill of an overseas merchant, whose credit standing would not be known in the City, discountable on the London money market, a London merchant bank would put its signature on it, thus 'accepting' (i.e. guaranteeing) it. Once accepted by a merchant bank, a bill of exchange would qualify for the 'finest' rate of discount (or lowest interest charge) at a London discount house.

In 1832, Nathan Rothschild could already claim* that drafts on London were widely used to finance trade that never touched the UK and add, 'this country in general is the Bank for the whole world ... all transactions in India, in China, in Germany, in Russia, and in the whole world, are all guided here and settled

* Before the 1832 Committee of Secrecy on the Bank of England Charter (Minutes, Question 4799), quoted by Wilfred King, *History of the London Discount Market* (London, Routledge and Sons, 1936), p. 264.

through this country'. The discount houses, descendants of the earlier firms of bill brokers, continued well into the nineteenth century to discount inland bills passed to them by the country banks. But by the middle of the century the volume of inland bills was declining and the discount houses were becoming more dependent on overseas bills. To start with, the discount houses' funds were provided by British lenders. But since London had the only money market where massive sums of money could be profitably invested for very short periods, by the middle of the century it was attracting funds from all over the world.

The Bank of England's prime role in this international money market was as lender of last resort. From the late 1820s onwards it stood behind the discount houses prepared *in extremis* to rediscount the houses' better-quality bills. Because the Bank was prepared to do this the houses were able to finance their massive bill portfolios with money that could be withdrawn virtually at a moment's notice.

The Bank of England was initially prepared to rediscount the houses' best-quality bills (the ones on which default was least likely) because it was profitable. Slowly and painfully the Bank learnt that it could, through its function as lender of last resort, control the stability of the money market. It did so only after the City and the entire banking system had been shaken by a number of serious crises. The one which has seared itself most deeply in the City's memory occurred in 1866 when Overend, Gurney and Co., the largest discount house, failed with liabilities of £18 million. When the firm first got into difficulties, it appealed for help to the Bank of England. It was rejected, partly because of an old quarrel with the Bank, and partly because the Bank did not consider the bills in its portfolio to be of sufficiently high quality. When the house crashed, the Bank had to pay out £4 million in one day to try to prevent the panic from bringing down other City houses in its wake.

In the international long-term capital market, the two key institutions were the merchant banks and the Stock Exchange. The merchant banks had been set up mainly by foreign immigrants during and after the Napoleonic Wars. In the long-term capital market they issued the great majority of foreign loans. The earliest merchant bankers had already gained experience of floating large loans by raising funds for the British government, especially during the Napoleonic Wars when the size of the National Debt had bounded up. With the end of the wars, houses like Barings and Rothschilds were also raising funds for foreign governments. The English houses which should have been best placed to become successful merchant bankers failed almost to a man. The house of Boyd, Benfield and Co., which was with Barings one of the biggest underwriters of government loans in the Napoleonic Wars, disappeared apparently without trace, while a high proportion of the immigrant bankers survived. Of the seventeen accepting houses, the City's top merchant banks, all but two (Arbuthnot Latham and Antony Gibbs) are directly descended from banks formed by immigrants.

The traditional explanation for the success of these foreigners in merchant banking and the British lack of interest is that the foreigners had a ready made network of overseas contacts. Certainly this was true in the case of Hambros or Rothschilds, or indeed the later arrival Morgan Grenfell, all of whom had brother banks in other capitals. But what of Brown Shipley, founded by the son of an expatriate Belfast merchant and a Delaware Quaker, or Marcus Samuel, set up by the son of a Dutch Jew, or S. G. Warburg, started by a Jewish refugee from Hitler's Germany? Or indeed why did the British merchants fail to take advantage of their perfectly adequate foreign contacts? It cannot be the complete answer. Perhaps simply being an outsider in the City makes a man run faster. If so, the next generation of City financiers could include an East African Asian.

The volume of overseas loans organized by these merchant banks was enormous. During the 100 years between the end of the Napoleonic Wars and the beginning of the First World War there was a growing stream of foreign issues, some on the London Stock Exchange, some issued directly by the merchant banks to other British banks and investors. In the early 1820s, a number of South American loans were floated, many of them disastrous, and in the late 1830s a succession of US state bonds, several of

which also defaulted. Yet despite these early setbacks the trickle
of foreign issues swelled to a flood. Between 1880 and 1914 well
over £2,000 million was invested abroad; in the 1913 peak
more than half of all British savings flowed overseas.

Borrowers continued periodically to default – with repercus-
sions in Britain. After the Honduras loan of 1879, floated to build
a railway to carry ships from the Atlantic to the Pacific Ocean, a
parliamentary committee was set up to look at foreign loans. In
an important declaration it rejected the idea that the Stock
Exchange Committee should be responsible for the quality of
securities dealt on the market.

Just as the Overend, Gurney crisis helped to push the Bank of
England towards taking ultimate responsibility for good order
in the money market, so it was the need to ensure stability in the
capital market that nudged the Bank towards accepting responsibility for good order in the City as a whole.

When the London market was threatened with the most
serious collapse of the century, a collapse which in the words of
the then Chancellor of the Exchequer would have made the
failure of Overend, Gurney and Co. appear 'but a trifle', it was
the Bank of England which had to organize the rescue. The
Baring crisis of 1890 followed a boom in lending to Argentina.
Barings, which had made the mistake of heavily committing its
own money in South American stocks, was squeezed by rapidly
tightening credit at home. With large blocks of temporarily
unsaleable loans on its hands, it was unable to meet its immediate
liabilities. A crash was avoided, but only by an unprecedented
display of co-operation among the City's banks, which the
Bank of England bullied into setting up a guarantee fund for
Barings of over £17,500,000.

DID THE CITY NEGLECT BRITISH INDUSTRY?

What possessed the British investor to lend his savings to governments and industries 4,000 or more miles away, rather than invest
it at home? The most convincing explanation is that the demand
was overseas. The third quarter of the nineteenth century, when

the main upsurge in foreign investment began, saw a vacuum in the stock market. UK government securities, which in 1860 still amounted to more than all the other securities quoted on the Exchange put together, shrank to only 5 per cent of the value of all quoted securities by the outbreak of the First World War. Moreover, the yield on government stocks never seems to have been very attractive compared with even the most impeccably secure foreign loans. But the real puzzle is why British industry did not compete more effectively for savings on the Exchange. The first barrier between industry and the Stock Exchange was erected in 1720, with the fiasco of the South Sea Bubble, when the so-called Bubble Act was passed, outlawing joint-stock companies set up without parliamentary permission. This was rarely granted: until the Act was repealed in 1825, the only way for companies to obtain the safeguard of limited liability and the power to raise capital by public issue was by the lengthy and expensive process of Act of Parliament.

The Act probably helped to create a gulf between the young Stock Exchange and industry. By the time industry did need to raise money through public flotation the Stock Exchange was better geared to channel money abroad or into government debt. One industry that probably suffered was insurance: fire, and even more life business both needed the framework of a company. But even without the Act, the early stages of the industrial revolution would have been financed mainly from family savings rather than on the Stock Exchange. Thanks in part to flourishing home and overseas trade, wealth was quite widely distributed and the scale of industry did not call for massive investment. The experience of the railways, which raised enormous funds in the 1840s, showed that when capital was needed at home, the City could mobilize it. It mobilized it with little help from those monarchs of the foreign loans market, the merchant banks. As Disraeli said of the railway boom:

What is remarkable in this vast movement is, that the great leaders of the financial world took no part in it. The mighty loanmongers, on whose fiat the fate of kings and empires sometimes depended, seemed like men who, witnessing some eccentricity of nature, watch it with mixed feelings of curiosity and alarm.*

It was well into the nineteenth century before company law reached a stage which made floating a new joint-stock company both easy and advantageous. The public showed a clear preference for shares in enterprises with limited liability; yet it was not until two Acts had been passed in 1855 and 1862 that it became possible for companies to obtain limited liability simply by registering, rather than by going through Parliament.

Towards the end of the century an increasing number of firms, mostly in heavy industry or brewing, did come to the London Stock Exchange. They still faced powerful deterrents. Floating a company was extremely expensive. In 1909, the minimum cost was put at £2,000, and it could easily be ten times that amount. The big merchant banks were not, on the whole, interested in domestic industrial issues. With foreign issues generally so much larger than domestic ones, it did not pay them, and besides, all their experience and training had been in the foreign loan market.

Doubtless a substantial reason for British industry's failure to make greater use of the London Stock Exchange was that it did not want to. Either it did not need the capital or it preferred to remain private and finance expansion from retained profits. Even in the years shortly before the First World War only about a tenth of real investment in Britain was financed by new issues on the London Stock Exchange. Yet the fact remains that even if Britain's industry was not eager to raise capital on the Stock Exchange, the merchant banks and the Exchange itself gave industrialists little encouragement. If for the large firm floating an issue was expensive, for a small company, raising public capital cheaply or quickly was virtually impossible. As long as the foreign loan market boomed, it paid the City to concentrate on this and leave industry to find its funds elsewhere.

In other countries, the obvious alternative would have been

* Benjamin Disraeli, *Endymion* (1880), Volume III, chapter 10, pp. 97–8.

the commercial banks. In Britain the clearing banks might have become industrial banks, with shareholdings in industry, as did the German banks; or they might have offered long-term loans, like the American banks. In the event they did neither. They concentrated on attracting deposits and perfecting their system of short-term lending. By the end of the century they had become cautious and conservative, more interested in building up their size and their branch networks than in finding new industrial outlets for their deposits.

This hardening of the arteries is surprising in view of the clearing banks' early aggression. It was not until 1826 that the Bank of England's monopoly of joint-stock banking was breached and not until 1833 that joint-stock banks (today, clearing banks) were allowed everywhere in England and Wales. Unlike the country banks the joint-stock banks were not allowed to issue their own banknotes. This had been the country banks' main source of profits. The joint-stock banks had to look elsewhere – and made their money by attracting the largest possible deposits and re-lending them at the best possible rate. To snatch deposits from the country banks and the London private banks they bid up rates on deposit accounts and even offered interest on some current accounts. Soon they realized that the best way to collect deposits from the largely unbanked middle classes was to create extensive branch networks across the country. As the century progressed and it became clear that the joint-stock banks had won their battle with the older banks, their interest in building up massive branch networks became predominant. One after another, joint-stock banks merged with each other or swallowed up country banks and private banks until by the 1920s the country's banking system was dominated by seven giant clearing banks, Barclays, Lloyds, Midland, Westminster, National Provincial, District and Martins.

The deposits for which the joint-stock banks competed so fiercely were re-lent not long-term but short – by discounting bills of exchange, or on overdraft. By the end of the century the banks had developed a highly efficient short-term lending system. Why were they reluctant to lend long-term to industry?

They could, after all, have earned more on their deposits by doing so. It may be that the experience of frequent banking crises had given the banks a passion for liquidity. But the more important reason was probably that most firms wanted only trading capital. Those that wanted investment funds on a large scale could usually find them from their profits.

Thus with both the Stock Exchange and the clearing banks the story seems to have been the same. Neither, in the nineteenth century, appears to have set out to interest industry in their services as providers of long-term finance. Moreover industry, by and large, did not want their help, for it was reaping the reward of leading the industrial revolution: its profits were generally substantial enough to pay for such investment as it wanted. Those enterprises which needed greater amounts of capital – the railways, brewers, steel firms – appear to have been able to raise what they wanted on the Stock Exchange. That British industry was not modernizing its plants like its foreign rivals in the later nineteenth century was no fault of the City's. But the gulf that widened between industry and the Stock Exchange and clearing banks by the eve of the First World War has taken a long time to close again.

THE TWENTIETH CENTURY: DECLINE AND RECOVERY

Thanks to decades of foreign lending Britain entered the First World War with overseas investments of some £4,000 million, giving her an annual income of over £180 million. It is now apparent how far the country had come to rely on this income; how it helped to conceal the extent to which British industry had fallen behind its competitors in Germany and the United States; and how the massive rundown of these investments to pay for munitions during the war could therefore leave the country more gravely impoverished than contemporaries could appreciate.

The First World War had a traumatic effect on the City. The German banks closed their branches; the London sugar market, largely run by Germans, was deserted overnight. Lloyd's suddenly found itself making a good profit as the main market for insurance against air-raid damage. The London money market was utterly disrupted. When war was declared some £350 million of bills of exchange, most bearing the name of an accepting house or clearing bank, were outstanding in London and only swift action by the government prevented a wave of bankruptcies. The London discount market by October 1914 was doing 5 per cent of its pre-war business, and rigid controls on issues of foreign securities dealt a hard blow to the Stock Exchange.

To some extent, however, the decline in overseas business was replaced by new UK issues, particularly of government debt. Thus the volume of Treasury bills outstanding shot up from some £15 million at the beginning of the war to over £1,000 million by the end, while the general public became accustomed to holding securities, as they were encouraged to lend to the country by buying War Loan. The now notorious issue of 5 per cent War Loan in 1917 produced the largest block of securities ever created. Converted into 3½ per cent stock between the wars, it has still not been redeemed. Inevitably this rise in government debt increased the authorities' control of the monetary and banking system.

But the most profound impact of the First World War on the City came from its indirect effects on the British economy and specifically on the balance of payments. The massive income from investments abroad on which the country had depended to pay for its trade deficit disappeared. The trade deficit remained. The government struggled to restore sterling's nineteenth-century role and to rebuild Britain's investment income. But it failed to grasp how far sterling's international supremacy had been the result of Britain's special pre-war position as the world's largest trading nation and biggest exporter of capital. Instead it subscribed to the popular view that sterling's strength depended on international confidence, which in turn was reinforced by the pound's free convertibility into gold.

So attempts to rebuild the prestige of the City after the war were based on attempts to return to the pre-war gold standard. Ironically, the partial return to the gold standard in 1925 left the country with an overvalued exchange rate and plunged the British economy deeper into post-war recession. Efforts to revive foreign lending had to be financed with short-term funds, which in turn could only be attracted from abroad by keeping interest rates high. This then added to British industry's post-war difficulties and helped to convince industrialists that their interests and those of the City were diametrically opposed – a conviction which they have still not altogether relinquished.

It was the domestic economy, not the international, which provided the main source of City activity after the war. As soon as wartime restrictions on the Stock Exchange were lifted, a flood of companies came to the market for quotation. In the 1920s a great many of the firms which later formed the backbone of British industry were first quoted – Imperial Chemical Industries, Beechams, English Electric, Morris, Ford, Bowater. But the 1920s were essentially a period of consolidation for City institutions, rather than innovation. At the end of the war the clearing banks' amalgamation movement had its last spurt, inspired by the belief that, in the post-war reconstruction, large industrial companies would need correspondingly large banks to lend to them. The movement was finally checked by the Colwyn Committee's report in 1918. A parallel movement was reaching its culmination among the insurance companies. Since the beginning of the century, fire insurance companies had been gradually buying up accident and proprietary life companies, and the giant composites which dominate the market today were taking shape.

Such innovation as did take place in the City in the inter-war era was frequently inspired by the authorities. Thus the Bank of England initiated the creation of United Dominions Trust, touching off the growth of hire-purchase companies, and of Municipal and General Securities (today known simply as M & G), the first of a plethora of unit trusts. The established institutions tended to regard the new arrivals jealously: thus the clearing banks refused to help the finance houses by allowing them access to their clearing facilities.

The clearing banks did however co-operate in setting up the Industrial and Commercial Finance Corporation following the Macmillan Committee on Finance and Industry's report in 1931.

The committee found a gap in financial services for medium-sized companies: companies that were too small to go public but too large to continue using family funds to finance expansion found it difficult to obtain additional long-term capital. It was to help fill this 'Macmillan gap' that ICFC was founded.

It was the worldwide depression in the 1930s which finally put paid to the City's efforts to recapture its international position of the previous century. Foreign lending virtually died out. The discount market, once the centre of international bill business, had already found itself driven to relying mainly on commercial and Treasury bills for business. When between 1929 and 1933, the number of commercial bills halved, several discount houses failed. Those that survived found interest rates ruinously low as a result of the government's 'cheap money' policy, intended to revive economic activity. To avoid extinction (and encouraged by the Bank), the discount houses made a series of defensive agreements with the clearing banks and among themselves. Thus the clearing banks agreed to buy their Treasury bills always through a discount house; and the discount houses avoided competing for Treasury bills, bidding for them jointly and then sharing them out by agreement, an arrangement which survived until 1971.

Britain recovered relatively quickly from the depression, and by the time the Second World War broke out, new British industries such as motor manufacture, electrical products and cinemas had once again restored City activity. But many of the defensive attitudes built up in the lean years of the late 1920s and early 1930s survived. They are only now beginning to disappear.

The impact of the Second World War on the City was similar to that of the First, but far less devastating. This time it was the Italian and the Japanese banks that closed their branches. The government continued its cheap money policy – and persevered with it until 1951. Again, the volume of public debt rose swiftly. Exchange controls were maintained far longer than after the previous war. Sterling did not become fully convertible for overseas residents until 1958, and it was still not freely convertible for UK residents when Britain joined the Common Market.

For City banks the establishment of sterling convertibility in 1958 was arguably the most important event of this century, for it heralded the rise of the London eurodollar market. The steady flow of US dollars to Europe had replenished the reserves of the European central banks and was starting to find its way into private hands. Interest rates in the US were held down by a US banking control, Regulation Q. European banks, particularly those in the City, were able to bid higher rates for these funds. Thus British banks, baulked in the use of sterling for financing third country trade by the curbs imposed on sterling in the squeeze of 1957, switched to these dollars. US capital controls, in particular Interest Equalization Tax, in effect closed New York to foreign borrowers. These borrowers, who included the growing numbers of US overseas subsidiaries, turned to London and other European centres. Merchant banks in Britain started arranging longer-term bond issues for them. At last London again had a currency in which to operate worldwide. Throughout the 1960s it continued to develop this market, the latest refinement being the eurocurrency syndicated loan market, an international market in medium-term lending.

The phenomenal growth of the eurodollar has brought to the City a new era of international prestige, largely insulating it from sterling's difficulties. It has also had a considerable impact on the City's traditional institutions, giving a new lease of life to the merchant banks and providing the key attraction for the host of foreign banks in London. Both merchant and foreign banks began during the 1960s to disrupt the cosily demarcated world which the clearing banks and other established financial institutions had created for themselves during the previous decades.

The clearing banks in particular had suffered from being repeatedly subject to ceilings on their lending. An observation by Heathcoat Amory, Chancellor of the Exchequer, in 1958 proved prescient. Quantitative bank control, he warned,* 'is vexatious and frustrating and makes for inefficient banking, notably because it obliges the banks to restrict competition among themselves

* Quoted by David K. Sheppard, *The Growth and Role of UK Financial Institutions 1880–1962* (London, Methuen, 1971), p. 11.

and yet exposes them to additional competition from outside institutions'.

Meanwhile domestic industry was increasing its demands on the City. Throughout the 1950s a stream of private companies came to the market, partly because of the unfavourable tax position of private companies but also to raise additional capital. These issues were often organized by provincial or West End issuing houses, many of which have since joined forces with the merchant banks.

More profitable still has been advising industry on takeovers and mergers. Before the middle 1950s this was handled by accountants, but the merchant banks spotted the opportunity to develop it and by the end of the decade had a virtual monopoly. Takeovers first caught their attention with the great battle waged in 1958-9 for the control of the British Aluminium Company, the country's largest producer, between Alcoa and the American firm Reynolds Metal of Virginia (with the British firm Tube Investments). BAC and Alcoa were represented by the old established merchant banks of Lazards and Hambros, Reynolds and TI by the newcomers Warburgs and Helbert Wagg. The Reynolds team emerged victorious with 80 per cent of BAC.

If takeover battles kept the City in the headlines, the growth of savings media kept the public interested. The post-war era saw the proliferation of institutions designed to collect funds from the small saver and funnel them into the stock market. Where a century ago the saver had little choice but to put his money directly into the market, or indirectly into government debt through the Post Office Savings Bank, today he can choose between investment trusts, unit trusts, life assurance policies and so on. This has given the stock market a far wider catchment area of savings and should therefore have made capital easier to raise.

Thanks to the growth of these savings media, and to the increasing coverage given to finance by the national press,* more people now have an interest in what the City does than ever

* The two are linked. The advertising revenue from unit trusts has largely paid for the increased size of the business pages.

before. The City, as this book argues, is now undergoing important changes in almost every area of its activities. Barriers of every kind are coming down: class and sex barriers are weakening, cartels (such as those which have so long restrained the banks and the money markets) are being dismantled, the system of credit control has been withdrawn, the intense specialization which has long been a peculiarity of the City is being diluted by mergers and by the arrival of new kinds of competitor. From being a sleepy, rather traditional place, the City is becoming alert and aggressive. The change is taking place faster in some institutions than others. The following chapters show which are changing most quickly – and which are still half asleep.

2
Branch banking

Without a doubt the clearing banks* provide people in Britain with a banking system as convenient, secure and sophisticated as any in the world. This is not just flag-wagging. In 1972 all of Britain's 'big four' banking groups were, in terms of deposits, in the world's top thirty. The largest, Barclays, was number four. They have a gigantic network of branches. A current-account customer† can walk into any one of 12,000 bank offices in England and Wales and, with his cheque card to guarantee it, cash a cheque for up to £30 on demand. It is virtually impossible for a bank customer to find himself more than a dozen miles from a branch. This means that he can travel anywhere with just a

* The clearing banks – Barclays, National Westminster, Midland, Lloyds, Williams and Glyn's and Coutts – are so called because they are members of the London Clearing House (see pp. 37–8). With the exception of Coutts they are financial conglomerates, providing basic and other banking services for British industry and individuals through their branch networks. Money market banking services, performed both by the clearing banks (usually through separate subsidiaries) and by merchant and foreign banks, are tackled in the next chapter.

† Of any clearing bank except Barclays, which does not provide its customers with a cheque card and whose Barclaycard only guarantees cheques at Barclays' counters.

cheque book – unlike the American who has to carry around a wallet full of credit cards or the Continental who needs a bundle of notes. If the banks are shut he can draw cash from automatic dispensers in every major city in the country. He has 'free' financial advice from his manager. Above all, he can still borrow on overdraft – the cheapest and most convenient form of personal bank borrowing anywhere in the world.

Yet even the casual observer of British banking in the 1960s must have been aware that bank customers were not wholly satisfied with the services they were offered. The clearing banks suffered repeated attacks from official bodies such as the Monopolies Commission and the Prices and Incomes Board, and from the Consumers' Association and the press. The Monopolies Commission, advising against the merger of Barclays and Lloyds, earned the banks' undying resentment by describing them as 'soporific'.

The description at the time was fair enough. The banks were inhibited from introducing any major innovations or changes by their cartel agreement, which fixed the rates they paid for deposits and the minimum rates that they charged for overdrafts. These rates, which were linked to Bank rate and therefore effectively determined by the Bank of England, were virtually identical. The amount which the banks could lend was also determined quantitatively by the Bank.

The banks, for their part, tended to see themselves in the main as public servants. Not only did they offer a number of facilities such as free bank manager's advice and cheap overdrafts which if costed properly were quite uneconomic. They carried out a variety of specific services for the government for which they received no direct reward: the administration of exchange control, for example, and the provision of cheap export credit. They were allowed by the government to subsidize these through their interest-rate cartel.

Not all the banks, it must be admitted, were content with this state of affairs. Midland in particular had pressed to be allowed to compete on rates in the early 1960s, and had been firmly refused by Reginald Maudling, then Chancellor of the Exchequer.

The Treasury at that time believed that bank competition would not result in cheaper credit for industrial customers. It preferred to allow bank depositors, most of whom were individuals, to continue subsidizing the interest rate on industrial loans.

By the late 1960s, it had become urgent for the banks to make the painful transition from public service to competitive enterprise. They had no alternative. The interest-rate cartel and the controls on lending had encouraged a host of competitors – merchant and foreign banks, building societies, National Giro – to chip away at their business. Despite the range of the banks' activities and their massive size, the competitors were being alarmingly successful. The clearing banks' share of total deposits declined steadily and much profitable 'near banking' business was slipping away from them altogether.

In the early 1970s two major changes occurred which should have gone some way both to halt the widespread criticism of the banks, and to arrest the decline in their business. In February 1970 the clearing banks published their true profits for the first time. Before then no bank knew for sure the profitability of its rivals, and bank shareholders had no accurate way of judging their management's performance. In September 1971 the Bank of England introduced a new system of credit control* which put an end to the banks' cartel and to the quantitative controls on bank lending.

In the first year of the new controls, a part of the banks' business began to improve: the money market part, described in the next chapter, rather than their traditional business of collecting deposits and re-lending them through their branches. But neither the new system of controls nor the publication of profits has halted the criticisms. In the banks' eyes many of their critics are unfair: they are trying to have it both ways. They urge the banks to retain the services they find convenient, ignoring the fact that many of these are uneconomic; and at the same time expect the banks to behave like commercial enterprises. But the banks for

---

* The new controls were first outlined in *Competition and Credit Control*, published by the Bank of England in May 1971. For a description of both the old and new systems of credit control, see chapter 8, pp. 207–11.

their part are also trying to have it both ways. Thus their idea of acting like commercial enterprises was dropping Saturday opening altogether, rather than finding a way of giving their customers – at a price – what they demanded. It is clearly going to take bankers a long time to stop thinking like public servants and to start thinking like businessmen.

The reason for the banks' continued difficulties, this chapter argues, is not that they are lazy or, as is too often claimed, managed by incompetents. It is that they are run by men who may be excellent bankers but who are not fitted by their experience for the job they now have to do. The clearing banks, massive financial conglomerates, are managed not by managers but by bankers. That is the root of their problem.

WHO THE CLEARING BANKS ARE

The names of the so-called 'big four' are household words: Barclays, National Westminster, Midland and Lloyds. Between them these banks handle four out of five personal deposit bank accounts in the country and an even higher proportion of company accounts. Though they dominate the market for basic banking services, the big four do not have a complete monopoly. There are a number of other banks which offer a comparable range of services: the Scottish banks, smaller deposit banks and to a lesser extent some of the merchant banks and foreign banks with London offices. The big four also face competition for various aspects of their business from building societies and National Giro and from companies specializing in factoring, leasing (both explained in chapter 3, p. 61), hire purchase and other kinds of industrial lending.

All the big four except National Westminster, which is building a new 600-foot tower, live in very similar head offices: solid temples designed to convey an impression of unshakeable stability, with marble pillars supporting a grandiose dome. They still have different characters. By big-four standards Barclays is the most aggressive. The Barclays group has long been the largest, though in 1973 it was being rapidly overtaken by National

Westminster. When the new National Westminster, formed in 1968 by a merger between National Provincial and Westminster, first threatened to overtake it, Barclays tried to merge simultaneously with Lloyds and the smaller Martins. When that was blocked on the recommendation of the Monopolies Commission it kept its lead – briefly – by buying Martins alone. It is also the innovator of the big four. It pioneered bank credit cards in this country with Barclaycard and had a decentralized system of control well before the other banks. Unlike the others, too, it has long had a controlling interest in its main overseas banking subsidiary, Barclays DCO, from 1971 owned outright and renamed Barclays International. This means that it presents a united image – Barclays' name appears above more branches than any other bank's in the world, and Barclays was the first UK bank with a substantial branch network in the United States.

The other three banks heartily dislike Barclays. To the outside world, Midland might appear to be Barclays' main opponent. It has tended to strike out in the opposite direction from Barclays and then be forced to turn back. Midland led the anti-Barclaycard lobby, and then when Barclaycard started (after five years) to make money, Midland joined a rival credit-card scheme, Access, with the other banks. Midland, too, has begun to move away from a centralized management system towards the Barclays model. But occasionally Barclays seems to have taken the wrong course and Midland the right one. At home Midland pioneered personal loans and has a wholly owned hire purchase subsidiary, Forward Trust, while some Midland branches have started to sell hire purchase across the counter. Abroad, Midland has rejected the policy of setting up direct overseas branches and instead has forged solid links with a powerful group of European banks.

National Westminster has a less clearly defined personality, perhaps because it is still engaged in sorting out the organizational problems created by the merger. But it has already emerged as Barclays' strongest challenger. In 1970 it quietly overtook Barclays in terms of parent-bank deposits.* It was National

* According to their annual accounts, 1970 and 1971.

Westminster that took the lead in setting up Access. It has the most diversified interests of all the banks, including its own merchant-banking subsidiary, County, and links with a number of foreign banks, including Chase Manhattan of New York, for some of its foreign business.

Lloyds, the smallest of the big four, has concentrated on wealthy personal customers rather than industrial clients. It benefits from its relatively compact branch network centred in the rich south of England. Like Barclays, it has always had international aspirations. It has a large minority holding in the overseas bank, National and Grindlays, and has full control of Bank of London and South America, which it has renamed Lloyds and Bolsa International and intends to convert into an operation on the lines of Barclays Bank International. So far, however, Lloyds has failed to develop a coherent policy to make the most of its strengths. Indeed, its indecent eagerness to merge with Barclays in 1968 suggested an incipient death wish.

The big four have interests in most of the other British deposit banks. But in general they regard these interests simply as trade investments. Lloyds owns 16 per cent of the Edinburgh-based National and Commercial Banking Group, by far the largest of the banks competing with the big four. This group owns the largest bank in Scotland, Royal Bank of Scotland, as well as Williams and Glyn's in England, formed out of Glyn Mills, Williams Deacon's and National Bank in 1970. In terms of deposits National and Commercial is little more than a third the size of Lloyds, and it has to run harder to grow as fast as the other banks: in Scotland the distribution of its branches is directed towards rural areas, and in England it just does not have enough of them.

Also north of the border is Clydesdale Bank, owned by Midland, and the venerable Bank of Scotland, founded in 1695 and now seemingly heading into Barclays' eager arms. Barclays already has a 35 per cent interest and many bankers believe (despite stout denials by both parties) that it is no more than a matter of time before Barclays takes full control.

Elsewhere on the Celtic fringes two of the clearing banks have

Northern Irish subsidiaries: National Westminster owns Ulster Bank, and Midland owns Northern Bank. Both are based in Belfast but have branches in Eire. There is really only one other regional bank, Yorkshire Bank, owned by four clearers.

Stronger competition comes from the Co-op Bank, 'money shops', and several companies offering banking services. The Co-op Bank is owned by the Co-operative Wholesale Society and offers a conventional banking service. 'Money shops' are owned by large financial groups, including United Dominions Trust and the US First National City Bank. They offer a simple banking service aimed mainly at working class customers. Finally there are 'fringe banks' run by smaller companies such as Cedar Holdings and First National Finance. Of these a number had to be rescued from collapse in December 1973.

Finally a couple of curiosities: in the antique Coutts, formed in 1692, they will give you – if you insist – a quill pen to sign your cheques. The bank has a select air about it (the only one of its nine branches outside London is in Eton) which belies its ownership by the proletarian National Westminster. More precious still is C. Hoare and Co., a private bank which only stopped having its statements written in longhand in 1962.

The really serious competition for the personal deposits which are the lifeblood of the clearing banks does not come from other commercial banks at all. Four other main kinds of institution offer what amounts to a simple personal banking service, which all have one substantial advantage over the banks: their more convenient hours. Two of these are savings banks: the Trustee Savings Banks, which have 1,500 branches scattered across the country with 8·5 million active accounts, and the National Savings Bank, formerly the Post Office Savings Bank, which operates from the 23,000 post offices. Neither are permitted to lend and only the TSBs offer cheque books.

The TSBs could become more serious competition if they were allowed to offer personal loans and become members of the London Clearing House. But the two competitors that the clearing banks fear most are the building societies and the Post Office's National Giro. Both enjoy privileges denied to the banks. The building societies have special tax concessions which allow them to offer standard-rate taxpayers better interest than the clearing banks. Giro has been heavily subsidized by the government.

Traditionally building societies have been the haven for long-term savings. In recent years, however, they have found that demand for home loans has forced them to accept short-term money too, bringing them into the banks' province. They now provide what amounts to a deposit account on which after-tax interest is about 3 per cent higher than the banks pay. As a result, while deposits of the London clearing banks rose by two-thirds between 1961 and 1971, those of the building societies nearly quadrupled.

National Giro is also a potential threat but for a different reason. What frightens the banks here is that it has broken their monopoly of transferring money. It offers both personal and business customers a money transfer service which it claims is more convenient and appreciably cheaper than the banks'. It does not lend money directly, although loans are made through it by the hire purchase company, Mercantile Credit. But complicated forms, badly briefed counter staff and poor advertising have set Giro off to a slow start. In 1973 it was still losing money.

HOW THE BANKS ARE MANAGED

Looking at clearing-bank management, two things immediately stand out. One is that the boards of directors of three out of the big four are comprised almost entirely of men with no experience, past or present, in banking. The other is that the men who actually run the banks, the general managers, have little experience of anything else.

The gentlemen/players distinction survives. The boards of the big four are composed overwhelmingly of gentlemen who have either distinguished themselves in fields such as industry, politics, the Civil Service and the armed forces – but hardly ever in banking; or they have come from old banking families whose banks have long since been swallowed up. Taking Lloyds as an example, no less than nineteen of the thirty-four members of its 1971 board had titles. Three directors (none of whom had titles) worked full-time at the bank. Rarely do these directors play any executive role within the bank: until recently even the chief executive – the chief general manager – could not expect a seat on the board.

The general managers, by contrast, are recruited entirely from the ranks. They come from the same pool as the thousands of branch managers all over the country, though they may have been singled out at an early stage and given a spell at head office. These men are very able bankers: they have had to be to get to the top of a massive organization. They have frequently been sent by their banks on management courses, and even occasionally on high-powered business courses in the US. But inevitably they are handicapped by their lack of industrial experience. Their whole career has been within the clearing banks – and within the same bank at that. Their training is slanted towards decisions on banking matters, such as the creditworthiness of customers, rather than on management matters, such as the cost-effectiveness of a computerization project.

There are three important qualifications to this. Firstly, the chairmen of the big four are all full-time executives, and three of them are experienced bankers. Both Anthony Tuke of Barclays and John Prideaux of National Westminster come from old banking families. The Tuke family bank was one of the private banks that combined to form Barclays. Anthony Tuke's forthright father, known as the 'Iron Tuke', was chairman of Barclays from 1951 to 1962. John Prideaux's family bank is Arbuthnot Latham, a minor accepting house. (His mother was an Arbuthnot.) Apart from war service, John Prideaux spent his entire life from the age of eighteen working for it. In 1970 he took over the chairmanship of National Westminster from David Robarts, the scion of another old banking family.

Eric Faulkner of Lloyds is also a banker but without family connections. He joined Glyn, Mills (now incorporated into Williams and Glyn's) after Cambridge and worked his way up through the bank to become chairman in 1965. He was made chairman of Lloyds rather by accident in 1969. The bank's first choice, the chairman-elect Sir Reginald Verdon Smith, stood down following criticism that Bristol Siddeley (of which he was also chairman) had overcharged the government on aircraft-engine servicing contracts. This unfortunate episode enabled Faulkner to reach his present position. The non-banker chairman is Sir Archibald Forbes, at Midland. A Scottish accountant, he had a successful career in industry before becoming chairman of the bank in 1964.

The second qualification is that Barclays does not fit into the pattern of figure-head directors. It has organized a system of local head offices each with its own board. Through these boards members of the 'special list' – composed of the cream of university graduates and scions of the old banking families that formed Barclays – can bypass the hierarchy, and may ultimately become executive directors on the main board. The local-board system, a decentralized system of control, enables Barclays, the only one of the big four to be formed from private banks, to ensure that it is run by executive directors rather than general managers. It has the added advantage of preserving respectable jobs for the private bankers' descendants.

The third qualification is the one that will become most important in the future. The banks are increasingly being forced to employ specialists who do not fit into their caste system, and still less into the sort of salary structure that clearing banks think appropriate to people in their twenties and thirties. The instinct of the banks is to try either to train their own men to do new jobs, or hive off the new functions which call for these specialists into a separate subsidiary. This way the pay scales are not undermined. But this does not always work. The banks have had limited success in training their own men in marketing and public relations, while their attempts to set up computer systems with their own staff have been, in most cases, disastrous.

At present the key man in the banks' hierarchy remains the branch manager, the GP of the financial world. He is also one of the banks' two big staff headaches.

Look at his job. He has long had to run an office efficiently, to advise on personal financial problems, to judge credit risks and to sort out companies' balance sheets. Now he is expected to act as salesman for the bank too. Yet he has virtually no training – bar experience – for the job. Banks openly admit that they are finding it increasingly difficult to get branch-manager material, mainly because of the decline in the status of banking as a profession and of the spread of university education. Banks' rigid salary scales make it almost impossible for them to attract graduates, and in private bankers complain bitterly about those they do get. Already it is becoming extremely difficult for the banks to man their branch networks. In ten years the situation will be even worse.

The other staff problem of the banks is the marked increase in militancy since the second half of the 1960s. The banks, faced with their first ever strike by members of the National Union of Bank Employees, were forced to recognize it alongside their home-grown 'unions', the staff associations.* Until now, NUBE has been relatively docile. But if it does not deliver better salaries, other unions may step in. The unionization of insurance workers – led by Mr Clive Jenkins – is already under way.

The clearing banks, then, have a grave management problem. This is not at all a criticism of the way the men who run the banks from day to day perform the tasks they have been set. The senior management have rarely been prepared, by experience or training, to guide a massive financial empire. As for the branch manager, his job is virtually impossible.

HOW THE BANKS MAKE THEIR MONEY

The essentials of banking have not changed in three centuries. Banks borrow savings mainly from their 13 million or so personal customers, lend them mainly to companies and run a money transfer system which allows their customers to make payments without using cash. In addition, banks increasingly offer a wide range of related services. For individuals they will do anything from keeping valuables safe to acting as executors;

* Barclays, however, has recognized NUBE since before World War II.

for companies, anything from managing payrolls to share registration.

In the way the banks offer services there are two major illogicalities. The banks treat their company customers almost exactly as they do their personal ones: very often both borrow and deposit on just the same basis. And a large proportion of bank services are 'free' – which means in practice that they are subsidized by overcharging for others.

(a) Banking

Some 35 per cent of adults in Britain have a bank account. To persuade someone to leave his hard earned savings with it, a bank offers two inducements: convenience and interest. Its profit (or a great part of it) derives from the difference between the amount it pays for money and the amount it lends it out at. There are basically two types of account: current and deposit. Clearing-bank current accounts offer no interest, but only the convenience of being able to write a cheque and use the banks' other money transfer services.

In principle, personal and industrial customers pay for their current accounts in almost exactly the same way though the rates charged vary. For both, the banks calculate interest of between 4 and 6 per cent on their average balance and allow this against a charge of about 7–10p on each cheque. For industrial customers, the banks then translate this figure into a percentage of turnover on which they base future charges. Charges vary from nil to 25p per £100 of turnover, depending on the work involved, the balance maintained and on how much the bank wants the company's business.

In 1973, there was a radical change in the way in which bank charges applied to personal customers. Embarrassed by their high profits – entirely the result of high interest rates – the clearers competed to cut their charges. Before, some 25 to 30 per cent paid no charges at all. Besides those with large current accounts, these were managing directors of important companies, people with long family connections, and certain financial journalists.* In 1973

* Not us.

this select group was joined by 80 per cent of National Westminster's customers – anyone with a minimum balance of £50 on current account. The other banks quickly followed with schemes of their own.

The net effect of these schemes is to make those who use their accounts rarely subsidise those who use them a lot. The banks would have been fairer to offer interest on current account, as does the Co-op Bank. Their defence is that customers are not taxed on the notional interest allowed, but would be on interest payments.

There are no charges on deposit accounts but a personal cheque cannot be drawn on them. As money has to be paid in and withdrawn over a bank branch counter, they are less convenient. Interest is fixed at $1\frac{1}{2}$–$1\frac{3}{4}$ per cent under 'base rate'.*

The banks offer personal customers a number of variations on these two types of account but the bulk of the deposits of the UK clearing banks – some £17,000 million in 1972 – are still in current or deposit accounts, with the proportion in the latter about 60 per cent in late 1973, and rapidly rising.†

Until the new credit controls were introduced, each bank not only offered the same rate on all types of deposit, but the same rate as its rivals, a rate linked to the now abolished Bank rate (though the Bank of England always preserved the fiction that it was chosen voluntarily by the banks). Now each bank is free to offer whatever rates it likes for deposits, and within the first year of the new régime, deposit rates began to diverge. Each bank ties its deposit and overdraft rates loosely to a base rate decided by itself. So a $\frac{1}{2}$ per cent rise in a bank's base rate generally means an automatic $\frac{1}{2}$ per cent rise in its deposit rate and all its overdraft rates.

When most people think of banks, they think of overdrafts. There are only three ways any bank anywhere can lend money. It can grant a loan; it can discount some form of bill;‡ or it can

* Fixed by the banks on the basis of supply and demand for funds.
† The clearing banks accept deposits for fixed periods at higher rates of interest through subsidiary companies and, since September 1971, directly. These 'money-market' deposits inflate the proportion of cash on deposit account. This aspect of the banks' business is discussed in chapter 3.
‡ For an explanation of bill finance, see p. 57.

extend an overdraft. In Britain all three methods are used, but the overdraft is overwhelmingly the most common. It does not matter whether the customer is a student wanting £25 till his grant comes through, a draper wanting £5,000 to finance a new line of summer dresses, or British Leyland wanting another £10 million to pay its tax bill. All get (or in the case of the student, perhaps do not get) an overdraft. The overdraft is a remarkably flexible instrument and has helped to make short-term borrowing in Britain cheaper and more convenient than anywhere else.

How it works is well known. A customer, either an individual or a company, is given an overdraft limit for a certain period (usually a year) and can draw up to that amount whenever he wants. Interest is calculated daily (so that he only pays for the amount of credit actually used) at a rate fixed in relation to base rate. Rates for personal borrowing range from 2 to 5 or 6 per cent over base rate, with favoured customers (or customers borrowing for favoured projects) paying rather less. For commercial and industrial companies the rate might be as low as 1 per cent over base rate. This bottom rate is called the 'blue chip' rate.

The overdraft is intended for short-term needs and is theoretically repayable on demand. In practice it is often used to finance long-term projects because it can be 'rolled over' from one year to another. A bank frequently requires what it calls 'security' against a loan. This is a claim against some asset of the borrower, often property, which it can sell should he default on the loan. In Ogden Nash's words:

> Most bankers dwell in marble halls,
> which they get to dwell in because they encourage
> deposits and discourage withdralls,
> and particularly because they all observe one rule
> which woe betides the banker who fails to heed it,
> which is you must never lend any money to anybody
> unless they don't need it.*

* Copyright 1935 by Ogden Nash. This poem originally appeared in the *New Yorker*.

There is still a lot of truth in this.* But in recent years there has been a shift in lending criteria. Instead of looking at the borrower's assets the banks now ask about his earning power. Often a bank will lend unsecured on the basis of an individual's expected future earnings, or a company's cash flow.

Attachment to the overdraft system distinguishes British domestic banking techniques from those of almost any other country. In the United States banks usually make loans for specific periods. In France, most short-term lending involves some kind of bill. Why are the English clearing banks so fond of the overdraft? It is not because it was their invention: a form of overdraft was introduced by the Royal Bank of Scotland in the 1720s. One of its greatest advantages is its simplicity. Initially there is no paperwork. There is no formal loan agreement (overdraft permissions are generally set out in a letter but may well be purely oral) nor any negotiable paper such as a bill of exchange. An overdraft, whether secured or unsecured, is fundamentally a statement of faith in the borrower's honesty and financial reliability. Compared with other systems of lending the overdraft is remarkably convenient. American banks get into extraordinary contortions with their loans. Not only do loans become tied up with sheaves of legal documents but the actual agreements are tortuous: there is, for example, the system of compensating balances whereby the borrower has to lend back (at no interest) a certain proportion of the funds borrowed.

The overdraft allows the clearers to preserve the fiction that their loans can be recalled on demand. This, they pretend, protects their depositors – the primary duty of a bank. There are, however, two obvious flaws in this argument. Banks already lend their depositors money medium-term through their subsidiaries. And whether the banks like it or not, overdrafts *are* used for

* A bank overdraft is very much the prerogative of the well-to-do. A survey carried out for the Crowther Committee on Consumer Credit of 1971 revealed that bank overdrafts, the cheapest form of credit, were used by 22 per cent of borrowers in the AB social brackets and by a mere 1 per cent of those in the DE brackets. By contrast, check trading, one of the most expensive ways of borrowing, was used by 18 per cent of those in the DE classes and by only 2 per cent of the ABs.

longer-term finance. The problems this creates are trenchantly described by Donal Carroll, formerly governor of the Bank of Ireland.*

The problem here is that the customer sees overdraft permission as part of his capital and is inclined to feel that he can use it for any purpose. For example, a seasonal overdraft can very easily be used to avail of the opportunity to buy more plant. In a very few years a regularly renewed overdraft permission becomes a necessary part of the permanent capital of the customer. He has, therefore, too little incentive to reduce his commitment out of the earnings of the asset which it has been used to purchase. This is a bad financial discipline which is not in the customer's own interest.

From the point of view of the bank, in these days when the quantity of credit outstanding may have to be regulated, there is always a vast pool of unused overdraft permissions which are difficult to control. Furthermore, the increasing use of the overdraft tends to undermine the customer's desire to keep a credit balance. And credit balances are, after all, the life blood of the bank.

The Irish banks led the British banks in switching these rolled-over overdrafts into term loans. But especially since the new credit controls, the clearing banks have been switching more and more of their overdrafts into term loans, mostly channelled through their subsidiaries (discussed in the next chapter) but also increasingly through the parent banks. The parent banks also lend for fixed periods under two special schemes. First, the banks have been bullied into making a certain proportion of their funds available for shipbuilders for up to eight years, and exporters for up to five years (ten years in practice) with the credits guaranteed by the government. At the beginning of 1974 a total of about £1,700 million was lent in this way. Secondly, through the personal loan schemes money is available for personal borrowers for up to three years, often unsecured. Interest is fixed by the bank itself and the rates are invariably considerably higher than over-

* Interviewed in *The Banker* (September 1968).

draft rates: profitable business and growing fast, though the total volume of such lending by the London clearing banks was still small in late 1973. Indeed *all* personal lending is small in relation to the total – amounting to only about 21 per cent. Excluding loans for house purchase (mostly to staff) it is even lower – 14 per cent.

More recently still, the clearing banks have started to lend money through credit cards, an American invention, made necessary in the US by the absence of overdrafts and the limited acceptability of personal cheques. In this country it was pioneered by Barclays with Barclaycard and followed in 1972 by the other banks with Access. The interest rates on Barclaycard and Access are even higher than on a personal loan and far higher than on an overdraft. Lending through credit cards is still in its infancy but it will have to grow if the cards are to be made to pay more than their running costs.

Credit cards are also one of the three ways – apart from physically shifting cash around – by which the banks can move funds. The others are cheques, and credit or debit transfers.

The banks are the channel through which new notes and coins are distributed round the country and dirty notes removed. But the basic aim of any bank is to cut down the amount of cash that has to be carried around. The cheque, originally a written instruction to a goldsmith, is their traditional solution.

A cheque can be written on anything* though it upsets the banks' computers if the magnetically coded cheque books provided by the bank are not used.

Computers have enabled the banks to clear bounding numbers of cheques, which have to be returned to the bank on which they are drawn. Total cheque clearings through the London Clearing House rose by 63 per cent between 1961 and 1971 to 729 million a year, while the amount exchanged rose by 248 per cent to £843,626 million during the same period. In 1971 the banks cleared internally a further 307 million cheques, worth £186,500

---

* Witness the court case about a cheque written on a cow. 'Was the cow crossed?' 'No your Worship, it was an open cow.' A. P. Herbert, *Uncommon Law* (London, Methuen, 1970), pp. 201–6.

million, which were drawn and paid into different branches of the same bank. The London Clearing House operates the 'town clearing', a sort of wholesale high-speed clearing for very large cheques drawn on some City branches, and the 'general clearing' for banks all over the country. The cost? Despite computers most banks reckon it at about 10p a cheque.

The personal cheque is widely acceptable in Britain, and becoming more so thanks to the cheque card which guarantees cheques of up to £30. But because cheque clearing is so expensive and cumbersome the banks are backing two alternatives, the credit card* and the credit transfer.

The battle between the cheque card and the credit card has now reached a most interesting stage. Barclays issues only a credit card; the other four banks still provide cheque cards, but also offer their joint credit card, Access. The banks' dream is to use credit cards through computer terminals in, say, retail shops, which would allow instant and reliable money transfer. But at present and in the foreseeable future, cheques still have the edge over credit cards in security, convenience and acceptability. Even in America, where credit cards are firmly entrenched, cheque clearings are rising faster than ever.

Before credit cards replace cheques, the banks' other substitute, the credit transfer, is likely to be well established. A credit transfer sounds more complicated than it really is. Intended mainly for business customers, it merely means that the customer instructs his bank to add a sum to someone else's account and deduct it from his own. A debit transfer is simply the reverse – an account holder agrees to let a body like the local electricity board debit him automatically when bills fall due. Standing orders are credit transfers made at regular intervals. The beauty of credit transfers is that they can be transacted entirely on computer. Ultimately a company customer of a National Westminster branch in Shropshire will be able to instruct his bank

* There are two kinds of credit card: a bank card, intended for all types of transaction, and a travel and entertainment (or T and E) card, intended mainly for luxury items, hotel bills and so on. The best-known T and E card is American Express.

manager to credit an employee with an account at Barclays in Norwich. The Natwest computer will simply feed the instruction into the Barclays computer. No bit of paper will have to be sent across the country. Already the system is both cheaper and quicker than the cheque.

(b) Fringe services

Besides banking, banks have long offered customers a number of fringe benefits. Now, however, the banks are rapidly expanding these ancillary services, especially to companies.

For personal business, these services are really 'loss leaders'. They are still the main way the banks compete between themselves for personal deposits, as they remain unwilling to compete energetically on price. They are also their main defence against the increasing competition from other institutions like the building societies and National Giro. It is rather like IATA airlines trying to woo new passengers from each other and from charter flights with prettier hostesses and more exotic sandwiches.

'You get more than a cheque book when you open a bank account' bank advertisements tell their personal customers. And they do. They can buy shares from a bank. They can get an accountancy service and legal advice. They can use its strongroom to deposit valuables. They can get it to act as executor or trustee. They can call on the range of services of bank subsidiaries, including unit trusts and hire purchase. And they can still get free personal financial advice from the branch manager.

Useful though these services may be to the personal customer, they have serious drawbacks for the banks. They are frequently unprofitable. In the merchant banks the saying is, 'all advice is free until it is taken'. The clearing banks' unique service, the branch manager's advice, is effectively free whether it is taken or not. Even with their newer personal services the banks have often failed to charge an economic price. Cheque cards are a case in point. Many bankers feel now that the banks should receive some sort of compensation for the risk they have to take in guaranteeing cheques. But once a service has been offered for nothing, it is impossible to start charging for it without antagonizing customers.

This unprofitability would matter less if the services were effective as 'loss leaders'. But it is questionable whether they have in fact attracted many personal depositors away from the banks' competitors. The services for which the banks do charge are often worse than customers can buy for the same money elsewhere. And such meagre market research as the banks have published suggests that what their personal customers want most are more convenient opening hours. A survey conducted by Williams and Glyn's shortly after the banks decided to close on Saturdays revealed that nearly half their customers wanted the banks to remain open on Saturdays, while nearly 30 per cent wanted longer opening hours generally.

Company services, by contrast, are profitable. The banks charge for them at an economic rate, which explains why they have been so eager to develop them. Many new services, too, use time on the banks' expensive computers which would otherwise be under-used. Thus the banks are offering to control inventories and to organize payrolls, taking over the whole business of making up wage packets. Ultimately they would like to offer a complete computerized management information service.

Most of the more sophisticated company services offered by the big four are still organized through separate subsidiaries (see pp. 69–71) though gradually the parent banks are starting to offer them themselves. Some of them have been trying to provide what has previously been the province of the merchant banks – specialist financial advice. National Westminster has its own merchant bank, County, and Midland bought control of Samuel Montagu. Williams and Glyn's is building up merchant-banking services of its own. The banks have also branched out into near-banking activities such as hire purchase, factoring and leasing; and into non-banking ones, such as insurance broking. The quality of the more routine of these services is fully comparable with those of the bank's competitors. The bank-owned hire-purchase companies, for example, have as good profit and growth records as the others. But in merchant banking, requiring initiative and even inspiration, the clearing banks are left far behind. The basic reason is simple. The best merchant bankers in the City will not work for the big clearers because they neither pay enough nor give them enough freedom of action.

EVERYONE'S AUNT SALLY

Banks are everyone's Aunt Sally. It is easy to take a tilt at them. And the aspect that almost everyone from the man in the street to the Monopolies Commission chooses to attack is their lack of competitiveness. This is an easy line, and is certainly still valid. But with the end of the cartel and publication of profit figures, it is no longer the banks' most crucial problem. Even before the new credit controls were first announced in spring 1971, the cartel had begun to disintegrate on the lending side while on the borrowing side the banks had long been offering market rates for large deposits. Bank competition is still hardly cut-throat, but it has come a long way since the mid-1960s. Increasingly the banks *are* competing – with other financial institutions and to a lesser extent with each other. The problems that the banks have hardly started to tackle are the consequences of becoming competitive commercial enterprises. Moreover many of the attitudes which the banks acquired in the long years when it was harder to compete – or when there was less incentive to do so – have survived the death of the cartel and continue to flourish.

One pre-cartel habit which the banks have found hard to drop is that of hiving off new and rapidly growing activities into subsidiaries. Under the old system of credit control this made some sense. Now it makes none – apart from dodging the difficulty of fitting the subsidiaries' specialist staff into the parent banks' salary structures. What it has done is to exacerbate the banks' management problems. Not only does it make it harder for the branches to see themselves as sales points for all the banks' services, but it also discourages the banks from giving as much management attention to their subsidiaries as they need. Only two of the clearing banks have organized their management structure to reflect the importance of subsidiaries: Barclays, whose central board directs the group as a whole but not the day-to-day operations of the parent bank; and Williams and Glyn's, whose executive directors are responsible for each major activity and sit on the main board. Both banks have adopted noticeably more coherent policies than their competitors, Barclays in pioneering statewide banking in the US and Williams and Glyn's in introducing new services in the UK.

Reorganizing their subsidiaries is not the only problem which the end of the cartel has made more obvious. No less serious has been the banks' inability to charge economically for their personal fringe services, their unwillingness to rationalize charges for handling current accounts into a fixed and published scale and their continued failure to make best use of their branch networks. These have inexorably become more expensive to run and harder to man. The banks' response to both difficulties has been to employ women and introduce computers. Neither expedient, as the banks are the first to admit, solves the problem.

There are, indeed, only two answers. One is to make better use of the branch networks, to make them pay more. The banks have a 'shop' in every High Street, which could be developed as a sales point for these specialist services. For all the lipservice which the banks pay to marketing, they have so far largely failed to do this.

The second answer is to streamline the way in which bank branches are run. Even when the banks make better use of their branches, they are still likely to find that they have too many of them. Several senior bankers have declared that the banks must consider cutting back their branch networks. Leonard Mather, then chief general manager of Midland, even likened the banks' situation to that of the railways with their uneconomic branch lines,* implying that the banks would have to do a Beeching. (In such an event Lloyds would be best placed; it has Lord Beeching on its board.)

Mr W. B. Davidson, a former chief executive of National Westminster, has suggested that branches should be split between wholesale and retail banking. Commercial services could be offered from large city branches, leaving private business to

* Presidential address to the Institute of Bankers, May 1970.

smaller offices.* And Mr Mather has proposed a rationalization which would group branches under one manager at a larger central bank. Many branches which do little more than take in cheques and dispense cash could operate with just an office manager, who would pass on any customer wanting specialist services, including lending, to the manager of the central branch.

In 1973 Midland had still not adopted this sensible advice, and Mr Mather had been elevated to vice-chairman.

Even if the banks only manage to build up a modicum of managerial expertise at head office and instil a little cost control at branch level this will still make a tremendous difference. The room for improvement is truly staggering. At the time of the PIB report Barclays admitted that it was about 10 per cent over-staffed in the clerical grades. Since Barclays had tried harder to cut clerical costs than anyone else, the other banks were probably worse. Recently some attempt has been made at cost control: National Westminster, like Barclays, has set up a work measure-ment programme. Indeed all the banks have been putting more effort into job evaluation, management by objectives and pay-ment by results. But in 1979 – three years after PIB – the National Union of Bank Employees found that its hopes for a productivity agreement with the banks foundered because the banks had no way of measuring productivity. This is serious, for if the banks are to afford the higher wages demanded by an increasingly mili-tant staff they must learn to use their people more efficiently.

The central problem of the bank manager remains. How should the banks approach the twin problems of finding better men to run their branches, and making their task less impossible? Part of the answer is to streamline bank branches, concentrating com-mercial services into large city offices, leaving personal business with smaller branches, and grouping several under one manager with higher qualifications and status. But there is also a clear need to redefine the bank manager's job, to split the banking and managing functions. Banks might consider the success of US stockbrokers Merrill Lynch, whose branch managers play no

* Talk to the Institute of Bankers, February 1970.

part in the firm's investment decisions. Their responsibility is their branch's profits and on that basis they are paid.

If managers are to be made more responsible for the profits of one or more branches then it is all the more important they should be relieved of some of their present duties. A fixed (and published) scale of charges and standardized lending procedure would help simplify personal business. The one thing the banks must be careful not to throw away is financial advice for their customers, for this remains their exclusive advantage over all their competitors. But they should ask themselves whether this task should not be carried out by a specialist 'financial counsellor' as in large US banks rather than by the branch manager. Perhaps the branch manager's time would be more valuably spent managing his branch.

3
Money market banking

London's claim to be the leading world banking centre rests on a group of some 200 'money market' banks. They have widely different origins. They range from the historic house of Rothschild to the Bank of England's new next door neighbour, Republic National Bank of Dallas. What they have in common is that they have all, especially since the early 1960s, become involved in money market banking. This involves borrowing huge deposits from companies – typically £1 million to £10 million at a time – and re-lending them in equally massive chunks, either to other companies, or on the money market. Through the money markets too the banks lend any spare funds to other banks . . . and borrow other banks' funds when they find themselves caught short.

Most of these banks, which fall into five main groups, started life doing something very different, and most of them still have a wide range of activities outside the money markets. Thus the first group, the merchant banks, offer companies services of various kinds and carry out activities ranging from bullion broking to data processing; many of the second, the British overseas banks, have extensive branch networks abroad; and the third group, the foreign banks, of which the most important are American, usually operate as ordinary branch banks in their own countries. Not all have found altering the direction of their business easy. Only the last two groups, the clearing-bank subsidiaries and the consortium banks, have been set up expressly to undertake money market business.

There are two sides to this business in London: sterling banking, where the borrowers are British local authorities and companies; and international eurocurrency banking, where the borrowers are foreign and overseas corporations (but sometimes British). The international side is easily the larger. Both sides – and this is what has attracted so many different types of bank – have been among the most highly profitable and rapidly growing areas of banking.

The essential difference between all these banks and the clearing banks is the source of their deposits. While the clearing banks collect their funds mainly through their branches in small amounts from millions of personal customers, the wholesale banks either take large deposits from companies or borrow them on the money markets described in the next chapter. They may have branch networks abroad, and even the odd branch in Britain, but these are secondary to their money market banking operations. The way they raise funds affects the way they lend. As their deposits are generally for fixed periods, the money market banks usually lend for fixed periods and not on overdraft like the clearers.

Until the late 1950s the banks which were important were those with the largest networks of branches. Normally a branch network was the only way to attract a large volume of deposits. This remained true as long as the bulk of deposits came from personal customers, who cared more about the convenience of having a branch on their doorstep than the interest they received. But more and more, everywhere in the world, companies were becoming major lenders. It is their deposits that give a bank without a branch network a chance to rival a branch bank. For company depositors are far less interested in convenience than in earning the highest possible rate of interest.

In Britain, from the late 1950s on, a number of special factors allowed these wholesale banks to compete with the clearing banks for company deposits by offering better rates. One was the clearing banks' cartel on interest rates, in which the overseas and merchant banks were not included. Another was the demand for funds from local authorities, prepared to pay high rates for money for short periods. A third was the speedy development of new money markets, which allowed these non-branch banks to lend funds they could not immediately use, and to borrow when they were temporarily short. This meant that they could use their funds in the most efficient way and allowed them to pay the highest possible rates of interest. And finally there was the growth of the eurocurrency market, which provided them with another source of funds which they could lend to overseas customers who were not subject to the restrictions on sterling lending.

It is to the activities of the money market banks, especially in eurocurrencies, that London owes its rebirth as the world's most important international banking centre. Self-congratulatory though the City feels about this, it has been more reticent about the relatively small part played by the British banks in this revival. Specialist banking in London is dominated by foreign, and especially American, banks. Indeed about half the invisible earnings from banking of which the City so proudly boasts are generated by foreign, mainly American, banks.*

To some extent, this American domination is inevitable. It is simply a reflection of the worldwide domination of US commerce and industry. An important part of the work of American banks in London is serving the overseas subsidiaries of their customers at home. But US domination is also a sign of weakness caused by the split in the structure of British banking. It reflects the failure of the clearing banks to put their weight behind what is now banking's biggest growth area. Because government restrictions prevented them from going into wholesale banking

* No firm figure is available. This rough estimate is based on the sort of profit foreign banks should be getting from the size of their deposits – excluding US bank repatriations – plus commission earnings on trade finance.

directly, they had to enter it by the back door – through their subsidiaries. But they only did so when their competitors were already well entrenched, and they did so on too small a scale and with inadequate staff.

It reflects, too, inadequacies in the organization of the other British specialist banks. These are to some extent the result of their diverse origins. The merchant banks are too small to make loans off their own backs on a large enough scale. The British overseas banks have the necessary resources, but these tend to be tied up in branches in the 'wrong' places, the Commonwealth and the developing world rather than the growth points of Europe and America.

With the new bank controls announced in spring 1971 the clearing banks and the specialist banks were put on the same footing. The way is now open for the clearing banks to put their vast resources directly into wholesale banking. It is still too early to see whether they will succeed. But unless they do, Britain's future as an international banking centre will be increasingly in American hands.

THE MERCHANT BANKS

The leading merchant banks have probably had more romantic nonsense talked about them than any other group of companies in the world. It should therefore be said straightaway that merchant bankers are no longer the kingmakers of Europe; that even the largest houses are lightweights compared with the international deposit banks; and that they are hard pressed by increasing competition from their less glamorous competitors. And despite the fact that the banks, as a group, enjoyed outstanding profit and growth records during the 1960s, there are signs that the 1970s may be more difficult.

There are two distinct sides to merchant banking. One is wholesale banking, in which the merchant banks compete with the other groups of banks described in this chapter. The other is providing industry and personal clients with financial services which do not involve the banks in lending their own money: the main ones are acceptance and issuing business, investment management and the newer moneyspinners, takeovers and mergers.

Indeed takeovers and mergers were the largest single source of profits for some banks in the 1950s and 1960s. For years the banks have had, in Sir Edward Reid's famous phrase, to live on their wits rather than their deposits. Of course, many of the banks have long lent their own money on a small scale. But it was only with the development of the money markets that they could emerge as major bankers. This change has brought with it a dilemma: while being big is a positive handicap in providing some financial services, in banking it is vital. In terms of their capital base, the merchant banks are tiny compared with the clearing banks, the American banks and the British overseas banks. The difference is not only one of size. It is also one of attitudes and interests. The person adept at pushing through a contested takeover differs in training, skills and character from the person whose job is to take decisions on whether a company will be able to pay back a £30 million loan in three years' time. The first is interested primarily in making sure that his client wins; the second, in making sure that his depositors do not lose. Knowing how to raise money, long the merchant banks' special skill, is quite different from lending money wisely.

To sum up, three problems now confront the merchant banks. Will they become big enough to be competitive wholesale bankers? If they do, will they sacrifice their skill at performing non-banking activities? And can they develop the abilities needed to be good at lending their own money?

Given the vast range of activities in which merchant banks are involved, and the fact that no two are quite alike, it is hardly surprising that there is no authoritative list of all merchant banks in the City. Perhaps some 100 institutions like to call themselves merchant bankers. Of these, the 18 most exclusive belong to the Accepting Houses Committee and are called accepting houses. Another 60, of which 54 are based in London, belong to the less exclusive Issuing Houses Association and are called issuing houses. Some banks belong to both. To 'accept' a bill of exchange is in effect to guarantee it (see below), while 'issuing' means arranging an issue of shares or bonds on a stock exchange. But membership gives no particular rights, since non-accepting houses can accept bills, while nearly half the issues (by number, though not by value) on the London Stock Exchange are organized by stock-brokers. Besides, accepting is now only a small part of a merchant bank's business, while most issuing houses do many other things apart from making new issues.

The descriptions below take the ten largest accepting houses roughly in order of size. The ranking is imprecise, partly because merchant banks still do not have to publish full profit and reserve figures; partly because, though two merchant banks may show similar balance-sheet totals, the spread of their activities and the way in which they are run may still be very different; and partly because taking group and bank assets gives a different ranking. Vying for top of the list are Hambros and Hill Samuel. Hambros, a confident and energetic Victorian bank, became a public company in 1936. The group is still, however, controlled by the Hambro family, under a system which its chairman, Jocelyn Hambro, dubbed 'enlightened nepotism'. Jocelyn's cousin, Charles Hambro, has now taken over the day-to-day running of the bank.

Hill Samuel, marginally the smaller on 1971-2 group assets, is a newer creation. It was formed in 1965 by a merger between the old City bank of M. Samuel and the West End issuing house Philip Hill, which had previously swallowed up two other City houses, Higginson and Erlangers.

Jocelyn Hambro and Sir Kenneth Keith, chairman of Hill Samuel, are very different people. Hambro is an urbane ex-Coldstream Guards officer with a distinguished limp and an impressive ability to keep a diverse team of people working in harness. Keith is one of the City's most successful outsiders, controversial and abrasive. Like God, he is on the side of the big battalions. He believes that merchant banks must become substantial wholesale banks if they are not to be swallowed up by the clearers and the Americans. As part of this strategy he tried (and failed) to merge with Metropolitan Estate and Property Corporation, the property giant, in 1970. He tried (and failed again) to merge with Slater Walker Securities in 1973. The next move is unclear. While Keith has pursued sheer size, Hambro has concentrated more on building up a range of non-banking activities to cushion lean banking years.

Kleinwort Benson is headed by Gerald Thompson, but the influence of its former chairman, Sir Cyril Kleinwort, is still in evidence. It has wider trading interests than most other merchant banks, and is particularly involved in eastern Europe. It has good profit and growth records, but ran into serious problems with its efforts to buy into advanced technology with an investment in the computer firm of Autonomics. It lost £1·25 million in this venture in 1971.

Schroders lives in a smoked-glass building in Cheapside, and is liked and admired in the City for doing most things well and nothing too aggressively. Schroders is a holding company which controls J. Henry Schroder Wagg in London and J. Henry Schroder Banking Corporation in New York. The New York operation, nearly as large as the London bank, was set up in the 1920s at the request of Benjamin Strong, then head of the New York Federal Reserve Bank. He was a great admirer of British merchant banks and wanted one of them to come and teach the Americans about acceptances and international short-term money markets. Head of the group is Michael Verey who took over when Gordon Richardson became Governor of the Bank of England in June 1973. Schroders is particularly strong in corporate finance and investment management.

Samuel Montagu is one of the few merchant banks with a link with a clearer, as its parent, Montagu Trust is owned by Midland. Midland has, however, failed to integrate Samuel Montagu into its operations and apart from a joint-venture capital subsidiary, the two banks appear to operate quite separately. Montagu, the world's largest gold-dealing firm, is probably the largest foreign exchange dealer among the merchant banks, but wishes that these were not always the only things most people remembered it for. It only broadened into general merchant banking after the Second World War. Much of the group's profits now come from insurance broking. At the end of 1973, the bank had no chairman. The Hon. David Montagu resigned after Midland bought full control.

Lazard Brothers is now part of the Pearson empire, which also controls the *Financial Times*. The New York investment bank, Lazard Frères, with which Lazards was once linked, still works closely with it. It has an important new issue business and still a number of large industrial clients. Lazards became entangled in the Rolls-Royce débâcle of 1971. Not only did it raise a £21 million rights issue for the company less than three years before it went bankrupt but Lord Kindersley, one of its own men, was chairman of Rolls-Royce at the time the disastrous RB 211 contract was signed. Chairman, since 1973, is Daniel Meinertzhagen.

Morgan Grenfell tells young men who come to it for jobs, 'We're not one of the largest banks, but we are one of the nicest to work for.' It was one of the last of the larger banks to come to life, and to appoint the men who actually ran it to the board. It is part of an international family of banks: a third of its capital is held by Morgan Guaranty of New York and it owns a bit of Morgan et Cie. in Paris. Lord Catto became its chairman in autumn 1973.

S. G. Warburg is very much the creation of one man, Sir Siegmund Warburg, a voluble German who arrived in Britain in 1934 with less than £5,000 in his pocket. His bank won its spurs in the Great Aluminium War of 1958–9 when it engineered the takeover of British Aluminium by the American Reynolds, with the UK firm Tube Investments, fighting off a rival bid from Alcoa, represented by Hambros and Lazards. Warburgs had pioneered corporate advice in the 1950s: in the 1960s, the bank was one of the pioneers of eurocurrency finance and is, with Rothschilds, the largest British-owned eurobond issuer.

N. M. Rothschild was the last of the major merchant banks to publish its results: when it did, it emerged as one of the medium-sized accepting houses. It is however one of the banks that has made a great deal of its money on takeovers. Although there are now non-Rothschild, non-Jewish directors, the bank is still very much a family, Jewish affair, run by Jacob Rothschild.

William Brandts has had difficulties. For 150 years it was a successful family bank. Then in the early 1960s it got embroiled in the de Angelis salad oil affair and had to be rescued by the overseas bank National and Grindlays, which bought two-thirds of its capital. The troubles continued. It had a terrible time at the hands of the Takeover Panel, being suddenly told to find £5 million in cash to underwrite a bid. Grindlays helped it again. Then in 1972 Brandts had further difficulties with doubtful debts in Argentina. Finally National and Grindlays had had enough. It bought full control of Brandts.

Baring Brothers, once included in the Duc de Richelieu's list of the great powers of Europe, is today no longer one of the top ten accepting houses. True, its size is probably understated by its published assets. But it has shown little ability to innovate and prefers to make a virtue of staying small. 'We've got a nice building, plenty of money and we eat very well,' is the Barings attitude. 'Why should we risk it all by trying to grow faster?' At its head, until he went off to be Ambassador in Washington, was Lord Cromer, a former Governor of the Bank of England. He was succeeded, after some discreet in-fighting, by John Baring.

Then there are a number of smaller accepting houses: Brown Shipley, which has a joint banking subsidiary with the US brokers Merrill Lynch, distinguished itself by once employing Edward Heath, and Guinness Mahon by being financial advisers to Bernie Cornfeld's Investors Overseas Services. Guinness Mahon was merged into Lewis and Peat and renamed Guinness Peat in December 1972. Rea Brothers is run by Walter Salomon who might, if it did not sound so improbable, be described as a poor man's Siggy Warburg. Like Warburg, he came to London before the war and built his bank up from scratch. Unlike Warburg, who acquired his seat on the Accepting Houses Committee by buying the older bank of Seligman Brothers, Salomon was elected to the committee. The most recent member, Singer and Friedlander, joined in August 1973.

Slater Walker is not a member of the exclusive Accepting Houses Committee. The Walker was Peter Walker, subsequently the Conservative Secretary of State for the Department of Trade and Industry, but its architect has been Jim Slater, now head of the house. Slater's astonishing growth in the late 1960s and early 1970s has been built largely on share dealing and asset stripping. His success as a share dealer became largely self-generating. Once it was known he had bought a block of shares in a company their price tended to rise automatically. Asset stripping – buying sleepy companies, selling off their more valuable and underutilized assets – was usually not carried out by Slater himself, but by satellite companies, such as John Bentley's Barclay Securities or Christopher Selmes's Drakes Trust.*

Also not yet on the committee is Keyser Ullmann. Under the former chairman of the Conservative Party, Edward Du Cann, it grew at astonishing speed in 1972 by dint of a series of deals with other financial institutions. First the Prudential bought a 20 per cent stake in Keyser Ullmann. Next Keyser Ullmann took over the property firm of Central and District. And then it joined forces with Dalton Barton, a firm of West End financiers run by an ambitious and softspoken Mancunian, Jack Dellal. In December 1972 it diversified further, buying what was left of Bernie Cornfeld's British subsidiary, International Life Insurance.

The latest accepting house is Singer and Friedlander, owned by the insurance-broking group of C. T. Bowring. It is one of the few merchant banks to realize that there is more to Britain than the City: it specializes in services to medium-sized companies and has set up four provincial branches, each headed by a managing director or local director of the main bank. Robert Fleming, still a relatively small bank, has long specialized in portfolio management. Its first big venture into the rough and tumble of takeovers landed it in the middle of the Pergamon/Leasco affair as the advisers to Robert Maxwell. Still on the fringe of the merchant-banking world, but growing at a rate the accepting houses might envy, is First National Finance. Run by Pat Matthews, son of an East End antique-furniture reproducer, First National Finance has a substantial merchant and investment banking business. But its real success has been in lending to property developers and builders at steep rates of interest.

New 'merchant banks' are constantly sprouting. Some flourish.

* How asset stripping works is explained in chapter 5, pp. 126–7.

A very few will grow into the Rothschilds of tomorrow.*
Others will go bust . . . or end up in the Old Bailey.

The ancestry of the new merchant banks varies. Sometimes a
couple of merchant bankers, frustrated in one of the older firms,
get together and raise enough capital to start their own bank.
This was how Cripps Warburg began, founded by two ex-War-
burgs bankers, George Warburg (Siegmund's son) and Milo
Cripps, joined shortly afterwards by George Newell of First
National City Bank. It is backed by Williams and Glyn's. Others
start in the grey area between financing and merchant banking, or
are set up by companies outside banking which need a captive
banking subsidiary which can compete for deposits. Some are set
up by enterprising outsiders, often dealers in shares, who spot a
gap in the services provided by the older banks and set out to
plug it.

These smaller and newer merchant-banking operations can
continue to make an excellent living by specializing in services
which more established banks have not been providing ade-
quately. For a variety of reasons, the conventional merchant banks
do not want to copy them. They do not want to move into asset
stripping because it would damage their relationship with their
large industrial clients. They do not want to lend to the general
public, as this would mean hiring more staff and completely
changing the rationale of their operations.

So the larger merchant banks face a dilemma. Should they
continue to rely on their old recipe of offering advice on how to
find money, rather than providing it themselves? Or should they
concentrate on developing their banking activities? The first is
unlikely to offer them much prospect of growth. But if they
choose the second course, they find another problem: they are
too small to compete effectively.

To see why, one has to appreciate the need for size in wholesale banking. The existence of the money markets has made it

* Myth has it that Rothschilds' own prosperity had seamy origins. Nathan
Rothschild is supposed to have received advance information of the British
victory at Waterloo, gone to the Stock Exchange and sold stocks heavily. This
precipitated rumours of a British defeat, prices slumped, and Rothschild stepped
back into the market and made a killing.

possible for the merchant banks to compete with the branch banks, by providing merchant banks with an alternative, if expensive, source of deposits. But the money markets do not affect the size of the merchant banks' capital resources. Banks generally hold that it is ultimately the size of their capital base that determines how much they can safely borrow and lend. There is no hard-and-fast rule, but generally banks do not take in deposits more than twelve times their capital and reserves. So while the merchant banks have been able to enter the banking field on a substantial scale, they cannot hope to compete effectively with the clearing banks, particularly in sterling business where the clearing banks borrow over half their funds interest-free through current accounts.

In eurocurrency banking, the dice are not so heavily loaded against the merchant banks. They pay as much for funds as their competitors. All borrow on the eurocurrency market. But again the amount they can safely borrow and re-lend is limited by their capital and their reserves. Here they do not face the direct competition of the clearing banks; but ranged against them are the substantial forces of the British overseas banks, clearing-bank subsidiaries, consortium banks formed especially to tap the eurocurrency market and, most important of all, the American banks. This last group has one overwhelming advantage: a network of branches in the US to fall back on if the eurodollar market turns sour.

In the eurocurrency market, the merchant banks have tried to cope with their size problem in two ways. They have found partners among the American banks to form consortium banks. Thus Hambros joined with three American banks to form Western American. And they have developed the syndicated loan system, which means sharing out large loans among syndicates of banks.

Neither has been completely satisfactory. With the consortium banks, the merchant banks have generally been too small to put up most of the capital – or take most of the profits. Syndicated loans pose problems for the borrower, who has to wait until the loan has been syndicated to find out how much he will have to pay for his money. From the point of view of the merchant banks they have also been a disappointment. The real profits are to be made in organizing the syndicate, but the merchant banks have in general been less successful at that than the American and consortium banks. And because of their capital limitations, they can only take up relatively small shares.

Becoming big enough to compete with other money market banks is fraught with difficulties. But can the merchant banks rely on their other services to go on growing? Accepting and issuing, both once major merchant-banking activities, certainly no longer look like major growth areas.

Accepting is a way of providing a three-month loan by guaranteeing bills. The bill itself is like a postdated cheque. Instead of paying for goods immediately, the buyer gives the seller a bill of exchange which says that he will pay (usually) in three months' time. If the seller wants the money immediately, he swaps the bill for cash with a discount house. Since the discount house has to wait three months for the money, it gives him a little less than the face value of the bill, the difference being the interest on what is in effect a three-month loan.

In order to make a bill more attractive to the money market it may be taken to a merchant bank to be guaranteed or accepted. Then if the issuer of the bill goes bankrupt the merchant bank will buy it back. In return for guaranteeing the bill, the merchant bank charges a commission varying from 1 to 3 per cent depending on its judgement of the bill's soundness. A bill bearing a well-known British bank's guarantee not only qualifies for the finest rate of discount (i.e. the lowest interest charges) in the money market, but if held by a bank, it also counts towards its reserve assets, and if held by a discount house, it can be pledged against a loan from the Bank of England. (See next chapter.)

Acceptance business, which had virtually died out in the late 1950s, was revived in the 1960s because for a long time it escaped the restrictions imposed on other forms of credit. With the extension of credit ceilings to acceptances, this rapid expansion was checked. But there are ways in which it could grow in the future. The new bank controls of 1971 made accepted bills an extremely attractive asset for a bank to hold, as they now counted towards banks' reserve ratios. There have also been attempts to develop an acceptance business in eurocurrencies, but these have not been particularly successful.* Merchant bankers freely admit that the system of acceptance is preposterous. Why should ICI or Shell have to have a bill guaranteed by a bank it could buy up many times over for the bill to count as a reserve asset? The system would look less like a Victorian relic if the commission rates on acceptances were more widely differentiated. As it is, there is precious little spread between what a top blue-chip company has to pay for the privilege of having its bills accepted, and what a really dubious company† in serious danger of collapse has to pay.

Whatever enlightened merchant bankers think of acceptances, the Bank of England encourages them. And as long as it does so they are unlikely to lose popularity. Nor, however, are they ever likely to become more than a useful sideline.

Issuing business has also flourished in recent years. New issues in 1972 totalled £1,096 million, compared with £605 million in 1962.‡ This is one of the two main areas in which merchant banks' corporate finance departments operate (the other is mergers and takeovers) and might account for as much as a fifth of these departments' income. A bank making an issue may be floating a private company on the Stock Exchange for the first time or raising additional capital for an established public company. In either case the banks face competition from stockbrokers, who usually offer a cheaper service. The banks, however, have probably been increasing their share of this business. They claim to be able to offer companies better advice than the average new-issue broker.

Many industrialists harbour deep suspicions about the way merchant banks price issues. If an issue is priced too low it will

---

* The apparent failure of eurocurrency acceptances shows how superfluous a bank guarantee is on the short-term debts of reputable companies. A market in eurocurrency commercial paper (discussed in chapter 4), which needs no bank guarantee, emerged in 1970-1.

† Occasionally, as in the case of Rolls-Royce in early 1971, some merchant banks do not seem to be able to tell the difference between the two.

‡ Source: Midland Bank.

be oversubscribed and the borrower will be paying more than he needs to for his money. The bank is open to the charge that it has allowed the issue to be oversubscribed so that it can pocket the interest on funds left with it for a few days by disappointed applications. The truth is probably that the major merchant banks do try to price correctly. At least one provincial issuer ruined his business in the late 1960s by getting a reputation for consistent underpricing.

Businessmen also complain that merchant banks overcharge for making issues. The banks deny this, claiming that issuing is not particularly profitable. But since banks rarely publish a scale of fees, customers feel that they are charged on a basis of what the market (i.e. they themselves) will bear.

The banks claim that the problem with adopting a fixed scale of charges for any of their corporate finance work is that a large part of it is done free. A bank may groom a company for flotation for several years on the assumption that the fee it gets at the end will make it all worthwhile. But merchant banks themselves are confused. Singer and Friedlander, which specializes in medium-sized issues, found that it had to draw up a scale of fees for its internal use so that the ultimate fee charged bore some relation to the amount of money raised for a company.

The number of domestic new issues handled by merchant banks probably rose throughout the 1960s. But there were few really large (and therefore profitable) issues. The biggest growth area was in international new issues, in eurobonds. These are simply bonds denominated in eurocurrencies, issued by international companies and public utilities. Though British investors have been in effect barred from buying these by exchange control and British issues have been infrequent, both Rothschilds and Warburgs have built up substantial eurobond business.

It is, in short, hard to see either acceptance or issuing business as major profit earners in the 1970s. The merchant banks' revival since the war has been founded on the other main aspect of their corporate finance work, takeovers and mergers. This is where the banks' biggest profits were made in the 1950s and 1960s. The fee of £250,000 that Hill Samuel received for GEC/AEI is an example of the rates that prevail for handling large takeovers, while fees of £50,000 to £100,000 are quite usual for takeovers of £25 million or more. Hotly contested takeovers also command higher fees. There is a catch. The charge is for success, for few merchant banks would charge an established customer more than a nominal fee for a deal that failed to come off. Thus Lazard's and Williams and Glyn's waived the fees for the abortive merger between P and O and Bovis in 1972.

In takeover business the merchant banks now have no serious rivals.* Stockbrokers also handle new issues and other banks are involved in eurocurrency banking or accepting. But neither have shown willingness or ability to get into takeovers. There are several reasons. The clearing banks' main difficulty is in attracting the right people. This is partly because they do not pay enough, partly because of their monolithic organization and partly because they are not fun to work for. For the stockbrokers the problem is more that a company could hardly feel happy talking about its takeover plans with a firm whose *raison d'être* is advising people on what shares to buy. This conflict of interest also exists in the merchant bank, for banks act as investment advisers too. But reputable merchant banks make strenuous efforts to keep investment and corporate finance departments quite separate.

Profitable though takeovers and mergers have been, the post-war reorganization of British industry that generated them may be nearly over. The era of the great takeover battles, when a company would put in one bid after another, driving its prey's share price sky-high, is coming to a close. There is growing evidence to suggest that mergers actually reduce industrial efficiency.† Merchant bankers acknowledge that companies are becoming more ready to withdraw their bids if the share price moves too high. And that means no reward for the bankers.

Another possible outlet for takeover skills is the trans-national

* There are dangers in this. When Robert Fleming refused to continue as Pergamon's advisers in the Pergamon/Leasco merger, no leading merchant bank would take its place. Eventually William Brandts, owned by National and Grindlays, agreed to do so after the intervention of Grindlay's chairman, Lord Aldington, who felt it was wrong of the City to close ranks in this way.

† See chapter 5, p. 126.

merger, particularly within the enlarged Common Market. But so far such mergers have been few and far between.* There is another difficulty. Handling mergers in Europe, as in America, requires legal skills rather than market ones. In the US mergers and takeovers are heavily circumscribed by the Securities and Exchange Commission regulations. In Europe the complexities of several different sets of company legislation have much the same effect. Legal skills are something which the merchant banks have yet to build up.

All the merchant banks offer a range of other services besides these main activities and have specialized in one or more of them. Thus all big merchant banks manage other people's investment portfolios, advising pension funds, unit and investment trusts (and a few rich private individuals) where to put their money. For most this is a major profit-earner. But for Robert Fleming it is its bread and butter. Though Flemings employs only 170 people, in 1972 it managed over £1,500 million.

There are several important sidelines. Leasing and factoring were both growth areas in the second half of the 1960s. With leasing, a bank buys an aircraft, ship or piece of industrial equipment and rents it to the company that is going to use it. This has tax advantages. British Rail, for instance, plans to lease equipment worth £115 million, over a fifth of its investment programme, between 1971 and 1975 from a company backed by a group of City bankers. With factoring, a bank takes over the debts of a firm and gives it immediate cash, less a fee. And then there is what is known as venture capital – the investing of a merchant bank's own money in a small company with the hope of making large profits if the company grows successfully. Few of the merchant banks' venture-capital operations have in fact been particularly successful; some, such as Kleinwort Benson's adventure with Autonomics, have been disastrous.

* Memorandum on the Industrial Policy of the Community by the EEC Commission, 1970, which looked at 3,000 mergers in fifteen sectors of EEC industry between 1961 and 1969. Of these, 1,861 were mergers between two companies in the same country. 1,035 were between firms from outside the Community and firms from inside. Only 251 were mergers between companies in two different Common Market countries.

While these are the main activities of merchant banks they are by no means the only ones. Among the bigger banks it is possible to find houses engaged directly or through subsidiaries in commodity dealing, property development, computer data processing, foreign exchange dealing, metal merchanting, insurance broking and underwriting, bullion market broking and dealing, life assurance and oil exploration. This range is remarkable, particularly considering the size of a merchant bank's staff. Even Hambros, the biggest bank, only employs 1,200 people.

For both their banking and their non-financial services, the banks' main clients are industrial companies, British and foreign. Yet despite their dependence on industrial clients, the merchant banks have so far failed to conquer the suspicion with which many British industrialists regard them. It is extremely difficult to pinpoint the origins of this suspicion or to say whether it is justified. That it is so widespread, however, should be enough to worry the merchant banks.

What is it that British industry so dislikes? At one level it may simply be a manifestation of class hostility, an emotional dislike of confident and articulate young men. The banks' rapid expansion in the 1960s has forced them to give considerable responsibility to people in their twenties and early thirties. This has put them among the best places in the City for a clever graduate to find congenial and exciting work. But it has also meant that businessmen who have spent their lives building up their company find themselves being advised by men half their age with no practical experience in industry.

The banks' system of charging is probably adding to this hostility. A businessman, accustomed to controlling his costs, is understandably nervous of buying a service without knowing exactly what it will cost him.

But this could hardly explain it. One way this distrust is frequently expressed is in vague accusations that merchant banks 'don't really understand about industry'. This point was put with rather more sophistication by John Davies, then Secretary of State for Trade and Industry, at the twenty-fifth anniversary dinner of the Industrial and Commercial Finance Corporation (ICFC) in November 1970:

> But I would like to ask you tonight whether the City of London has sufficiently modernized its structure and its facilities to meet the present-day needs of industry. Is it fully ready to meet the increased responsibilities which will devolve upon it following the disengagement by Government from intervention in industry? . . . There are many institutions, for instance in France and Germany, which have now acquired most, if not all, the skills and expertise which you in the City of London have developed. But they have in some cases gone further – not just by learning each other's languages. They are prepared to acquire technical expertise to enable them to assess and advise on proposals for new investments put to them by industry.

Three criticisms of merchant banks' relationships with industry are commonly confused. There is first the feeling that banks ought to become more involved in industry by taking larger equity shares in companies. Then there is the belief that merchant bankers should take more part in running companies at board level, as bankers do in Germany through the advisory board system. And finally there are complaints that industry does not get the quality of financial counsel it needs from its merchant bankers.

British banks have not traditionally taken equity stakes in the companies they lend to. Their recent experience has not been happy. In the late 1960s there was a brief period when many merchant banks saw venture capital as the moneyspinner of the future. Some set up special departments to handle it, others separate subsidiaries. Montagu joined with Midland in Midland Montagu. Each bank tried out a different formula, the most usual one being to lend to small private companies planning to expand in return for a share of their equity. Bankers used to wax lyrical about it: 'We think of ourselves as making people's dreams come true.'

But the banks' venture-capital subsidiaries certainly did not make *their* dreams come true. They had hoped to better the record of Industrial and Commercial Finance Corporation, a company owned by the clearing banks which has been lending to small companies since the last war. Why did the merchant banks fail? There are a number of reasons. With the slow growth of the British economy in the 1960s there were only a limited number of suitable industrial situations for venture-capital operations. It may be, too, that the banks did not define clearly enough what they wanted to achieve with their venture-capital subsidiaries, and so did not set out to achieve it in the right way. ICFC has learnt over the years to work very closely with companies it invests in, and has branch offices all over the country with intimate knowledge of local business conditions. Among the major merchant banks, only Hill Samuel, Keyser Ullmann, Rothschilds, Singer and Friedlander and Samuel Montagu have more than one branch in the provinces.

Nor have the banks' attempts to involve themselves in industry by taking seats on the boards of companies they lend to been resoundingly successful. The banks have tended to move onto company boards only after they suspect that the company is in trouble. Having a banker on the board is by no means a sure recipe for recovery.

Banks' attempts to involve themselves directly in industry, either through buying equity shares or by sitting on company boards, have not notably improved industrial performance. But why should anyone expect banks to involve themselves directly in industry in these ways? In some continental countries, where banks are very much the main source of industrial finance, there may be a case for banks taking some part in industrial management. If Britain, in the Common Market, moves in this direction, then the case for more direct bank involvement may become stronger. But at present the only rationale for more direct bank involvement seems to be that Britain has an outstanding record in finance and a relatively poor one in industrial management: therefore why not involve financial experts more closely in management?

Easily the most serious criticism is the third one: that industry is not getting the financial discipline it needs because banks do not know how to give it. There are a growing number of instances where merchant banks have lost money to companies whose weaknesses should have been apparent to anyone who had made a careful study of their accounts. Part of the banks' problem is that they simply do not have the staff available to scrutinize the companies to which they lend, or for which they raise capital.

Staff shortage is only part of the problem. There is also a question of attitude. The merchant banks have not yet thought out where their responsibility as providers of finance ends. By and large they see their role as finding the borrower his funds in the cheapest way: they are retained by a firm and their duty is towards it. What the firm does thereafter (or even whether it should get the money in the first place) is not the merchant banker's business.

This attitude, born of years of advising people on where to find money rather than actually stumping up their own funds, is becoming less appropriate as the banks move from providing financial services for industry to lending to companies on a growing scale. The dangers of this attitude are compounded by the tendency of other City banking sectors – notably the clearing banks – to rely on the merchant banks' judgement of companies' creditworthiness. And it will become still less appropriate if the merchant banks expand their equity interests in industry.

BRITISH OVERSEAS BANKS

The British overseas banks are a relic of the empire. A century ago banks with such exotic names as the Ionian, the Ottoman and the Hongkong and Shanghai ran branch networks in the countries of the Empire and its allies, and financed trade between them and Britain. Then, as emerging nations either nationalized their branches (as in Egypt or Tanzania) or took a controlling interest in them (as in Zambia or Libya), the overseas banks were forced to look elsewhere. Today most have either disappeared or become transformed. Thus the Ottoman Bank has been split up; its branches in Turkey were conceded to the Turkish government, the rest to other banks. Ionian Bank no longer has any interests in Greece and is a small London merchant bank. Hong-kong and Shanghai has transferred its headquarters from London to Hong Kong (not Shanghai), where its business is centred. Only a handful have lived to carry on anything like their original overseas bank business, and these have survived partly because they have forged links with clearing banks, which have used them as ready made overseas branch networks, and partly because they have moved into the eurodollar market, reorientating themselves towards London.

There are a few exceptions, such as the Australia and New Zealand Bank and the National Bank of New Zealand, both of which still run their networks in Australasia from London head offices. These banks have not been forced to diversify into euro-currency business because of the greater political stability of the areas where they operate. But given their lack of interest in the eurodollar market, it is hardly logical for them to keep head offices 12,000 miles away from their branch networks.

The rump that can still fairly be described as British overseas banks is made up of four main groups: Barclays Bank International (formed in 1971 when Barclays Bank took complete control of Barclays DCO); Lloyds and Bolsa International (also formed in 1971 when Lloyds Bank Europe was merged with Bank of London and South America, and now owned by Lloyds); National and Grindlays (which is independent, but in which Lloyds also has a large interest); and Standard and Chartered Group, formed in 1970 by the merger of Standard Bank and Chartered Bank (which remains independent of other groups).

Each of these groups has retained an extensive overseas branch network in the countries in which it originally specialized. Thus Barclays has branches in Africa – particularly in South Africa – and the Caribbean. LBI retains Bolsa's network in South America, as well as a handful of branches in fashionable European towns originally set up by Lloyds for its wealthy customers. National and Grindlays still specializes in India and Pakistan and has some branches in east and central Africa. Standard and Chartered combines Standard's branches throughout Africa with Chartered's Far Eastern network.

On the face of it these far-flung branch networks look like an ideal springboard for international corporate banking. The American bank with the most extensive network, First National City, of New York, has a mere 300 or so offices overseas, counting those banks in which it has a majority stake. The British overseas bank with the most extensive network, Standard and Chartered, has over 1,360 branches.

But these branches tend to be in the 'wrong' places: mainly slow-growing, politically unstable developing countries. Even where they are in the 'right' places they are geared to provide local retail banking and trade finance. The banks have been slow to convert them to provide the sophisticated industrial banking services required by international business. These branches provide a declining proportion of the banks' profits. In the case of National and Grindlays the proportion of profits generated in London rose from 35 per cent in 1965 to 55 per cent in 1971.

As profits from overseas branch networks have dwindled they have been replaced by profits earned in London by borrowing on the eurodollar market to finance foreign trade and overseas investment projects. The discovery of the eurodollar market has been the salvation of the overseas banks, providing them with an independent source of funds. The early development of the eurodollar market was to a large extent the work of Bolsa and in particular of its former chairman, Sir George Bolton.

Eurodollars, however, are not an ideal substitute for retail deposits. Not only do they cost more, but rates are much more volatile. So the overseas banks were forced to look for financial support from other sources. At the same time the clearing banks, whose own efforts to build up networks of overseas branches had been unimpressive, began to look for ways of offering their customers international connections: hence the close links with clearing banks.

Of the four groups, Barclays Bank International now boasts the best-distributed branch network: it has a chain of retail branches in California which alone puts it among the top 500 American banks and, taking advantage of the fact that only foreign banks can open branches in more than one US state, it is spreading into New York and Massachussetts.

Lloyds is now in the incongruous position of having an interest in two overseas banking groups. In the middle of 1973, it bought full control of Lloyds and Bolsa International, in which Mellon National Bank of Pittsburgh is the other main shareholder. But it also has a stake in National and Grindlays. Lloyds owns 41 per cent of a holding company which in turn controls 60 per cent of the bank, the other 40 per cent being owned by First National City Bank, of New York. Lloyds denies that this is an illogical situation, although the two groups compete in the money markets and First National City Bank is LBI's main competitor in South America. Most people in the City assume that sooner or later Lloyds will either sell out its interest in National and Grindlays, or buy full control.

The only overseas bank independent of the clearers is Standard and Chartered. It has a branch network which rivals that of Barclays International. It is the least integrated of all the overseas banking groups, formed, as both banks admitted at the time, to fend off any possible bid from a clearing bank. Three years after the merger, Chartered and Standard were still operating from separate offices at different ends of the City, running some competing money market departments, with most of their branches still operating under their original names.

If you confront directors with the slowness of integration they nod politely in agreement and top up your glass. In 1973 the group was led by Sir Cyril Hawker, an energetic septuagenarian, previously chairman of Standard, with George Pullen, chairman of Chartered, as deputy chairman. Sooner or later the group will have to be pulled into one unit.

What will become of the British overseas banks? It has yet to be demonstrated that a bank can survive as an independent money market bank, that is, without some source of deposits other than the money markets. So despite the growing proportion of these banks' profits coming from eurocurrency business it is unlikely that they can be viable as independent units. But then (with the exception of Standard and Chartered) they are not independent now. It seems inevitable that they will be completely swallowed up into other commercial banking groups. What is not yet clear is the role these banks will play within the larger groupings. Perhaps the best hope for them is that they will develop into international merchant banks. In several countries they have been able to maintain control of their merchant-banking operations despite losing their commercial business. This would fit in well with the banks' skills and their access to the money market.

CLEARING-BANK SUBSIDIARIES AND FINANCE HOUSES

Clearing banks are involved in money market banking in three ways. First, there are Barclays' and Lloyds' links with the British overseas banks, just described. Secondly, most of the clearing banks began, after new credit controls were introduced in late 1971, to do some money market banking themselves. But the bulk of their operations is still carried on through their hire-purchase and money market subsidiaries. In the fifteen years before the publication of *Competition and Credit Control* the clearing banks were apt to hand any new or exciting activity over to a separate subsidiary.* The first example of this was in the 1950s, when the banks watched a whole range of hire-purchase companies spring up and corner the market for consumer lending and then, just as the consumer boom was fading, hurriedly bought into these various finance houses. In the 1960s the banks made the same mistake. They sat back and watched the mushroom growth of money market banking. Eventually they began to participate in the new markets, either by setting up new subsidiaries (as did Midland with the Midland Bank Finance Corporation) or by transforming existing ones (as Lloyds did with Lloyds Bank Europe). Sadly, by the time their

* Had they any choice? The answer depends on whether one believes that the clearing banks – not the authorities – were mainly responsible for the continuance of the cartel (see chapter 2). Given the cartel, setting up subsidiaries, subject neither to rate controls nor, initially, to lending ceilings, was the only way the clearing banks could compete with the hire purchase companies and money market banks. It was the cartel itself that brought these into existence.

subsidiaries had begun to participate fully, lending ceilings were being imposed on the wholesale banks. A latecomer, like the Midland Bank Finance Corporation, found it was only allowed to lend £5 million to the private sector.

The structure of the clearing-bank subsidiaries still reflects these origins. There is a set of finance houses or hire purchase companies, mostly acquired in the late 1950s, and a set of money market subsidiaries acquired or developed during the late 1960s.*

Barclays has no hire purchase subsidiaries proper. Until 1972 it had a 28 per cent holding in United Dominions Trust, the largest finance house, but this was sold when UDT became a bank itself. Barclays kept a small interest in Mercantile Credit but was, in autumn 1973, trying to sell this. Its main money market subsidiary is Barclays Bank (London and International).

National Westminster's finance-house group is Lombard North Central. Its money market business is done mainly by two subsidiaries: International Westminster (which also runs a small branch network in Europe) and County Bank (which also does merchant-banking business). This split creates problems: it means that County does not normally do eurocurrency lending because that is carried out by International Westminster. Forced out of eurocurrency banking County has had to build its reputation on merchant-banking business. It has not yet shone.

Lloyds formed a sterling money market subsidiary, Lloyds Associated Banking Company, in 1970 and in late 1972 proclaimed that it would build this into a full-scale merchant bank.

The justification for separate clearing-bank subsidiaries to carry on hire purchase and money market business died in 1971 with the introduction of the Bank of England's new credit controls. During 1972 the clearing banks took the first timid steps to merge subsidiaries with parent banks – or sell them.

---

* The hire purchase subsidiaries borrow their deposits directly from companies, or on the money markets, or occasionally from a handful of retail branches. They lend them to individuals as personal loans or to finance hire purchase deals, and to companies as term loans, or to finance plant and equipment bought on instalment credit. The money market subsidiaries raise their money on the money markets or by borrowing from their parent banks' company customers. They lend it to local authorities and to industry as term loans.

Several finance houses are not owned by banks, and some of them have obtained bank status including United Dominions Trust, Mercantile Credit, First National Finance Corporation, Julian S. Hodge and Co. and Lombard North Central. UDT and FNFC in particular are trying to build up their retail banking business.

FOREIGN BANKS IN LONDON

Half of Britain's invisible earnings from banking are generated by the 200-odd foreign banks in London. They employ over 10,000 people and their number has more than doubled since 1960. They range in size from First National City Bank, of New York, with nearly 1,000 staff in its London offices, to a representative office of the Bulgarian Foreign Trade Bank, run by a Mr Dimeter Kalinov and his secretary. There are so many US banks round about the Bank of England that Moorgate has been nicknamed 'Avenue of the Americas'. The Japanese are the next largest group, with virtually all the major banks having branches. The Communist bloc is well represented: Moscow Narodny has 250 staff here and Bank of China over 100. The last major industrial country to open full branches in London is Germany. These were closed down in 1914 and for years only a few representative offices were subsequently reopened, although in 1973 Deutsche Bank, Dresdner Bank and Westdeutsche Landesbank Girozentrale all opened branches in London.

These banks have come to London for a number of reasons. Sometimes it is purely prestige. But most are doing one or more of three things: they are financing international trade; they are providing an information and liaison service; or – and this is where most of their invisible earnings are generated – they are carrying out international money market banking business, typically financing US corporations in Europe. Lastly, with the introduction of the new banking controls in 1971 some foreign banks are beginning to build up their UK domestic banking business.

The importance of each type of business varies from bank to

bank. Where there is just a representative office, it will simply give information to potential customers. Its main job will be to generate business for its parent bank. The London branches of the banks of developing commodity-producing countries, such as the Ghana Commercial Bank, are mainly concerned with financing commodity trade. For the banks from developed countries, international money market business is the most important. US banks may be borrowing eurodollars to increase the deposits of their parent banks, or to re-lend to international companies. The Brazilians may be borrowing to finance industrial development in Japan . . . and Swiss banks may be lending the (possibly illgotten) gains of their anonymous clients.

Easily the largest single contingent of foreign banks is the American. There are some fifty US banks, accounting for three-quarters of the deposits of foreign banks in London and generating foreign earnings of around £50 million a year.* A few have been in London since the 1920s, but the real onslaught did not begin until the 1968 squeeze in the American economy, when US banks began to borrow eurodollars on a massive scale to supplement their loanable funds at home. These banks have already had a tremendous impact, both on the development of the eurodollar market in London and on British banking practices.

It is largely because of the investment that the American banks have made in London that the eurodollar market has stayed here. They have brought to the market a number of American banking techniques. The most important is the term loan: in euro-currency British banks follow the US practice of making loans for a specific period rather than extending an overdraft.

With the new banking controls of 1971 American banks were beginning to compete not only in the international money markets, but in areas where British banks had long had a domestic monopoly. The merchant banks are facing an American challenge in their provision of company services; the clearing banks are finding a few American competitors opening retail branches of their own and touring the country, recruiting industrial clients.

* See footnote, p. 47.

'EUROBANKS'

The crucial influence that the new foreign banks in London are having on the City is in the formation of an entirely new kind of bank. For want of an accepted term, these could be called 'euro-banks'. By late 1973 there were some thirty of them in the world, of which three-quarters were in London. They are already proving the main innovatory force in international banking in the 1970s. These banks rely solely and exclusively on the euro-currency markets for their funds. However, they have the capital backing of one or more giant banking groups, which means that they can put together bigger loan packages for longer periods than any other type of commercial bank in the world.

Often these banks are formed by a consortium of other banks, usually from several countries. For example Western American was set up by three American banks and Hambros; Midland and International Banks, the oldest and largest (by total assets), was formed by Midland Bank, Toronto Dominion, Standard Bank and Commercial Bank of Australia; and Orion was created by National Westminster, joining with Chase Manhattan, West-deutsche Landesbank Girozentrale and Royal Bank of Canada, later joined by Credito Italiano and Mitsubishi. Often one bank has set up a eurobank as a specialist subsidiary to carry out this kind of business: among others Bankers Trust, Manufacturers Hanover and Marine Midland control eurobank subsidiaries.

The larger of these eurobanks can lend $30 or $40 million off its own back. But usually loans are syndicated. The bank that is organizing the loan, called the 'lead' bank, contacts up to fifty other banks, inviting them to participate. The lead bank may carry a large part of the loan itself. The rate will usually be tied to the six-month eurodollar rate, and the loan will generally be for three to ten years. The sums involved are enormous. The largest eurocurrency loans to date, late 1973, were three of $1,000 million each, including one to the UK Electricity Council.

What is most impressive of all about the new eurobanks is that the first consortium banks for medium-term lending were only conceived of as recently as 1967. Now most of them are beginning to wonder whether carrying out a narrow banking function is enough, or whether they should be offering an international merchant-banking service, raising and managing funds for giant international companies in a host of different countries.

Many bankers are convinced that the future of banking lies in this kind of multinational venture. If companies are to become more international, the argument runs, then so must banks. They therefore see these eurobanks developing into international wholesale banks, offering both longer-term loans on a massive scale and other banking services, company advice and so on. At present, it looks as though this is where the biggest growth area in international banking will lie.

Will these international money market giants continue to base themselves in London? The growth of money market banking in London has so far been dominated by the American banks. The British banks in the field are either too small to compete with the Americans on an equal footing or are tied in one way or another to the clearing banks, which have yet to demonstrate a real aptitude for anything other than the day-to-day business of retail banking. Until the merchant banks find ways of increasing their capital and coping with the problems of size, and until the clearing banks organize themselves to operate an efficient international banking service, London's future as the leading international banking centre remains insecure.

At some time the American banks might easily decide that they could deal in eurocurrency markets more conveniently from some other capital. Although other markets have sprung up in centres like Frankfurt and Singapore, nobody seriously believes that the American banks would yet prefer to site the bulk of their eurocurrency operations there rather than in Moorgate. But what if they could operate from New York? The parent American bank could then control its lending direct. In mid-1972 there were the first signs of what might become just such a movement: a eurodollar market was developing in New York. And early in 1973 the US announced that it intended to lift some of the regulations – such as Interest Equalization Tax – that had stimulated the growth of the market in the 1960s.

4

The money and foreign
exchange markets

Money markets thrive on adversity. Nothing seems to stimulate them more than government regulations, cartels and restrictive agreements designed to keep them under control. For money markets are mechanisms through which money is channelled from lenders to borrowers. Try to dam the flow . . . and it trickles round another way. Thus the tremendous growth both of sterling and of international money markets in the 1960s was, to a large extent, encouraged by the attempts of the British and other governments to keep the lenders and borrowers apart.

Abstruse though they sound, money markets do quite a simple job. But before looking at what they do and how they do it, it is important to understand their structure. Until the end of the 1950s, there was really only one kind of money market in the City: the discount market, run by the discount houses, and closely controlled by the Bank of England. During the 1960s, a whole new group of money markets sprang up, the so-called parallel markets. These are commonly divided into two groups, depending on whether they deal in sterling or eurocurrencies. The sterling parallel markets include the local authority, the sterling inter-bank, the finance houses, the certificate of deposit (or CD) and the intercompany markets. Some of them evolved to escape the regulations and cartels by which the discount market was trammelled. The eurocurrency markets, for which London is the main dealing centre, grew up to dodge attempts of national governments to keep lenders and borrowers apart. These parallel markets are run by money brokers. The main customers of the discount market are the clearing banks, and the main customers of the parallel market the non-clearing banks described in the last chapter.

Thus the split between the two types of money market corresponds to the split between branch banking and money market banking. By the time the new Bank of England credit controls in 1971 rendered both splits illogical, the two types of market were already beginning to merge. Now the demarcation line has become blurred. What happens to interest rates or to the volume of borrowing and lending in any one market ultimately affects all the others. And the distinction between institutions in each market is fading: discount houses are buying money brokers, clearing banks are dealing directly in parallel markets. But the demarcation line was still clear enough in 1973 for this chapter to follow it. The chapter also describes another type of market, the foreign exchange market. This is not strictly a money market, but is operated by some of the firms of brokers who run the parallel markets, and was the origin of the techniques used in them. Together these markets are the lynchpin of London's banking business.

There are about 1,500 people in London who spend their day buying and selling money. About half of these work for 250 banks and finance companies, and the rest for the discount houses and money and foreign exchange brokers. To the outsider it may sound odd to talk about buying and selling money. But when a banker talks about 'money', he means specifically money borrowed for a very short period. So if he talks about 'buying overnight money', he means borrowing it (or buying the use of it) till tomorrow. The price is the interest. So in a money market, people borrow and lend money for relatively short periods.

The actual sums involved look enormous. The usual unit for deals between banks is £250,000. However, provided one does not want the money for long it is surprisingly cheap: £1 million, borrowed overnight (the shortest possible period) at 8 per cent costs less than a good electric typewriter – £219·18. To borrow overnight is by no means unusual: most of the funds on the London money market are borrowed for less than a week.

But what can you do with £1 million till tomorrow? The money markets use this very short-term money to do two jobs. First, they lend it to the banks to help them balance their books at the end of each day. If a bank finds it is a bit short, it goes to the market and borrows enough to tide it over. If it finds that it has spare cash, it makes a profit by lending it on the market.

Though very short-term money is useful to a bank, it is not much use to anyone else. So the second function of a money market is converting it into longer-term money that can be used by industry and the government.

This conjuring trick is done in a different way by the discount market and the parallel markets. In the discount market, it is the discount houses themselves that convert this short-term money into longer-term loans. The discount houses borrow the spare cash of the banks, mostly 'at call' which means that the banks can have it back whenever they want it. The houses then lend it to the government and to companies, usually for three months.

In the parallel markets, the trick is done by the banks. But they can only do it because they have the parallel markets to fall back on. In parallel market banking the banks borrow from financial institutions, such as pension funds, and industrial companies, usually for fixed periods of anything from a month to several years. They may borrow directly, or through the money market. They lend to company customers or to local authorities, for rather longer periods. Thus a bank may lend for five years to one company and keep borrowing six-month money from the market to finance the loan. As long as it can borrow short-term from the market, it can safely go on lending for these longer periods.

To look at, the parallel markets are more lively and successful than the discount market. The people who run them reflect the difference. Although the atmosphere is now changing, discount house men are a dignified breed who work some of the shortest hours in the City and who still enjoy the daily rite of putting on a silk top hat to call on the clearing banks and the Bank of England. Despite this genteel atmosphere the discount men are, like everyone else in the City's money markets, doing much the same job as a bookie.* The dealers in the money-broking firms which run the parallel markets actually look like bookies. They are younger men, rarely from old City families. They spend their days in front of a switchboard, shouting prices into telephones. In contrast to the all-male hierarchy of the discount offices, some of the dealers and several of the directors in money-broking firms are women.

In the 1960s, the sleepy atmosphere of the discount houses was reflected in the stagnation of their business. Throughout the decade their total assets only crept upwards. The discount houses' stock-in-trade, their business with the clearing banks, barely grew. Meanwhile the growth of the parallel markets and the money brokers was dramatic. The sterling parallel markets started from scratch and overtook the discount market, while the parallel market in foreign currencies, the eurodollar market, became the largest international money market the world has ever known. But it is wrong to attribute the faster growth of the parallel markets wholly to the fact that they are run by more aggressive people. Until 1971 they had the crucial advantage of being free from the controls, described below, that hampered the discount houses.

By the early 1970s the discount houses had woken up and moved into the parallel markets. The two markets began to merge, a process taken further by the introduction of the new system of credit controls. For both the discount houses and the money brokers, this breakdown of the old demarcations makes the future look uncertain. The discount houses have found their

* More accurately, they are like bad bookies in that they take a view on the market, rather than trying to balance their books.

profits decimated in the new competitive atmosphere. And the money brokers are wondering whether the explosive growth of the parallel markets will continue, now that the restrictions under which they were born have been removed; and whether another new market will spring up the next time the Bank tries to keep borrowers and lenders apart.

THE DISCOUNT MARKET

A discount house's day nowadays begins at about 9.00 when the CD dealers start. The traditional bill business gets under way at 9.30 with calls, usually by telephone, from the banks who have placed money with it 'at call' and now want it back. By mid-morning a large house might find that it needs £20 million if its borrowings are to cover its investments by the end of the day. During the morning, half a dozen of its men put on their top hats and stroll round to the money departments of the four main clearing banks and some of the other banks with which it does business, to find out whether they expect to call back even more of their funds – they have to do so by noon – or whether they expect to be able to lend substantial amounts back to the discount houses. Quite junior men in the house may go on these rounds, and the conversation is as likely to be about cricket and the laziness of British workmen as about the bank's requirement. Still, the tradition survives largely because everybody seems to like it.

Meanwhile some of the house's directors will be looking at its investment position, perhaps wondering whether the price of government bonds is about to fall and whether it would be safer to switch into shorter-dated gilts. Around midday a senior man from the tiny house of Seccombe, Marshall and Campion* will ring up each house to sound out its position and to discover whether it is likely to be short of money later in the day. Seccombes acts as 'special buyer' and its chairman, Hugh Seccombe, is the Bank's link with the market.

Lunch for the partners will be a lengthy and high-calorie affair,

* See chapter 8, p. 201.

with a couple of guests, usually bankers. Afterwards the banks will be evening up their balances and the house should find money flowing in as the banks lend it their spare cash. If by mid-afternoon, however, it is clear that the house is not going to be able to borrow enough from the banks to make its books balance, Seccombes will tell it what the Bank wants the market to do. Usually the house will be allowed to sell Treasury bills to Seccombes; but if the Bank wants to squeeze credit it may be forced to borrow either from the clearing banks (with which it has agreed overdraft limits), or even more expensively from the Bank of England itself.

This help from the Bank is the discount houses' most important privilege. It puts them in a unique position. It allows them to perform their conjuring trick of borrowing money at call – for a short period of uncertain length – and investing it for three months and longer.

Sometimes, of course, the discount houses' conjuring trick goes wrong. It only fails if they misjudge the trend of interest rates and hence the value of their investments. It failed for National in the late 1960s when the value of its portfolio of government bonds plummeted. It was made very difficult for all the houses after 1971, when they have suffered from the fluctuations, in gilt prices, resulting from the Bank's new policy of non-intervention in the gilt-edged market. But a major reason why the discount houses can borrow amounts which in terms of their capital bases look dangerously large is that they know that one way or another the Bank of England will see that they do not go bankrupt.*

There was a long period in the 1960s when the discount houses found themselves rather in the doldrums. Their special relationship with the Bank was not an unmixed blessing: one reason why the houses took so long to move into the parallel markets was because they were afraid the Bank might not like it.

But the special relationship was not the primary reason for the

* Anyone who thinks of the panic that followed the collapse of the discount house of Overend, Gurney and Co. in 1866 will understand the Bank's reasons (see chapter 1, p. 8).

houses' slow growth. More important were a couple of restrictive agreements between the houses and the clearing banks, legacies of the 1930s era of cheap money. Under these agreements, the banks agreed to lend the houses a certain proportion of their funds as 'basic' money at a very low rate of interest. In return the discount houses agreed not to compete with the clearers for commercial funds by offering higher rates of interest than the banks charged under their cartel. This meant that the discount houses enjoyed a substantial source of cheap funds. But for reasons explained below, they could not offer high enough rates to attract deposits from the faster-growing non-clearers, and their funds rose only slowly.

Then in 1971 these restrictive agreements were swept away in the new credit controls. With these the Bank conferred on the discount houses yet another special privilege. Money that the banks lent to the discount houses at call was to count as part of the banks' reserve assets.* This was sure to be a strong incentive for the banks – clearers and non-clearers alike – to place spare funds with the discount houses rather than on the parallel markets.

The chief beneficiaries of this revival are the twelve members of the London Discount Market Association, by whom most discount market dealing is carried out. They vary in size from Union Discount, which had balance-sheet totals of £542 million at the end of 1972 and accounts for rather under one-third of the business of the market, to Seccombe, Marshall and Campion with a 1973 balance sheet of £69 million. All discount houses, however, have certain things in common. They are all small, intimate firms, dealing in enormous sums of money. Even Union only employs about seventy people excluding the staff of its broker subsidiary, but its balance sheet would make it about as big as a medium-sized bank.

Union lives in a gloomy, wood-panelled office in Cornhill. It is rather like General Motors in the US: it has so much of the market that to increase its share would be embarrassing. It has suffered from a long run of non-executive directors, while its

* See chapter 8, p. 210.

chairmen have traditionally been installed by its chief customers, the clearing banks. The last one was Eric Faulkner, now chairman of Lloyds, while its present chairman, Alexander Ritchie, is a full-time executive director of Williams and Glyn's. Under his leadership, however, Union has been transformed. Several Union managers have been made directors, and it is now possible to get a board-level decision in less than a fortnight.

National Discount, though one of the largest houses, was the sick man of the market all through the 1960s. After its disastrous experience with its bond portfolio it was rescued by Gerrard and Reid in 1969. The new company, Gerrard and National, comes a close second to Union in size. With its main driving force, the jovial and rubicund Kenneth Whitaker, JP, Gerrard has been the discount market's big post-war success. It also gives one of the best lunches in the City.

Alexanders, the oldest, is a rather conventional house: for example it has not ventured into money brokerage. It had until 1972 an excellent profit record and its managing director, Ivan Smith, has a reputation for being one of the market's most competent technicians. Allen Harvey and Ross has young directors, and is one of the very few discount houses with an all-executive board. It has been the maverick of the discount world. If the market experiments with a new type of business, Allen Harvey is frequently the pioneer. It threw itself into trading in certificates of deposit, now one of the market's great success stories, at a time when most other houses were still hesitating.

Cater Ryder tried to take further than the other discount houses the idea that its job was to provide bank customers with a complete range of money market services. At one stage it had under one roof not only its discount market operations but dealers in all the parallel markets and in foreign exchange. It found, however, that it could not make this mix work. By 1972 the broking and discount divisions had once again separated.

Smith, St Aubyn is about the same size as Cater. Its members have the reputation of being gifted amateurs and it owes a lot to its portly chairman Duncan Mackinnon. Clive Discount was the first house to be taken over by an outside company. Until it was bought by Sime Darby in 1972 it had a patchy profit record, but had made money out of its broker subsidiaries.

Gillett, to the outsider, is the crustiest, most hidebound house in the City. But until 1973 it had maintained a fine profit record. In 1971 it bought up the Kirkland Whittaker group of money brokers, a new group with a young and aggressive staff.

A smaller up-and-coming house is Jessel Toynbee. Apart from its 40 per cent stake in Charles Fulton, one of the largest of the money brokers, it is a rather conservative house, with a solid profit record until the disasters of 1973.

About the same size is King and Shaxson, another conservative house. It did however have the distinction of starting the first gilt-edged unit trust.

Easily the smallest independent house, in terms of 1972 balance-sheet totals, was Seccombe, Marshall and Campion. Besides being 'special buyer' to the market, it carries out some ordinary business.

Finally, Norman and Bennet became the twelfth member of the market in 1972. With Clive, it is the only member of the market to be controlled by an outsider, Wood Hall Trust.

Apart from the discount houses proper three other types of institution carry out money market business: the two discount brokers (sometimes called running brokers); the 'money trading banks'; and what are confusingly called the 'money brokers'. The first are 'junior' discount houses (this is how Gerrard and Reid and Norman and Bennet started); the second an assortment of wholesale banks that have traditionally carried out part of the business undertaken by discount houses, namely dealing in short-term securities; and the third, six firms of stockbrokers (not money brokers at all) that use money borrowed from banks to trade in gilts and so can smooth out gilt trading. The first of these institutions have limited rediscount privileges at the Bank. The others do not.

All these discount houses borrow the bulk of their money from banks, mainly from clearing banks. A small amount, which the houses would like to see grow, is borrowed from companies. They borrow almost all of it at call, and re-lend by investing in five main types of longer-term debt: commercial bills, Treasury bills, government stocks, local authority bonds and certificates of deposit. These investments are usually offered by the houses to the banks as security for their loans. The mix of investments varies from house to house, but all houses are required by the Bank of England to limit the amount of their funds they keep in non-public sector debt.

Commercial bills were the discount market's main asset during the nineteenth century. In the 1960s they again became important, as restrictions on clearing-bank lending forced companies to make greater use of commercial bill finance. The last chapter explained how bills were guaranteed or 'accepted' by merchant banks. There are two kinds of commercial bill: those that have been guaranteed by a bank (bank bills or bank paper) and those that have not (trade bills). Bank bills can be either 'eligible', which means they have been accepted by a substantial British bank and that the Bank of England will lend cash to the discount houses against them* or they may be non-eligible, which means they have been guaranteed by a smaller British bank or by a foreign bank. However reputable the foreign bank, the Bank of England xenophobically refuses to lend against the bills they have accepted.

Treasury bills are similar to commercial bills in that they are also three-month loans: but with Treasury bills the borrower is the government. As with eligible bank bills the Bank will lend cash against them.

The discount houses buy their Treasury bills through a ritual called the tender. Every Friday the Bank of England offers a batch of Treasury bills to banks, discount houses and government departments. The amount varies, but a typical offer would be £150 million. The discount houses always bid for more bills than have been offered, and this is the key part of the tender. It means that whatever happens the government knows that it can always sell all its bills. This, more than anything else, is why the Bank grants the discount houses their special privileges. An odd feature

---

* In the textbooks these bills are described as 'eligible for rediscount' at the Bank. This means that they can actually be swapped for cash at the Bank. In practice the Bank almost invariably lends against the security of the bills.

of the ritual is that the clearing banks rarely tender for bills. They usually buy them all from the discount houses.

Discount houses also lend to the government by buying government bonds. It is here that they make their big profits or – as in 1972 and 1973 – big losses. Because they are longer-term securities, the prices of government bonds tend to fluctuate more than those of other discount market assets. Since the government decided to stop supporting the gilt-edged market, these fluctuations have become still wider and the houses' investments in bonds a more speculative component of their portfolios. A discount house that gets its bond portfolio right can make far more money on it than on all its other operations put together.

The last two types of security – local authority bonds and certificates of deposit – have provided the discount houses with a way into parallel market business. When the parallel markets grew up in the early 1960s the discount houses found that they could not offer sufficiently high rates to keep the bulk of their non-clearing-bank funds. This was because the interest on the things they put their money into – the types of security described above – was almost always lower than the 'free' market interest rates. They therefore had to look for a security that would offer higher rates. Local authority bonds (often called 'yearling bonds' because they were originally issued for a year) were the first. They have not been particularly successful, because the local authority parallel market, described later, is more convenient both for borrower and lender.

Sterling CDs, by contrast, have been enormously successful, and are the discount market's fastest-growing asset. They work like this. A large company has £250,000 spare on which it wants to get the highest possible rate of interest. It thinks that it will not need the money for a year and since it can earn a higher rate the longer it lends it, it puts it on deposit with a bank for the whole year. But it is possible that it might need the money earlier. So when it puts the money on deposit it gets a certificate of that deposit in return. This says that £250,000 has been left at such and such a bank at a certain rate of interest until a date one year hence. If the company needs its money earlier it takes the certificate along not to the bank (which has by now lent the money to someone else and so does not want to repay it) but to a discount house. The discount house buys the CD at the going market price, thus providing what is called a secondary, or trading market in CDs. The money it uses to buy the CD is – as with all discount-house money – borrowed at call from the banks. The conjuring trick has worked again: the company can get its money whenever it wants . . . and the bank knows it has it for a year. In fact the CD has turned out to be so convenient that banks use it between themselves. What happens then is that one bank issues a CD to another. If the second bank wants its money back it takes the CD to the discount market. If banks want to lend to each other for short periods they do so on the inter-bank market, but they tend to use CDs for longer periods.

CDs have given the discount houses their most important direct way into parallel market business. But the discount houses operate in the CD market in a different way from the money brokers. Whereas the money brokers simply match would-be sellers with would-be buyers, the discount houses buy and sell CDs as investments. More important, when CDs were first issued the houses agreed to act as 'market makers' in them. This means that they will always quote a price at which they are prepared to buy or sell CDs. That the discount houses are prepared to perform this jobbing role in CDs has given the fastest growing of all the sterling parallel markets a vital element of interest-rate stability.

Finally the discount houses carry out a small but growing amount of foreign currency business. They do the same job in the dollar CD market as in the sterling market, and they discount bills of exchange denominated in foreign currencies.

Discount houses are virtually unknown outside London. No other major financial centre bothers with them. Are they really necessary, or are they just an expensive eccentricity kept alive by their special relationship with the Bank of England? Certainly from the Bank of England's point of view they are useful. Quite apart from holding substantial sums of public debt, they provide a channel through which money can be pumped into the banking system quickly, or syphoned off.* If one accepts the principle of a money market, that it is useful to employ short-term funds that would otherwise be lying idle, then a discount market provides a valuable service. In other centres it is carried out by the banks. In 1959 the Radcliffe report on the Working of the Monetary System concluded its analysis of the discount houses' business by saying, 'It would not be beyond human ingenuity to replace the work of the discount houses; but they are there, they are doing the work effectively, and they are doing it at a trifling cost in terms of labour and other real resources.'

The houses, were still there at the end of 1973, but their future looked much less secure. Trying to run a bond portfolio in a time of steeply rising interest rates is dangerous and expensive: over 1972–3, the discount market probably lost its entire reserves. That left the houses unable to exercise their principal skill of taking risks, and more dependent than ever on their client status with the Bank. The Bank may decide that the houses have outlived their usefulness. In 1973, it began dealing directly in the parallel money markets. As this develops, it will have less need to control the banking system through the discount houses.

THE PARALLEL MONEY MARKETS

While the activities of the discount houses in the 1960s were restrained by the cartels and ceilings of the old system of credit control, new parallel markets were springing up to find ways round these. They have survived the abolition of the system which brought them into existence, and indeed have continued to flourish because they provide extremely cheap and convenient machinery for borrowing and lending large sums of money.

The essence of a parallel market is that money is borrowed and lent between institutions, companies and banks, unsecured, without the guidance and control of the monetary authorities. Thus the Bank of England does not act as lender of last resort to anybody in the City's parallel markets, as it does to the discount houses in the discount market. In some centres the bulk of this

* This important process is described in detail in chapter 8.

inter-institutional borrowing and lending is done directly between banks or companies. In London the bulk of it is done through the money brokers. While the discount houses make their profits on their own investments, the money brokers' job is simply to match up would-be borrowers and lenders, charging a small commission on each deal.

It is largely because the broking system is more widely used in London that the City has developed such a complex and sophisticated system of parallel markets. London brokers quote much narrower margins than their counterparts elsewhere. And in turn the sheer size of the London markets has allowed the brokers to thrive. As the brokers are beginning to buy interests in other brokers abroad and to set up subsidiary companies to deal in other centres, London is becoming the centre of an international network of broking offices.

Several of the main money brokers are descended from foreign exchange brokers. Others have a different line of ancestry: they were local authority brokers, formed in the mid-1950s to channel funds into local authorities. They are fiercely competitive. For money broking is the City's Wild West, where few holds are barred. Most discount-house men have been with their firm all their lives, but the money brokers' job market is a Mad Hatter's tea party with dealers constantly on the move from one firm to another. They move for vast and spiralling salaries – and if they are still not satisfied, they go off and set up on their own. A good average dealer, aged nearly thirty, would get about £15,000. But while top dealers are paid more than anyone else in the City, with the exception of a few merchant bankers and stockbrokers or jobbers, they probably need it. Their professional lives are short.

The broking companies themselves are a disparate lot. A few are large, able to place money in any market and to deal in foreign exchange and sterling alike. These firms employing 100 or more people and with a chain of offices and subsidiaries around the world are by far the biggest operators of their kind anywhere. At the other end of the scale there is the man alone in a dingy office trying to put together a few deals. Because in sterling business there is no formal organization of brokers and no restriction on entry, there is no firm figure for the number of money brokers in the City: but about thirty firms like to describe themselves as such. Of these, six of the largest have links with discount houses, and thirteen, the members of the Foreign Exchange and Currency Deposit Brokers' Association (FECDBA), deal in foreign exchange.

Largest of all the brokers are probably Charles Fulton and P. Murray-Jones. The chairman of Fulton's is Stephen O'Brien, an ordained priest: Fulton's has always taken more care of its reputation than the average broker. P. Murray-Jones lives in a Queen Anne House opposite Rothschilds and is part-owned by Gerrard and National. It has ten foreign offices, owing its rapid expansion largely to the autocratic Paul Murray-Jones.

In both these brokers, discount houses hold only minority stakes; but four other brokers are – or have been – wholly owned by discount houses. For Cater (Brokers), once wholly owned by Cater Ryder, this posed problems: there was a clash of personalities, and in the end Cater (Brokers) left FECDBA.

Clive Discount, which owns two broking houses, Guy Butler and Long, Till and Colvin, also ran into trouble. Long Till, local authority brokers, had been used to charging higher commissions than other broking houses, and Clive persuaded it to cut commissions and trade more aggressively. Virtually all the firm's senior staff objected and left. Union Discount's money-broking subsidiary is Roberts Union, a firm whose image does not match the rather sober reputation of its parent. Finally Gillett has bought one of the newest brokers, Kirkland Whittaker.

There are several brokers with no links with discount houses. The largest one, Short Loan and Mortgage, which specializes in local authority business, R. P. Martin, which went public in 1973, and Harlow Meyer, owned by Vavasseur. Latest member of the association is Tullett and Riley.

Apart from a few stockbrokers with money-broking departments, of which Phillips and Drew is probably the largest, and one or two foreign money brokers, there are a score of other small brokers. The best of these are perfectly sound. But there are also a hoard of fringe operators, many of them suspect if not downright fraudulent, such as the European gentleman with a dubious title who appeared at intervals in 1970, or the small broker operating from his flat behind Harrods. The rest of the market detests the shadier smaller operators: they give the larger firms a bad name.

All the big firms of money and foreign exchange brokers are linked by direct telephone lines to the main London banks. Each has up to eighty dealers constantly on the phone, ringing round the banks to find potential customers, and when they find one, scouring the other banks for a 'match'. Deals on both the foreign exchange and money markets are made on the phone. Written confirmation follows, but usually after the deal has been completed.

The parallel markets are made up of five sterling markets and the eurocurrency market. The five sterling markets are distinguished by their borrowers. On the local authority market, local authorities borrow largely from the institutions but also from banks, companies and a few private individuals. On the sterling inter-bank market, banks borrow from each other. On the finance-house market, the hire purchase companies borrow from a group of lenders similar to those on the local authority market. On the sterling CD market, banks borrow from companies and other banks. And on the intercompany market companies borrow from banks and each other. On the eurocurrency market, the largest, and in many ways the most complicated of all, banks borrow from each other in eurocurrencies.

Of the five sterling parallel markets, three owe their existence directly to government controls on the UK banking system. Thus the local authority market was born in 1955, when the government tried to reduce local authorities' borrowing by closing the Public Works Loan Board. In an effort to find a way round the squeeze, local authorities stepped up their borrowing direct from the private sector.

By 1972 the local authority money market, once the largest of the parallel markets, had been overtaken by the CD market. Of the total local authority loan debt of some £18,000 million,

£2,000 million was borrowed for periods of less than a year, representing what is conventionally thought of as the local authority money market. The smallest lump of money that is usually lent on this market is £25,000, and blocks of £1 million and more are common.

Shortly after the emergence of the local authority market, the inter-bank market grew up. Banks had found in the local authority market their first alternative outlet to the discount market for spare funds. The inter-bank market offered them an alternative way to even out spare cash among themselves. To do this through a discount house meant that they were paid only the discount houses' low rate of interest on call money. So to the amazement of the discount market they began to lend straight to each other. Side by side with the growth of the local authority market has been a corresponding expansion in inter-bank dealing. The total volume of funds deposited by banks directly with each other fluctuates wildly and is swollen by some double counting. But a typical figure in mid-1973 would have been some £4,000 million if inter-bank CD dealings are excluded. Under the new controls it has grown rapidly. The money is all very short-term – much of it overnight. The lumps tend to be a little larger than on the local authority market, with £250,000 the usual minimum.

The newest of all the sterling parallel markets, the inter-company market, emerged in 1968-9 as a way round the tough controls on bank lending imposed after the 1967 devaluation. Because of the rigid ceilings on bank lending, companies found it almost impossible to borrow through their bankers, who in turn were unwilling to pay high interest rates for money which they could not lend. During earlier credit squeezes a few large companies began to lend to each other on a small scale. Now this blossomed into a new parallel market which survived the end of the squeeze. No one knows its size for sure, but a fair guesstimate would be around £100 million in late 1973. The finance houses' market is very like the inter-bank market, except that the borrowers are finance houses instead of banks and the lumps are rather smaller. In the course of 1972 it began to merge with the inter-bank market as a number of finance houses acquired bank status.

Fastest growing of all the sterling parallel markets is the sterling CD market. The discount houses are all involved in the CD secondary market as traders, buying and selling secondhand CDs for their own accounts. Money brokers, by contrast, buy and sell these CDs for clients – sometimes dealing with discount houses and sometimes with banks and large companies. The total value of sterling CDs issued in mid-1973 was over £5,000 million.

All these markets intermesh. To take a simple sterling deal, a large company might lend £100,000 to County Bank which issues it with a CD. County then looks at the local authority market, decides that rates there are too low, and instead lends the money for a week on the sterling inter-bank market to another bank that is short of cash. A week later, local authority rates have improved, and County lends the £100,000 to Manchester City Corporation. Meanwhile the large company has brought forward an investment project and needs its £100,000 to cover the down payment on some machine tools. It sells the CD to Union Discount, which might either carry it to maturity or sell it to any of the banks in London – except County Bank. All these transactions, with the possible exception of the CD deals, will have taken place through a money broker. He sits on the end of the phone switching the funds from one market to another as rates move.

The origins of the eurocurrency market are rather more complicated. The first eurocurrency, and still by far the most important, is the eurodollar. For any currency to become 'euro' it must quite simply be owned by a firm or individual resident outside the country where the currency was issued and lent to another non-resident. Take, for example, a Middle Eastern oil sheik who has been paid $5 million in royalties by Standard Oil Co. (New Jersey). These funds were dollars when they were still on Standard Oil's New York bank account. But provided the sheik lends them to someone else not resident in the US, even to an overseas branch of an American bank which lends them back to its New York office, they remain eurodollars. They only become ordinary dollars again if he uses them to invest in American domestic securities or to buy some American product.

It was an American banking regulation which first helped to create the eurodollar market.* It came to Britain partly because London banks were among the earliest to find uses for these spare dollar balances. Not all were British. One early operator was the London-based Moscow Narodny Bank, which for political reasons wanted to employ its dollars outside the US and so helped supply dollars to the market. Since then markets have grown up in perhaps a dozen other financial centres and in other eurocurrencies. In Paris there is a small market in eurosterling (never europounds) and in Singapore a market in Asian dollars. But the City's dealing skills have helped to ensure that the lion's share of eurocurrency dealing goes through London.

The eurocurrency market is gigantic. By the end of 1973 the total pool of funds must have been about $135,000 million,† of which about 65 per cent would be dollars. This vast pool of money flows freely between the main financial centres. No one really knows how to control it. Already it is larger than the entire Gross National Product of Britain. Just under half this $135,000 million appears on the books of London banks. But unlike the parallel sterling markets, the eurocurrency market is in no way a UK domestic market. In fact, though London happens to be the main centre, foreign exchange controls prevent British companies from making much use of it.

This $135,000 million, the main eurocurrency market, is mainly a short-term inter-bank market. Banks borrow from each other lumps of $1 million up to about $10 million for periods as short as overnight or as long as five years. Most borrowing, though, is for six months or less. In theory there is nothing to stop a company with spare funds from placing them on the market, but a FECDBA restriction described later prevented the main brokers from accepting this 'commercial' money. A company therefore

* See chapter 1, p. 18, for its origins.
† Bank for International Settlements' annual reports give the best account of the market's development and the best estimates of its size.

has to place the funds with a bank which, after taking its 'turn', then lends them out on the market in its own name.

Equally if a company wants to borrow in eurocurrencies, it cannot do so directly from the eurocurrency market. This would mean borrowing from a bank; and banks insist on lending to companies through conventional banking channels. The company must go instead to one of the three other 'euro' markets: the eurobond market, the eurocurrency syndicated loan market or the embryonic eurocommercial paper market. The same institutions – big companies and public utilities – borrow on each. On the first, individuals are the main lenders, on the second, only banks, and on the third mainly banks. All these markets are run directly by banks. Brokers are used only rarely.

The eurobond market grew up in the early 1960s when the US Interest Equalization Tax closed New York to foreign borrowers. Eurobonds are just like ordinary bonds except that they are denominated in eurocurrencies: they are ten- or fifteen-year loans to a company on sale to the general public. The general public in this case usually means numbered accounts in Swiss banks and British investors are rare, deterred by UK restrictions on overseas investment. Certain foreign and some UK banks specialize in managing issues of eurobonds.

London has had limited success in eurobond issuing. In 1972 three UK-based issuers were in the top ten: S. G. Warburg, N. M. Rothschild and the London affiliate of the New York investment bank, White Weld. The eurobond market revolves mainly round half a dozen continental centres and its principal clearing houses are in Luxemburg and Brussels. Since there are so few British investors or borrowers, it is on the face of it hardly surprising that much of the business should go elsewhere. Yet curiously London is the base for the main secondary market, the market in secondhand eurobonds. This is run by a small group of London banks and stockbrokers.

The syndicated loan market only began to flourish in 1968. Until then most bank loans in eurocurrencies were rarely for more than a couple of years. This sort of loan might have been made by one bank – a large US bank, for example – or it might have been managed by a bank which would organize a syndicate of other banks to share it. By 1968 these methods were proving inadequate. Companies wanted larger and longer loans. One way to provide them was through consortium banks, described in the money market banking chapter. Another was to improve the syndicated loan technique, for example by readjusting the interest rate every six months to tie it to the eurodollar rate. Now virtually all the specialist banks in London take part in these loans and a secondary market has emerged in which they can sell off their shares to other banks. By 1973 the size of this market greatly exceeded that of the eurobond market. One leading issuing bank privately estimates that $15,000 million was raised on the market in 1973.

The most recent and so far the least successful eurocurrency market is that in eurocommercial paper. On it companies borrow for three months by issuing a promissory note (a sort of IOU, or promise to pay). Schroders and White Weld jointly organized a few issues of eurocommercial paper in 1971–2, as did the New York investment bank Goldman Sachs, but the idea was not an immediate success.

All these eurocurrency markets have developed despite the the fact that it often costs companies more to borrow on them than on domestic money and capital markets. The reason companies continue to do so is very often simply that the eurocurrency markets are the only place where they can find money on the scale they need. It may be quite impossible to raise funds on the domestic market at the time the company requires it. For unlike all domestic markets, the eurocurrency market has so far grown up entirely outside the control of any central bank. It is the supreme example of how domestic credit controls induce people to find ways round them. No doubt by the time the world's central banks have evolved an efficient way of controlling the banks' eurocurrency operations, the focus of the international capital market will have shifted elsewhere – to an intercompany eurocurrency market, perhaps?

THE FOREIGN EXCHANGE MARKET

The grandfather of all the parallel money markets is the foreign exchange market. London's is comfortably the largest in the world. On it some 230 London banks, authorized by the Bank of England to deal in foreign exchange, trade one foreign currency for another, usually through one of the thirteen foreign-exchange broking firms, the members of the Foreign Exchange and Currency Deposit Brokers' Association.

The foreign exchange market is riddled with restrictive practices. There are fewer than there once were, but those that remain arguably restrict both the growth of the London market and the range of services it provides. If the remaining restrictions are not soon removed there is a real danger that they may eventually lead to the creation of new markets outside the control of FECDBA, or even outside London.

For it is through FECDBA that these restrictions are enforced. Backed by the Bank of England and the foreign exchange committee of the clearing banks, it is one of those closed shops of which the City is so fond. A broker has to join it to be allowed to operate in the foreign exchange market. But joining is extremely difficult: there have only been four new members since 1951 when the foreign exchange market was reopened after the Second World War. Brokers justify this by recalling the chaos in the market between the wars, when the foreign exchange market was overbroked, and too many brokers were competing for a living. The Bank of England and the foreign exchange committee of the banks decided to make sure that this did not happen again.

This restriction on entry to the ranks of foreign exchange brokers has at least had the merit of keeping the market 'clean': brokers obey the rules. Less can be said in defence of the other major restriction operated by FECDBA, at the behest of the Bank and the clearing banks. This in effect prevents non-banks, large companies for example, from dealing directly on the foreign-exchange and eurocurrency markets, as they can on the sterling markets. In practice, whenever a company wants to borrow in a foreign currency or put money on the eurocurrency market, it has to do so through a bank.

If ICI wants to place $5 million on the London eurocurrency market, it has to do so through a bank which takes a commission for making two phone calls. If, however, Dow Chemical, a much smaller American company, wants to put $5 million on the eurocurrency market, it can do so through its own banking subsidiary in Switzerland. As the international banking business of the multinational giants grows, companies like ICI will either copy Dow and set up their own banking subsidiaries or insist that they be treated in the same way as a bank.

Until late 1973 another restriction prevented brokers in London from dealing in foreign exchange with banks abroad. A broker could only arrange exchange deals between authorized banks in London. In return a London bank would only deal in foreign exchange with other banks in London through a FECDBA broker but it dealt directly with other banks all over the world. This restriction meant that all profitable 'arbitrage' business (that is, buying in one financial centre and selling in another in order to take advantage of international differences in interest rates) has been in the hands of the banks alone.

London brokers started in the late 1960s to set up a network of offices and subsidiaries around the world. They are mainly intended to deal in eurocurrency deposits, although some also handle foreign exchange. This means the brokers had started to find a way round this restriction.

Such restrictions have grown up because of the hold which the banks enjoy over the brokers, whose only customers they are; and more important, because they have the support of the Bank of England. FECDBA should remember that it was the discount market's restrictive agreement with the clearing banks, backed by the Bank of England, that encouraged the growth of the parallel markets.

The foreign exchange market's most obvious purpose is to exchange different countries' currencies as they trade with each other or make overseas investments. But it is also the mechanism through which the world money system is operated. Since the last war the exchange rates of the world's major currencies have usually been fixed against each other. They do, however, move in three ways. From day to day, even from minute to minute, they fluctuate against each other within a narrow band each side of their parity against the US dollar. Normally they are held between these limits by the occasional intervention of the world's central banks in the various foreign exchange markets. Thus it is through the London market that the Bank of England stabilizes the price of sterling. It does this by buying sterling if the pound falls too low and selling it if the pound rises too high.

The second type of price movement is when a currency is either devalued or revalued, which means that it moves to a completely new parity at which it is then once more pegged by the central banks. Since the early 1970s governments faced with the need to devalue or revalue have shown an increasing preference for the alternative of floating. This means allowing the pressures of supply and demand to determine the exchange rate from day to day. Generally the central bank intervenes from time to time in the foreign exchange market either to iron out fluctuations in the rate, or to nudge it in the direction the authorities think it ought to move. From June 1972 the British government allowed the pound to float downwards from its previously fixed rate of $2.60.

Currencies are not only bought and sold 'spot' for 'immediate' delivery – in practice, in two days. They are also traded 'forward', which means that though the price between the currencies, the exchange rate, is agreed now, the buyer takes delivery in one, three, six or twelve months' time. Through the forward exchange market, traders can insure against exchange rate changes. For example, a British company has bought some Swiss looms for which it will have to pay in three months. It fears that the pound may depreciate against the Swiss franc during this period. And so it buys 'forward' the Swiss francs it will need to make its payment. If most people believe that in the three-month interval the pound is going to depreciate against the Swiss franc, the importing company will have to pay a premium over the spot exchange rate for its forward francs, but it will at least know exactly how much it has to pay in sterling terms. If it waited till the payment fell due and bought the Swiss francs on the spot market, it would have had to gamble on the exchange rate. While exchange rates fluctuate, therefore, a forward market is essential for international trade.

Almost anyone who buys or sells foreign exchange has to take some view of the way in which exchange rates are likely to move. In this sense almost everyone is speculating. But a line is conventionally drawn between those who, like the loom importer, are using the market as an insurance against exchange rate changes, and those who are using it purely to make a profit and not to cover another transaction. In practice this distinction is highly arbitrary. For example many large companies delay settling their accounts abroad if they expect their own country's currency to appreciate, and speed them up if they are afraid of the reverse. Because Britain is so heavily dependent on foreign trade this phenomenon, known as leads and lags, can put very heavy pressure on the exchange rate.

Someone must speculate on currencies if forward exchange markets are to work at all. To go back to the loom importer: in order for him to buy his currency forward, someone – probably a bank – has to sell it, taking on the importer's exchange risk for the price of the forward premium. Still, the very term 'speculator' has an unsavoury and unpatriotic ring about it. Certainly if enough people speculate on a currency with a fixed exchange rate being devalued, it is not easy for the combined forces of the world's central banks to stop them proving themselves right. But anyone who thinks that this is the result of the malice of speculators rather than the inadequacies of the international monetary system should remember the fate of Shell International. It lost £22·5 million in the 1971 currency realignment.

No one has lost more through sterling's gyrations than the Bank of England. During periods of pressure on a currency a central bank is supposed to support the spot rate to keep it within the limits set down by the IMF. Before the 1967 devaluation the Bank also chose to support the forward rate. At the time this was heralded as an important statement of the nation's faith in the parity of sterling. Had the pound not been devalued it would have had the advantage of taking pressure off the spot rate without causing a drain on reserves. As it turned out, the Bank – that is the country – lost £356 million on forward contracts in this futile defence of sterling. In effect the Bank was speculating against devaluation. It got it wrong and suffered the largest speculative loss ever recorded on the foreign exchange markets.

Understandably, the traumatic experience of the 1967 devaluation has made the authorities far less willing to fight to save a shaky exchange rate. In June 1972 it took less than a week of severe pressure before the pound was allowed to float.

During these currency crises, the foreign exchange market is chaotic. But at any busy period a dealing room looks like a madhouse. The best description is that of the ex-dealer of a clearing bank:*

Calls from customers, calls from foreign banks overseas, calls from the brokers. Some merely seeking information, some seeking rates on which to base their day's work. There will be calls from Paris, Amsterdam, Copenhagen, Brussels, Hamburg and many other financial centres. Some with genuine propositions, some hoping for an advantageous quotation somewhere in the list. . . .

The babel rises a few decibels as the linguists join the chorus. Rates are being quoted in French, Italian and probably German. Each operator will be dealing with the requirements of his own particular caller, whilst keeping his ear often cocked to any possible changes in rates by his colleagues as they effect their deals and look for a covering operation elsewhere. . . .

The textbooks discourse widely and wisely on spot rates and forward rates. They delve deeply into the mysteries of arbitrage. Unfortunately, especially when dealing with exchange for a forward delivery, it rarely works that way. When one wants to buy dollars for, say, three months' delivery, one finds the broker offers in lieu some two months or

* Jack R. Higgins in a symposium, *A Day in the Life of a Banker* (The Institute of Bankers, 1963).

some six months, or he cannot offer the outright date, but can offer the swap.

What shall one do? Will one of the propositions fit the book? Many questions flit through the dealer's mind. Try another broker? But the first will already have scented blood and be out scouring the market for a chance to close up a deal. To put someone else in will accentuate the effect. Take him off? He might see the opportunity to deal and go elsewhere. Try Paris? They will read a change in the market and be nipping back on another line and clobber the market under one's nose. Try Germany? Might work against marks. Can the mark dealer help? Has he something on his books which will help the arbitrage price? Questions and answers are flitting through the dealer's brain and he alone must find the answer. Meanwhile he is probably dealing with a fractious importer who is demanding last night's closing price as shown in *The Times* for a cheque for $27.53 drawn on Milwaukee, Wis.

Now, as exchange rates become increasingly flexible and movements of foreign currencies become larger, the foreign exchange broker's job will grow more hectic. Of one thing you can be sure. The more chaotic the world's foreign exchange markets, the more money will be made by the men buying and selling in them.

5

The Stock Exchange

PUBLIC SERVICE OR GENTLEMEN'S CLUB?

Every stockbroker will assure you that the London Stock Exchange exists to serve the country.* To anyone who reads daily in the newspapers of takeover battles, daring coups by young financiers, and gyrating share prices, this assurance might sound unconvincing. And to anyone who suspects that top jobbers in a good year are the best-paid men in the City simply because they possess a superior gambling instinct, it might sound positively outrageous. But in a sense, the stockbroking community is right. The Stock Exchange does exist for the mundane purpose of channelling personal savings into industrial and commercial investment and of providing a market place for trading company shares. The criterion on which it should be judged is how well it performs these tasks.

The day-to-day business of a stock exchange is issuing and

* Well, almost every stockbroker. Graham Greenwell, senior partner of brokers W. Greenwell and a member of the Stock Exchange Council, wrote in a letter to *The Times* in June 1971 that the Exchange was a private gentlemen's club and not 'an institution which exists to perform a public service'. He could have been joking. But evidently the then Stock Exchange chairman Sir Martin Wilkinson did not think so. He was quick to disassociate himself from this view.

dealing in securities, which are of two kinds. In Britain, roughly one third (by market valuation) are fixed interest securities, some issued by companies (and called debentures, loans and preference shares) but most issued by the government (and referred to as 'gilt-edged'). These are, strictly speaking, stocks.* Shares (or equities or ordinary shares as they are known) are always issued by companies. Like fixed interest stocks, equities are bought and sold at prices which fluctuate constantly; but while fixed interest stocks pay their holders a known interest rate, equities pay a dividend which may be a different amount every half-year – or in a bad year nothing at all. Equity holders generally – though not invariably – have a vote in the company's affairs.

Taking the value of equity shares traded, a widely fluctuating figure, London always comes a poor second to the New York Stock Exchange, and is roughly level-pegging with the American Stock Exchange (also in New York) and Tokyo. It is, however, about as big as all the other European stock exchanges put together. London's substantial equity turnover has led many European brokers (and perhaps some London ones) to assume that it will be the main capital market for European industry. But before making this assumption, one should compare the amount of new capital actually raised on the London Exchange with that on European bourses. It is impossible to find comparable up-to-date figures. But it is fair to say that in the 1960s, relative to Gross National Product, the London Stock Exchange raised a smaller amount in new domestic industrial funds than its main rivals. †

This is due largely to the unwillingness of industry to raise new capital for investment, rather than to any defects in the mechanism of the Exchange. But on the other hand the mechanism is not capable of coping satisfactorily with two other relatively recent developments. These are the increasing domination of the Exchange by institutional investors, and the massive post-war increase in the volume of takeover bids.

---

* Confusingly, in the United States stocks (whether issued by companies or the government) are called 'bonds' and equities, 'common stocks'.
† See below, pp. 120–1.

The growth in investment channelled through institutions has put pressure on the Exchange's unique trading system. The Stock Exchange is the only one in the world where members are split into two groups, brokers and jobbers (though some other European exchanges are considering adopting the system). Clients buying or selling shares place their orders with the brokers, who are not allowed to deal directly with each other except in circumstances explained later in this chapter. The broker carries out his client's order through a jobber, who is not allowed to deal directly with the general public. The jobber deals in and holds shares as a principal – on his own account; the broker only buys and sells shares on behalf of his clients. The broker earns his living from the commission paid to him by his client each time he buys or sells on his behalf. The jobber earns his by quoting a selling price for a share slightly above the buying rate. The difference is known as the 'jobber's turn'.*

This trading system was developed when almost the only customers on the Exchange were private individuals. It still has many advantages. It enables a vast number of different shares to be traded: roughly 9,500 separate securities are quoted in London, far more than on any other exchange. It also makes it possible for small lots of shares to be parcelled into lumps large enough to be bought by institutions. And it provides a broad market in government securities, for London is one of the very few stock markets where the government sells debt directly to the public. This is a particularly valuable feature in view of the size of the UK National Debt, bigger in proportion to Gross National Product than that of any other major country.

The Stock Exchange likes to think of itself as the bastion of the small shareholder. The personal shareholder still plays a more important role than on many other exchanges. But in this century, mainly in the years since the war, funds invested on the Exchange have come increasingly from a quite different source. Private investors have switched their savings on a gigantic scale into a

* Jobbers point out that this turn is not necessarily clear profit. It would only be so if they could match each sale with a purchase. If they cannot they may find themselves holding a share whose price is falling.

variety of savings institutions. Life assurance, followed by pension funds, now accounts for the largest single chunk of savings on the Exchange. In the 1960s a tremendous growth took place in investment and unit trusts. In 1970 institutional investors accounted for some 40 per cent of all equities traded, 58 per cent of company fixed interest stocks, and 45 per cent of gilts.

Increasingly, then, brokers and jobbers have been dealing not with private individuals but with institutional investors. This has had far-reaching effects on the way that they conduct their business and on the market itself. For the brokers it has meant the expense of a large research staff and growing pressure to cut commissions charged for large deals. For the Exchange as a whole it has meant greater resilience in prices to good and bad news. But for the jobbing system, designed to handle the small investor and government debt, the rise of the institutional holder of equities has had the most dramatic effect. Despite a string of mergers which reduced the number of jobbing firms drastically, the jobbers have been unable to cope with the large blocks of shares in which institutions want to deal. This has in turn led to a growing number of institutional deals being arranged off the floor of the house.

Like institutional investment, the takeover battle is largely a post-war phenomenon; and as with the institutions, the Stock Exchange has not yet succeeded in adapting itself to cope with it. In the case of the takeover the problem has not been one of the mechanism of the Exchange but of policing takeover practices.

Originally, policing the Exchange was simply a matter of protecting customers from dishonest or incompetent brokers. In this, the Exchange has a sound reputation, aided by the enviable record of financial stability of broking firms – a record which contrasts sharply with that of New York. But ruling on the way takeovers and mergers are carried through is altogether a thornier and more delicate question. So far it has been carried out voluntarily – by the Takeover Panel. A powerful body of opinion both inside the City and outside believes that eventually the job will be done on a legal basis. In 1973 the government decided to take on one aspect of the panel's job, curbing 'insider' dealing.

THE EXCHANGE, THE BROKERS AND THE JOBBERS

In outward appearance, the Stock Exchange has been completely transformed since the mid-1960s. Until 1966 the Exchange was a nineteenth-century hall surrounded by buildings full of nondescript offices which housed the Stock Exchange Council and a couple of insurance companies. Then these buildings, next to the Bank of England, were torn down. They have been replaced with a 26-storey tower, completed in early 1970, to take the offices of the council, brokers and jobbers, and with a new trading floor of about 23,000 square feet, which opened in 1973.

The main reason for this rebuilding was to improve communications. Even on the temporary floor, where the market operated during rebuilding, these were far better than those in the old house, which were incredibly antiquated. Brokers and jobbers used to be called to the phone by top-hatted messengers (called 'waiters') who manned voice tubes from the phone room. Now any one of the 2,500-odd people who may be on the floor at a busy period can be contacted by his office by a 'bleeper' paging service. Some of the restaurants and pubs around the Exchange are also wired for the bleeper, so that the more convivial brokers can put in a full day's work in the bar of the Jamaica – and still remain instantly 'on tap' to their offices. Many of the larger brokers have gone one better, and equipped their staff with two-way radios.

The new house also boasts one of the largest private telephone exchanges in the world, big enough to serve a town of 30,000 people; and a market price display system which transmits share prices to 1,250 television receivers in the offices of brokers, jobbers and other institutions around the City.

The Stock Exchange's system of transferring shares and settling up after the transfer is completed is also being automated. This is possible because, like most American companies but unlike most European, British firms almost always have registered shares. This means that the names and addresses of all shareholders are kept on a central register, a card index or more usually a computer memory bank. Being listed on this register is the shareholder's title to his share, and transferring a share from one owner to another simply means altering the register on receiving the necessary written instructions. The merits of this system over the European alternative of bearer shares have long been argued. With bearer shares, the certificate itself is title to the share and transferring ownership means transferring possession of the certificate. The system of registered shares has many advantages. There is virtually no security risk, it solves the problem of shareholders who lose their certificates and it allows firms to mail their reports to shareholders. It also makes it easier for a firm which wants to take over another to find out who the shareholders are. But till now it has been more expensive to operate.

The Exchange now hopes to alter the system of settlement so that it can be put on computer. The new scheme, which should be in operation by 1975–6, is conservatively estimated to cost £8 million to develop. It should in the long run ensure that the registered share system is quicker and cheaper to operate than any other. At present, brokers and jobbers settle up every two weeks – the two-week period being called the account – and make their own arrangements for transferring the shares. The Exchange hopes to set up a central agency to which jobbers and brokers will report bargains, and which will then carry out a large amount of the transfer process automatically.

Running the Exchange is a council, made up of thirty-six practising brokers and jobbers. The council meets every week under the chairman, who since the summer of 1973 has been George Loveday. Chairmen normally hold office for about ten years, though there is no formal time limit. George Loveday is a partner in Read, Hurst-Brown. He and his deputies are the only members who devote themselves more or less full-time to the Exchange's business. Most of the real work of the Exchange, however, is carried out by the council's full-time staff, which in 1973 numbered 800, and by the various committees of the council. These usually meet at least once a week to consider such questions as whether a new company should be allowed a listing on the Exchange, whether new members should be admitted and whether brokers and jobbers are meeting the Exchange's solvency requirements. Technically members only have to vote on changes in the Exchange's deed of settlement. Major policy issues (such as whether women should be admitted) and decisions to change the rules of the Exchange (such as whether to allow brokers to advertise) are sometimes voted on by all members of the Exchange. In practice some important issues, such as the 1972 decision to cut commission rates, are resolved by the council, and some very minor ones, which involve changing the deed, have to be put to a full vote of members.

Whenever an issue has to be put to the vote, the smaller firms tend to dominate the outcome, for each member has a vote and small firms have more members relative to the amount of business they do than large ones. This has resulted in a number of reactionary and even dangerous decisions being taken in recent years on issues where the interests of the smaller firms run contrary to those of the larger. Members in small firms are widely believed to have carried the vote against allowing members to advertise, fearing that once the larger brokers could advertise they would steal their business. More worryingly, when a few broking firms ran into financial difficulties, after the collapse of the Australian mining boom, the council wanted to double the solvency margin of brokers. It was dissuaded by pressure from the smaller firms which felt they could not afford the extra margin – and from the country exchanges, which were then negotiating to merge with London. In the united exchange, formed in March 1973, the small firms and their members may have a still stronger voice.

The fault lies partly with the council, which has not given the Exchange a firm enough lead. In general, firms do not encourage their most active and capable partners to fill their time with council work. A third of the council retires each year, but is eligible for re-election. In 1972 the longest-standing member, Lord Ritchie, had been on the council since 1947 – and half the members had joined the Exchange before the Second World War.

In March 1973 the London Exchange had 3,536 members of whom 3,012 worked for the 168 firms of brokers, and 504 worked

for the 21 firms of jobbers. To become a member of the Exchange
you have to have been with a broker or jobber firm for three
years. Only a member can be a partner or a director of a Stock
Exchange firm. But it is possible to go onto the floor of the
Exchange on behalf of a firm without being a member: you
need only be an 'admitted clerk'. There are two species of admitted clerks, unauthorized (or 'blue button' after the colour of
their lapel badges) and authorized. Only authorized clerks can
trade. Until 1971 you had to be British to be a member. Now
foreigners are allowed to join. So are women. They became
members rather by accident, as a result of the merger in March
1973 of the London and the county stock exchanges, on some of
whose floors women could already deal. The merger gave another
1,000 members and 120 firms, nearly all brokers, the right to
deal on the London floor.

Almost all the brokers are partnerships. They vary enormously in size. The largest have branches overseas, forty or more
partners and a staff of perhaps 600. The smallest have two or
three partners and a couple of secretaries. Judging which are the
biggest is a matter of informed guesswork, as there are no published figures. It depends, in any case, on the measure used. In
terms of turnover the largest are certainly those which specialize
in gilt-edged securities, which are dealt in enormous blocks but
at very low commission. Biggest of all is almost certainly Mullens
and Co., the government broker (see chapter 8, p. 201). It is
probably closely followed by Pember and Boyle, which is also
very largely a gilt-edged broker.

On the more relevant measure of size of commission income,
the largest firm is probably James Capel, formed from a string
of mergers in the 1960s which it is still digesting. It is one of the
more international (or less parochial) firms, with offices in
the US and Luxemburg, and a rather young staff. Roughly
the same size are Messel, and Cazenove. Both are patrician;
Cazenove, which takes a positive delight in its reputation for
crustiness, has offices virtually indistinguishable from a St James's
Club. Also among the largest brokers are Sebag's, which built
up a reputation for dynamism in the mid-1960s, a reputation

slightly tarnished by the firm's involvement in the Australian mining boom – and the boom's subsequent collapse.

At the opposite extreme are two firms whose reputations are founded less on their partners' family connections and more on the dry modern techniques of share analysis. In the 1950s Phillips and Drew were one of the first firms to appreciate the importance of research into companies as a lure in the growing market of institutional investors. Its partners, mostly actuaries or accountants, quickly built it from a rather obscure medium-sized firm into one of the biggest. More recently the pace of research has been set by Hoare and Co., Govett which has developed mathematical techniques of stock analysis* further than any other broker. As well as having the largest research department of any broker, Hoare is also now one of the largest half dozen.

Among the other large firms Strauss Turnbull and Vickers da Costa have particularly large overseas interests, and Rowe and Pitman, besides handling probably the biggest ever new issue, J. Sainsbury, has made a speciality of put-through business, described below. Strauss Turnbull is well known as a 'market maker' in eurobonds (see chapter 4, p. 94), while Vickers da Costa is London's main specialist in Japanese securities. Vickers da Costa became a limited company in 1973.

At the other end of the scale there are eight or ten tiny firms with just a couple of partners.

Although both brokers and jobbers behave on the floor of the Exchange like overgrown schoolboys, setting fire to each other's newspapers and cutting off people's ties if they look too colourful, the brokers are regarded by the jobbers as rather sober. To

---

* Most analysts belong to one of two sects, the chartists and the fundamentalists. Chartists draw graphs of share prices from which they deduce complex inter-relationships between events and expectations which, they believe, determine whether the market or a particular share will move up or down. Their graphs reveal patterns with wondrous names like 'head and shoulders' or 'double bottom'. As – retrospectively – each shape can be interpreted in several different ways, the chartists are usually right. Their rivals, the fundamentalists, believe that it is the fundamentals of a company, its earnings, profit record, etc., that ultimately determine its share prices. Though the market may 'get out of line' for a while, all you have to do is wait for investment opinion to catch up. If you are prepared to wait long enough, they too are usually right in the end.

become a broker you have, since 1971, to pass a qualifying exam. It is the jobber who runs the biggest risks on the Exchange. A jobber is a compulsive gambler. When Goldie, the golden eagle, escaped from London Zoo one jobber in Akroyd and Smithers went short to the tune of £1 for every day it remained free. When it looked as though Goldie would never be recaptured, frantic calculations were made on the average lifespan of *aquila chrysaetos*.

Jobbers take massive risks, and can make equally massive profits. In a rising market they can hardly fail to make fortunes; in a falling one it is extremely difficult for them to make anything at all. This is because, unlike brokers, jobbers hold shares as principals. Each jobber carries a 'book' of shares, basing the price of any one share on the state of his book in it and what he expects its price to do. If he expects a rise, he will build up a holding; if a fall, he will try to avoid making a loss either by holding as little of the share as possible or even by 'going short' or by selling more of it than he holds in the hope that he will be able to buy it back more cheaply later on. Holding large blocks of shares is not only risky. It ties up jobbers' capital. In recent years jobbers have tried as far as possible to reduce the size of the position they carry over from one day to another.

Largest of the jobbers is Wedd Durlacher Mordaunt, which employs some 120 dealers; Jack Durlacher made enough out of the 1969 share boom to finance the late Jo Siffert's Formula One racing team. Next largest, and challenging Wedd Durlacher is Akroyd and Smithers, followed by Pinchin, Denny, which concentrates on company securities. Right at the other end of the scale is S. Jenkins and Son. Its staff consists of just that – now joined by a second son, and a Mr Howe. It specializes in greyhound racing shares.

THE TRADING MECHANISM

The system of broking and jobbing works – in theory – like this. A broker is given an order by a client to buy 1,000 shares in ICI. He goes onto the floor of the house and asks two or three jobbers the price of ICI. Whatever his view of the market, the jobber will always quote a price in the shares in which he specializes. One jobber might reply '280 282' which means that he will buy shares at 280 pence and sell at 282 pence. Another might say '282½ 284½' and a third '280½ 282½'. At this stage the broker will go back to the first jobber, being the one offering the shares at the cheapest price, and say he is a buyer for 1,000. Not until then does the jobber know whether the broker wants to buy or sell, or the size of the block of shares. If the block involved is very big, the broker may first ask the size of the market. The jobber might reply 'bid for ten, offered in twenty', meaning that he is prepared to buy up to 10,000 shares and sell up to 20,000.

Once the deal is agreed, both broker and jobber pencil it into their notebooks and go their ways. There is no other written record of their agreement: hence the Stock Exchange motto, 'My word is my bond.' When the two notebooks do not tally, as inevitably happens from time to time, broker and jobber have to work out a solution between themselves. Usually the jobber accepts the broker's word; but sometimes the two agree to split the difference.

How far what really happens diverges from this theoretical picture of dealing becomes clear in a moment. But it is worth digressing to look at the role of the jobber. Other stock exchanges seem to get along without him. Is he simply an unnecessary and expensive middleman?

Most other exchanges use one of two main trading methods. Small exchanges tend to use the 'call-over' system. This works rather like a London commodity futures market. An officer of the exchange calls out the name of a share and its current price, and members shout out their bids from the floor, if necessary agreeing on a new price to make a match. Inevitably this system sometimes leaves some shares unsold in the hands of brokers, who thus perform a jobbing function of sorts. The other main system, used in large exchanges like New York, is called the 'trading post' or 'specialist' system. Some brokers simply act as brokers; others act also as jobbers, trading with both brokers and the public and carrying books of shares. Each industry is traded at a 'trading post' or particular point on the floor of the exchange, from which the brokers 'specializing' in its shares operate.

Thus in practice, for the shares to have a continuous market, someone has to perform a jobbing role, carrying the shares for which buyers cannot be found and going short on the shares for which sellers have not yet appeared. It has, moreover, to be someone with enormous capital resources; even the New York 'specialist' system is under pressure as the specialists do not have the capital to carry shares in blocks of the size the institutional investors want to deal in.

The jobbing system is a luxury one. It probably makes the London market more expensive to trade on. But it means that there is always a market for every share. A jobber will always make a price in a share (even if it is a price at which no one wants to deal). He will always at some price find a share, however obscure, for a would-be buyer; he will always buy, at some price, any share, however stagnant the market in it.

But to return to the way the trading mechanism works: the theoretical picture has less and less in common with what really happens on the Exchange. In practice the broker may not find as many as three jobbers in any one share. He will certainly be hard put to it to find more. He may, indeed, set up the deal in his office, making only formal use of a jobber's services. Thus the trading mechanism of the Exchange has been coming under severe pressure. An increasing proportion of share-dealing is already bypassing the floor of the Exchange – and some may indeed soon bypass the brokers. What has gone wrong is that neither brokers nor jobbers have adjusted quickly enough to the rise of the large institutional investor.

For the brokers the most immediate effect of this rise has been to put pressure on them to readjust their scale of charging. At the moment their charges mean that the large institutional clients subsidize the small private ones. This helps to explain both the brokers' lack of enthusiasm for attracting private clients, and the institutional investors' desire to bypass the brokers.

Brokers charge by commission. On equity deals of up to £1·75 million this is on a sliding scale, but above that there is a flat commission rate of ⅛ per cent. The commission on small deals fails to reflect the difference in the broker's costs, while the commission on a large deal is extremely high, bearing no relation to the relatively small amount of work involved. Just how uneconomic small deals are can be seen by comparing the commission on buying £250 of a share and £25,000 of it. Both deals may cost the broker much the same to transact. But the commission on the first transaction is £4; on the second £156. To grasp how seriously the brokers overcharge their large institutional clients, compare the commission on buying shares worth £25,000 with that on £250,000 of the same share. On the first deal, the client pays his broker £156; on the second, £1,162. Yet, again, the difference in the work the broker has to do bears little relation to the reward.

The crux of the problem is that large brokers have had to provide a range of expensive new services to attract institutional clients, services from which private clients have benefited but for which they have not paid. Thus brokers have had to produce reams of paper about each industry's (and often each company's) prospects. They have to visit major firms at regular intervals. And if they want to be thought of as experts in a particular sector, they have to be in close touch with the directors of its companies.

Hence the marked decline since the last war of broker interest in private business. It is still true that for a small broker, private clients may be almost the only source of income, and that for any broker a client with about £20,000 or more to invest is worth having. But a large broker typically will hope to do about 75 per cent of his business with institutions. The increasing amount of discretionary business (where the customer turns over investment decisions to the broker's discretion) is making private clients' departments more important. But in many firms for a young man to be sent to the private clients' department is professionally rather like a spell in Siberia.

Most large brokers reckon they lose money on any transaction of less than £1,000. Is this threshold too high? The answer, judging by American experience, is yes. The only way to make personal business pay is to have massive volume. But unlike the mighty Merrill Lynch with its 200 branches across the United States, no British broker has been able to set up a nationwide network of retail offices to generate this.

One firm, Scrimgeours, tried and failed. In February 1968 it set about establishing a string of thirteen provincial branches. In November 1970 it withdrew. The operation was simply not profitable. The reason was probably just that the branches were in the wrong places. They had to be. The London Stock Exchange until 1973 had a gentleman's agreement with the country stock exchanges that each should not allow members to open within 25 miles of any other exchange without that exchange's permission. In practice this meant that members of provincial stock exchanges were allowed to open branches in London's West End – but that London brokers were refused permission to open in Coventry, less than 25 miles from Birmingham and in Minehead, less than 25 miles from Cardiff. Scrimgeours could hardly expect to succeed with branches in places like Penrith and Carlisle.

With the merger of the London and country exchanges, this demarcation agreement has come to an end. It remains to be seen, though, whether any firm of brokers will take advantage of this to establish a nationwide chain.

Even if Scrimgeours had been able to set up a viable branch network, it would still have been severely handicapped by the Exchange's ban on advertising. Until late 1973 brokers had a self-denying ordinance on advertising for business in Britain. New business was supposed to come from personal introductions, though if asked the Stock Exchange supplied a list of brokers who will accept personal business. There was a steady demand for this list, evidence of the number of would-be customers who had no personal introductions to stockbrokers, and of the need for advertising to make brokers' names known to the public. The ban was always absurd: not only were unit trust managers, portfolio advisers and other professional institutional investors allowed to advertise; so were US brokers in Britain. In 1972 UK brokers were allowed to advertise in publications circulating mainly overseas and finally, in 1973, in British publications too.

The ban only remained because small firms of brokers feared they would be at a disadvantage compared with their larger competitors without it.

For both brokers and jobbers, attracting the institutions has been expensive. Brokers have had to build up their research departments, jobbers their 'books'. In their efforts to improve their financial strength both have had two courses open to them: to merge, or to look for corporate money. Twenty years ago the brokers would have tried a third course: recruiting rich young men and selling them partnerships. When brokers lived off personal clients, rich young men with wealthy contacts were also useful for the new business they could attract. But the professional skills that brokers need to pull in institutional business are no longer the prerogative of the rich.

Until 1970 neither brokers nor jobbers could be limited companies. This meant that the easiest way to find new capital was to merge, and throughout the 1960s a succession of mergers thinned the ranks of both. The number of brokers fell from 294 in 1962 to 168 in 1973, even though the number of broking partners who were members of the Exchange held virtually steady, falling only from 1,921 to 1,768 over the same period. Since 1970 seven brokers have become limited companies, including J. and A. Scrimgeour, Sandelson and Co., Mitton Butler Priest and Hoare and Co., Govett. In December 1972 the Stock Exchange Council approved in principle a proposal that brokers and jobbers which had been incorporated could have their shares publicly quoted.

Among jobbers the pressure to look for more capital has been still stronger. All jobbers have to finance a larger 'book' and try to cope with much larger blocks of shares. They have found themselves without the funds to do so. To acquire them, seven of the twenty-one have so far become incorporated. Wedd Durlacher has a link with the merchant bank Rothschilds and Triumph Investment Trust holds shares in Smith Brothers. Others have merged. Among jobbers, the decline in numbers has been even more striking than among brokers – and more serious. The number of jobbing firms dropped from 187 in 1950 to 83 in 1962 to

21 in late 1973. Out of the 640-odd dealers that the jobbing firms have on the floor, some 90 work for one firm, Wedd Durlacher. The result has been that whereas ten years ago there would have been five or six jobbers making a market in a largish UK industrial company's shares, now there are perhaps three. In small, rarely traded shares there may be only one. There are now a number of important sections of the market, such as breweries and investment trusts, in which only two jobbing firms operate. Worse, jobbers often have price-fixing agreements and even pool risks and profits in a 'joint book'.

The jobbers who operate in the gilt-edged market have had further problems. The Bank of England's new credit controls have meant greater fluctuations in the prices of gilt-edged securities, and early in 1972 two of the nine jobbers in the gilt market went out of business and one withdrew to concentrate on equities. The Bank would dearly like to see new blood in this market, perhaps in the form of a jobbing firm backed by the capital of a consortium of other City institutions.

The whole jobbing system depends on competition to keep jobbing margins down. Since decimalization in February 1971 there has been a marked widening of the margins that jobbers normally quote. Before decimalization, the typical jobbers' turn in a well-traded share at £1 would be 3d. Since then, it has almost doubled to 2p. This rise in jobbing margins has angered many brokers, who are quite certain that the only reason the jobbers have been able to get away with it is because competition among them has decreased. But there is little brokers can do about it, except to try to divert more of their business away from the floor of the house. This they are increasingly doing, by a method known as the 'put-through'.

There are two kinds of put-through. Sometimes two clients simply want to exchange a block of shares, and ask the broker to organize it. Here the broker would only charge one commission. But though no two put-throughs are the same the much more usual type works rather like this. It starts with a selling order. An institutional investor, such as the Prudential, comes to a broker and asks to sell 500,000 Plessey shares. The broker will first establish a price, based on the market price. He may try to carry out the deal through a jobber, but this is a formality: no jobber would be likely to handle a block of this size. So he then rings round his other institutional clients to find whether any of them can buy enough Plessey shares to make up the deal. If it is a large order he may have a team of several dealers to do the phoning, and even split the transaction with another broker.

Once he has tracked down enough buyers, he tells a jobber and negotiates a turn. There is no agreed scale for this. The jobber has the right at this stage to take some of the shares onto his own book, and if the broker cannot match buyers and sellers exactly the jobber may help him complete the deal. The broker then goes ahead with the transaction. Here he takes a commission from both buyers and sellers. Considering the jobber has done virtually nothing, this is easy money for him. His justification is that if both client and broker default in a put-through, it is the jobber who carries the liability, and also that it is his market price that has provided the basis of the deal.

Not surprisingly, put-throughs are very popular with brokers and the proportion of deals done this way has grown steadily in the course of the 1960s. Though the actual number of put-throughs is small, the brokers most concerned with them put their value at between 5 and 10 per cent of all equity trading.

A few institutions have gone still further, and quietly arranged share deals which completely bypass the brokers and jobbers. It is impossible to know how large this business is. Stockbrokers say hopefully that it is tiny and not growing. But they should note that in Chicago a number of institutions have found it worth their while to pay a firm by the name of Tomasco Associates a flat fee of $10,000 to broke deals of this kind for them. Once the equivalent of Tomasco Associates appears in London, stockbrokers will know that this market is no longer tiny.

But a more immediate threat is the Accepting Houses Committee. In 1972 it set up a company called Ariel, which aims by the spring of 1974 to be running a computerized share-dealing system similar to one (Instinet) already established in New York. This works through terminals linked to a central computer. Once

Ariel comes into operation, the merchant banks and other institutional subscribers will be able to offer a share for sale simply by typing it into their terminals. They will be able to find the price of a share by asking the central computer what blocks of it are on offer. To trade, the subscriber will simply type an instruction onto his terminal, and receive a slip of paper telling him if the deal has been completed. The entire Exchange – brokers, jobbers and market floor – will be bypassed and its work done by a computer.

No one likes being told that their job can be done by a computer. The first reaction of many Stock Exchange men to the accepting houses' plan was to regard it as a bluff to put pressure on the Exchange to reduce its commission charges on large deals. If it was bluff it certainly succeeded. In January 1973, eight months after the accepting houses decided to go ahead with Ariel, the Exchange substantially reduced commission rates on company share deals over £50,000 and gilt-edged deals over £250,000. Ariel is still going ahead.

Brokers freely admit that they are still overpaid for trading in large blocks of shares. In theory there is no reason why brokers should not be paid on the basis of the work involved: so much per hour of executive time, such and such a fee for research carried out, and so on. But brokers are not anxious to make such a change. Nor are they enthusiastic about recent changes in the US which make commissions on deals worth more than £500,000 subject to negotiation. Given the choice, they would redraw their commission scale.

But whether or not scaling down top commission rates will be enough to keep business in the Exchange is another matter, for price is only part of the problem. It is also a question of the sheer inability of the jobbing system to cope with blocks of shares of the size the institutions want to trade in. As the volume of institutional business continues to grow, there is a real danger that business will move increasingly away from the floor of the Exchange. Although without massive capital backing Ariel will be no more able to hold shares than the jobbing system at present, it looks like posing a genuine and serious challenge to the Exchange. Ultimately the floor could become no more than a residual market for small business and personal clients, with most dealing taking place directly between brokers. If the computer trading system proves a practicable alternative, even the brokers may be increasingly bypassed. But for the Stock Exchange, that is a prospect too terrible to contemplate.

HOW NEW FUNDS ARE RAISED

Trading securities is only one side of the Exchange's work. Raising new funds for industry and the government by selling securities to the public is equally important: or logically should be. Yet the amount of time, energy and staff that members of the Exchange devote to raising new funds is a fraction of what they put into trading in existing securities. True, many brokers feel that new issues are the most interesting part of their work and some large firms, of which Cazenove is by far the largest, have specialized in them. A number of brokers have a separate department for handling new issues. But generally this department is tiny compared with, say, the research department, for by and large the new issues side of the brokers' business has not been promoted. They do not have young men scouring the country for companies which might be persuaded to raise funds on the stock market through them. And though the Exchange raises enormous amounts for the government by issuing gilt-edged (see chapter 8) its record in raising new industrial capital is very much less impressive.

The amounts raised both for the government and industry vary enormously from year to year, but by international standards London's record is not good. As the Governor of the Bank of England himself told a *Financial Times* conference on the City and Europe in December 1971:

> In terms of actual volume of funds raised by new capital issues, there is no ground whatsoever for complacency. In proportion to national income, the amounts raised on new capital issues by domestic borrowers (excluding government issues) has been lower in the UK than in the EEC on the average of the

last five years: considerably lower, not much more than half the level.*

London's record of floating new industrial and commercial issues seems all the poorer when one looks at the support given to new issues by its institutional investors. In 1970, admittedly an exceptionally bad year, the total value of equity issues on behalf of British companies was £87 million and of company debentures, £333 million. No less than £76 million and £330 million of these respectively was provided by the institutions. Indeed there is every indication that institutional investors would happily provide more if given the chance. They complain frequently of 'stock shortage', which means that there are not enough companies quoted on the Exchange to give them a reasonable spread of investments without having embarrassingly large holdings of some shares.

The mechanism for raising new funds in London is certainly more efficient than that in a number of European exchanges, and the cost of a new issue is not notably higher. The overwhelming reason for the relative smallness of amounts raised on the exchange is the low demand for investment funds from British industry.

If a company wants to raise money on the London Stock Exchange, it must apply for a quotation. There are several ways of doing so. While most exchanges have stringent size requirements before a company can be quoted, on London relatively small companies are traded. This means that almost all security trading in the UK takes place on the London floor (and that virtually all British shares can be bought on it). There are the provincial markets which in 1973 merged with London, but there is no 'over the counter'† market as in most other countries.

---

* See also *Capital Markets Study* (OECD, 1967), which shows that in 1960–5 domestic issues on UK capital markets as a proportion of Gross National Product were lower than in any major country except Greece.

† In an 'OTC' market, as it is known in the States, buyers and sellers deal directly with 'market makers' who quote prices for buying and selling each share, rather like a 'bring and buy' shop.

If a company simply wants a quotation and does not yet want to raise more funds (the most usual case being where a share quoted on a foreign exchange wants a London quote too) then it is simply 'introduced'. All this means is that if full particulars of the company's affairs are not yet publicly available, it has to publish them. While a quotation on the London Exchange implies that a company is providing adequate information about itself, it says little about the company's financial size or soundness: it is not a seal of approval. In practice there is no problem for companies listed on major US stock exchanges, but some European firms have often found it embarrassing to have to unveil their full consolidated accounts in public.

More usually a company which wants a quote is going public for the first time. The issue is usually handled by a merchant bank in co-operation with a stockbroker, although in the case of smaller companies a new issue is frequently handled by a stockbroker alone. There are two main ways of carrying out a new issue. The more usual is called 'an offer for sale'* where the company offers its shares to the general public. Advertisements setting out details of the offer and of the company's financial position are published in the papers.

However, the offer for sale is expensive for small amounts of capital. The cost of raising, say, £250,000 could be as high as 10 per cent. For smaller issues an alternative method called a placing can be used. Here the bulk of the shares are not offered to the public but 'placed' with institutional holders. A placing is cheaper than a public issue because it does not need to be underwritten. Underwriting means guaranteeing the sale of an issue. In an offer for sale, the issuing house, whether a merchant bank or a broker, gets underwriters – institutional investors like pension funds and insurance companies – to agree (for a fee) to buy any part of the issue that is not sold to the public. Thus even if the public does not buy all the issue, the company whose shares are being offered knows that it will get its money and the issuing house knows that it will not be left with the issue.

* A version of the offer for sale, which differs only in detail, is an 'offer by public subscription' or an 'offer by prospectus'.

A placing may seem a less democratic method of offering shares than an offer to the public. But it does at least avoid one of the less attractive facets of the new issue market – the 'stagging' of issues. Any issue has to be priced. Since this is an inexact science, many new issues are sold to the public at a far lower price than the public would be prepared to pay. Hence the market price quickly goes to a premium over the offered price. Stags are people who make a living by applying for shares at every suitable new issue, and then selling them off at a profit as soon as the market opens.

There is a simple way to curb stagging. It is to offer shares by tender. Would-be buyers write in the price they are prepared to pay for their shares and the amount they want to buy, and the shares are allotted at the lowest price at which there are enough buyers to sell them all. Tenders were quite popular in the late 1960s but subsequently went out of favour. There are two reasons for this. One is that issuers like to be able to groom the list of would-be holders of a share, to try to make sure that there is a fair balance of private and institutional clients. With a tender, issuers claim, there is the danger that a handful of institutions might put in the top bids for the entire issue, to make sure of being given a reasonable allocation, and end up owning the company. The argument that the Prudential or Slater Walker might not want the whole equity of J. Bloggs and Co. and might therefore be deterred from putting in unreasonable bids for excessive amounts of a share does not convince them. The second reason for the unpopularity of tenders is that issuing houses like to see a share go to a small premium after it has been floated. This is of course where stags make their money: the stag knows that the issuer is as anxious as he is to see the share go up a little when the market opens. A tender may make sure that the share floats at the price the market is really prepared to put on it. But that, as became clear in the late 1960s, means that a share is as likely to go down as up in its early days. No issuing house likes that idea. So the stags remain.

Companies quoted on the Exchange can, if their shareholders agree, raise more money in the same way as companies coming to the market for the first time. Otherwise the Exchange insists they go to their shareholders with a 'rights issue'. This is so called because the company offers its shareholders the right to buy more shares, generally at a cheaper price than the ruling market price to make them attractive.

Finally, companies can raise money not by issuing more shares but by issuing loan stock. With loan stock, an annual fixed rate of interest is paid, rather than a fluctuating dividend. Loan stock can be issued, like shares, by an offer for sale (where the stock is sold to the general public), by a placing (where it is sold to institutions) or by an offer restricted to the company's shareholders.

The choice between equity or loan capital is determined by a number of factors. Sometimes it depends on tax legislation. Thus the 1965 Finance Act made it cheaper to raise loan capital than equity, because equity dividends had to be paid out of taxed profits whereas loan interest was paid before tax.

The resulting balance between equity and fixed interest capital is known as 'gearing'. A company is said to be 'highly geared' if it has a high ratio of fixed interest capital to equity. Generally the more risky the business a company is involved in, the lower should be its gearing. A company which has a large – and fixed – amount of interest to be paid every year is more likely to be pushed into a loss in a bad year than one with a high proportion of equity capital on which it can reduce or if necessary pass its dividend.

TAKEOVERS AND MERGERS

Headline-making though they may be, mergers and takeover battles form a relatively small part of activity on the Exchange. They are no less important for that. They have radically changed the shape of British industry. Of the 2,126 manufacturing firms (outside the steel industry) quoted on UK stock exchanges in 1954, over 400 had been acquired six years later.* They have also confronted the Exchange with a whole batch of new and un-comfortable ethical questions.

Mergers and takeover battles are usually masterminded by the respective companies' merchant banks. Long before an offer is

* Ajit Singh, *Takeovers* (Cambridge, CUP, 1971).

made, senior men in the bidding company's bank will have spent days examining every available detail of the company being bid for, working out the price that their client can afford to pay, and discussing such finer points of diplomacy as whether the first approach should be made by the bank or the company, how directors of the company being bid for who are likely to object can be kept in the dark for as long as possible, and what should be said to whom and when. Throughout the bid, a reputable merchant bank has secrecy arrangements that make the Foreign Office look amateur. Bankers avoid naming their firm on the telephone, files are careful never to record company names and a minimum of staff are allowed to know of the bid.

If the firm being bid for is basically in favour of the deal, there will follow long negotiations between the two companies' bankers on what the terms of the offer should be. At critical moments, tempers may be diplomatically lost, but the bankers are professionals and the next week they are perfectly likely to be enjoying an amicable lunch together.

It is when a firm is determined not to be bought that a take-over battle ensues. The bidding company probably begins by making a 'silly bid' at a price level which is bound to be rejected. There are two reasons for this strategy. One is that it may be hard to find out enough about the bid-for company without forcing it to respond to a bid, which obliges it to send out a certain amount of information about its affairs to its share-holders. The other is that, as shareholders have grown more accustomed to takeover battles, they have come to expect not one bid but a succession of them. It may take several offers to persuade them to trade their shares.

For that is the object of the bid. The bidding company offers either cash, or more usually its shares or a combination of cash and shares, for those of the bid-for company. The company being bid for might, typically, have up to 25 per cent of its shares in the hands of institutions, and the remainder in the hands of private shareholders and of members of the board. The institutions play the game with sophistication, often delaying accepting the offer until the last possible moment and frequently having to be cajoled by the merchant bank to do so. So it is very often on the response of the private shareholder that the success of a bid stands or falls.

The takeover battle is an American and British phenomenon rather than a European one. There are a number of reasons. Industry in Europe is too firmly in the hands of banks and family trusts rather than a broad spectrum of private shareholders. Disclosure requirements are not strict enough to make it plain when a company is undervalued. And shares are generally held on a bearer system rather than a register which, thanks to its useful list of names and addresses, makes it easy for the bidding firm to bombard shareholders with bids. In Britain the takeover battle became common from the mid-1950s on. It could become less common during the 1970s, for two reasons. First, the concentration of large companies in Britain is already high by international standards. And second, the usual economic argument for encouraging mergers – that they promote industrial efficiency – is being increasingly questioned. There is growing evidence that companies merge not to achieve greater efficiency but to protect or increase their market share; and indeed, the company produced by a merger frequently appears to be no more efficient than the two firms from which it was formed. If companies themselves do not become disenchanted with the advantages once claimed for sheer size, it may be that the government will be tempted to step in to slow down the concentration of industry.

One kind of takeover acquired a special notoriety in the late 1960s. It was again an American import: asset stripping. If the takeover is the only way the City is prepared to discipline sleepy companies, asset stripping is the most brutal form of this discipline. This was the activity in which firms such as Barclay Securities and Drakes made their reputations. The stripper buys the company, sells off its under-utilized assets – usually property – to other companies who can use them more efficiently and closes down such remaining parts of the company as have no profitable future.

It may be true that asset stripping, by releasing assets which would otherwise be used less productively, contributes to a more efficient economy. Some of these strippers provide valuable managerial skills. But it is impossible not to question the enormous profits which accrue from what is sometimes no more than spotting a suitable firm, selling its land and laying off its workers.

Until 1959 the whole business of mergers and takeovers was largely unregulated. The Stock Exchange policed itself, working on the principle that its main duty was to protect its customers from dishonest or incompetent brokers. For reputable merchant banks there has always been an element of self-discipline in handling takeover deals, imposed simply by the danger of losing a reputation if the deal goes wrong. In the mid-1960s one of the smaller merchant banks, not normally involved in takeover business, strayed into the field. The international merger it tried to put together was an unpleasant failure. Since then it has not handled a single major takeover.

With the battle for control of British Aluminium in 1959 it became obvious that something stronger was needed. The US stock exchanges have been governed since 1934 by a body with legal powers, the Securities and Exchange Commission. The whole idea of statutory controls was – and still is – repellent to a large section of City opinion. The alternative has been the drawing up, by a working party set up by the Governor of the Bank of England in 1959, of the City Code on Takeovers and Mergers. Originally it seems to have been thought that the fact that the code had been drawn up on the Governor's word would be enough to make the City abide by it. By 1968 it was clear that some kind of supervisory body was needed to see the code was enforced; but it was not until 1969 that the present Panel on Takeovers and Mergers was finally set up, equipped with sanctions.

The code deals exclusively with the ethics of takeovers and mergers. Its principal aims are to ensure the protection of the shareholder and the fair conduct of bids. It insists that all shareholders be treated equally. This means, essentially, that those handling the bid are obliged to try to make the same knowledge available to all other parties, and are discouraged from profiting from their own inside knowledge.

Thus the code prohibits insider trading: no person or firm

involved in carrying out a takeover may use the knowledge acquired in the course of business for personal gain. It insists on disclosure: any person or company with an interest in the outcome of a takeover must declare dealings in the shares involved by noon the next day. And it refuses to allow a company to bid for part of another without bidding for the whole.

The panel is a two-tier body. There is the panel itself, chaired by a lawyer, Lord Shawcross, and made up of the heads of the main City bodies. And there is the executive, under its director-general, John Hull, a merchant banker seconded from Schroders. The executive carries out the panel's day-to-day business. It works very flexibly. Anyone who wants the panel's guidance can simply ring the director-general or another member of the executive and get prompt advice. The executive's verdict is not, however, final. It has in the past been overruled by the main panel.

The debate on how well-fitted the panel is for its job is still very much alive. There are a number of abuses which the panel fails to regulate. For example, there is 'massaging the price' in a takeover bid. As bids are generally made wholly or partly in a company's shares, it is in the company's interest to raise the price of its own shares to keep up the paper value of its bid for the other company. A company may not buy its own shares. Its 'associates' may – and this could even include the manager of its own pension fund – provided they declare the purchase. There is still no watertight definition of who is an associate.

More difficult to police has been the code's Rule 30 tackling 'insider dealing'. This prohibits anyone who knows that a bid is going to take place from dealing in the shares of the company being taken over. This has thrown up two major problems. The first is metaphysical: when does the company that plans to make a bid decide that it is going to make a bid and who is to prove it? The second is more concrete. Cases of insider dealing have passed the panel either without rebuke, or – as in five cases handled by the panel in 1971 – with a private ticking off and an order to give the illicit takings to charity. With so terrible a punishment awaiting people who infringe Rule 30, it is hardly surprising that insider dealing has remained rampant. However, in 1973 the panel and the

Stock Exchange council recommended to the government that insider dealing be outlawed.

Even if the panel had taken a sterner line with those who broke Rule 30, it would still have had grave difficulty in ensuring equality of information. Quite apart from officers in the companies themselves, there is a whole network of people within the City – stockbrokers, bankers, financial journalists – who are in a very much better position to know when to buy and when to sell in a takeover bid than the ordinary private shareholder. Their transactions do not have to be disclosed.

The code has already been refined several times. Other criticisms deal with the very form of the Takeover Panel. The mere fact that it is voluntary gives it powers which, paradoxically, are alarmingly extensive. It performs the role of a court without giving the defendant a court's privileges: there is no *sub judice* rule, and defendants have argued that bad press publicity has lost them their case; no legal representation is allowed, and if a member of a merchant bank is inarticulate he may lose his bank's case; and there is no appeal beyond the panel's own appeal committee. In the case of Adepton, the panel reversed a ruling of the executive, after the merchant bank involved had acted on the executive's decision. It is hard to imagine a court of law behaving so arbitrarily. Yet it was also out of the question for William Brandts to sue the panel for any loss that might have accrued as a result of having to put up £5 million in cash to comply with the code.*

The panel's sanctions are also, paradoxically, too strong. Because there is no system of fines it has little choice between a wigging and capital punishment. Its ultimate sanction (which is so extreme that it has never used it) is to request the expulsion of the offending firm from the powerful institutions that support it, which include all respectable City 'clubs', the Accepting Houses Committee, the Issuing Houses Association and the Stock Exchange itself. Such a penalty would spell disaster for even the most reputable firm.

So should the panel be replaced by legal controls in its entirety? City opinion is divided. A body led by David Montagu, chairman

* See chapter 3, p. 53.

of the Orion group, believes that legal controls will have to come sooner or later and will be hastened by British entry into the Common Market.* Others fear that the panel is in danger of becoming a cabal of the City establishment with one standard of morality for its members and another for those outside the charmed circle.

One aspect of the panel's work, the control of insider dealings, looks like being taken over by the Department of Trade and Industry. The Companies Bill, expected to be passed in 1974, is expected to make insider dealing a criminal offence, policed by the Fraud Squad. The DTI inherits the practical difficulties of defining insiders.

But the panel's voluntary policing of takeovers will remain. Here the panel does have two overwhelming advantages: its speed and its flexibility. It certainly needs many changes, of which probably the most essential is the infusion of new members from outside the City. To regulate something as elusive as the equal dissemination of information, it is better to have a body which can put adherence to the spirit of the code before an unyielding interpretation of its letter.

The trouble is that the choice always tends to be seen in terms of extremes, of legal backing or flexibility. But it is surely not beyond the ingenuity of the City and the government to devise a compromise, setting the present code (or a modified version of it) on a legal basis, with a system of fines for transgressors and a proper appeals mechanism through the courts, but still retaining speed and flexibility. If the Bank of England can enforce the exchange control regulations in a way which is widely admired, why should it be impossible to invent a satisfactory way to enforce the City Code?

* Letter to *The Times* (28 January 1971).

6
The insurance world

£4 MILLION A DAY

On the face of it insurance is one of the most successful sections of the City. Despite growing competition from New York and the Continent, it remains far and away the largest international insurance market in the world. The total net life and non-life premium income earned by Lloyd's in 1970 was £787 million; that of the insurance companies* in 1972 was over £5,000 million – altogether about a tenth both of entire world premium income and of the Gross National Product of the United Kingdom. It is also a big foreign currency earner. Indeed, insurance makes more in invisible earnings than the rest of the City put together – £300 million in 1972. It is also the largest single source of investment funds in the country. It finds a home for over £4 million of new money every day.

Insurance is sharply divided into two categories, non-life and life. Between the two there are very considerable differences.

---

* Premium figures of Lloyd's and the companies are not strictly comparable. Lloyd's premium figures are published three years in arrears. Those for the companies refer to the 286 British Insurance Association members only, which do however account for 95 per cent of the companies' business.

Not the least is the fact that the non-life market has, in the late 1960s and early 1970s, passed through one of the most confused and uncertain periods of its history. All three major categories of non-life insurance – fire, accident and marine – showed underwriting losses with varying regularity. There were a number of reasons, but one in particular stood out to those in the industry itself: inflation. For the underwriter, accelerating inflation is a particularly difficult problem to cope with. A risk on which the premium rate is fixed one year may not produce a claim for some time, and the claim may not be settled for several years more. By then prices may have risen far more than anyone could have initially foreseen.

If underwriting was all that insurers did, they would have been in an even worse way. Thanks to the ravages of inflation, they frequently got their sums wrong. Happily there is another aspect to insurance – investment. When you pay over a premium, it is invested by the insurer and its yield works as a longstop to the underwriting side.

As insurance moves into the mid-1970s, it looks as if the industry has begun to learn to live with inflation. Some branches have simply begun to raise premiums more readily and more frequently. But the insurance companies as a whole may be beginning to realize that though it is on underwriting that the really big profits – and losses – are to be made, it is less essential to make underwriting profits if investment can be relied on to provide profits overall. The same inflation that erodes the value of premiums and pushes up replacement and repair costs can also be relied on, by and large, to inflate the value of the industry's investments. Over the coming years the companies are likely to see themselves more and more as a collection of investment institutions, rather than simply as underwriters.

Life assurance is a very different activity from non-life. To start with, it is almost exclusively a form of investment, and so has been highly prosperous. The problem that faces the life assurers is not how to avoid underwriting losses, but how to make the most on their investments and thus pay their policyholders the best bonuses. The risk of dying has long been so closely calculated that short of an outbreak of Black Death it is virtually impossible for the companies to make an underwriting loss. Secondly, the nature of the business is different. Whereas you *insure* your car in case you crash, you *assure* your life even though you know you are bound to die sooner or later. Usually what you are saying to the company is, 'insure me against dying before I am, say, sixty. And in case I don't die by then, save my money, invest it and give it back to me.'

The total premium income from life assurance earned at home and abroad on the London market is over half as large as that from all non-life business, and tends to grow faster. Fire insurance, which includes both industrial and domestic fire business, accounts for about a quarter of the insurance companies' non-life premiums, and accident for nearly two-thirds, of which more than half is made up of motor insurance. Marine insurance is largely dominated by Lloyd's, but in aviation the companies claim to play the leading role.

There is one further distinction in insurance that should be explained here, and that is the one between direct insurance and reinsurance. Reinsurance is basically the taking-on of chunks of risks that have already been insured in Britain and abroad. It spreads the load more evenly and allows the cover for a large or particularly dangerous risk to be shared among a larger number of insurers. There are two main kinds of reinsurance: proportional reinsurance, where the reinsurer covers a certain proportion of the losses of the direct insurer, and non-proportional, in which the reinsurer covers all the losses of the direct insurer above a certain level.

London is still the world's largest international insurance market, although it has not been growing as fast as other centres. But overseas business still represents a very high proportion of transactions on the London market. In 1972 63 per cent of the fire, motor and accident premiums earned by insurance companies which are members of the British Insurance Association (almost all) came from abroad, and 13 per cent of the life premiums. About three-quarters of Lloyd's premium income is earned overseas.

Although London's share of world insurance business has been falling, it remains internationally important in three ways. First, it still leads the world in the markets of marine and aviation insurance. Second, London is still the only place in the world, apart from New York, which is truly an insurance centre. Zürich, for instance, is the headquarters of a number of extremely important insurance firms. But while most of them have branches in London, very few British insurance firms have branches in Zürich. As for New York, it is mainly a domestic insurance centre, taking the bulk of its business from the United States. And third, London is by far the largest reinsurance centre in the world. Lloyd's alone does more reinsurance than any other body.

At the heart of the insurance market are the underwriters, who assess risks and pay claims. Underwriting is carried on by two very different bodies: Lloyd's, which accounts for about a fifth of the market's total premium income; and the 750 British and foreign insurance companies (many of them very small) which account for the rest.

The insurance companies sell insurance to the public both directly and through part-time agents and specialist broking firms. At Lloyd's the broker is the only link between the underwriter and the insured. Then there are a number of firms providing specialist services such as loss adjusters and specialists in loss prevention and risk control.

THE UNDERWRITERS

(a) Lloyd's

Lloyd's is the oldest and most eccentric part of the insurance market. The companies regard it rather as one might a duck-billed platypus – as a creature whose antique form hardly justifies its successful survival into the 1970s. Certainly, if Lloyd's did not exist, no one would try to invent it. Yet it has been fairly successful over the last decade in maintaining its share of the British (though not the world) insurance market. Its net premium income declined as a proportion of total UK premiums in the early 1960s, but partly recovered by the end of the decade. In 1970 its invisible earnings overtook those of the companies, to reach

£121 million. That year Lloyd's accounted for just over half of all marine and aviation business underwritten in the UK, about a quarter of non-marine business other than motor, and just under a tenth of motor business.

Insurance at Lloyd's is transacted in five separate markets – marine, non-marine, UK motor, aviation and short-term life. Internationally, the aviation and marine markets are the most important. Marine insurance, Lloyd's staple diet since it began, is easily the slowest-growing section of the market, but still accounts for about 40 per cent of its net premium income. Premiums from non-marine business overtook marine in the late 1940s, and today are about one and a half times as large. The other three markets are the fastest growing. Lloyd's UK motor insurance premiums almost tripled in the decade from 1959 to 1969. Life assurance premiums, still a tiny part of Lloyd's total premium income, jumped tenfold – despite the fact that Lloyd's syndicates can only write life policies for seven years or less.*

Over half of Lloyd's business – and more in the non-marine market – is not direct insurance but reinsurance. The reason is essentially the way Lloyd's operates overseas. Unlike insurance companies, Lloyd's cannot set up subsidiaries to take on foreign business in countries which will not allow it to operate directly.

Ultimately, this may prove an advantage. As risks grow in size and it becomes more necessary to parcel them out among a number of different insurers, the demand for reinsurance seems certain to increase. At first glance, though, it is odd that Lloyd's should have allowed itself to become primarily a reinsurance market. It hardly, one would think, calls for the spot judgement, the pioneering spirit and the flexibility on which Lloyd's has always prided itself. By and large this is true of proportional reinsurance. It is not true of non-proportional reinsurance, in which Lloyd's specializes.

Lloyd's, as its members always proudly point out, is a pioneer both of insuring new types of risk, and of new techniques of insurance. There are still certain risks that can only find cover at

* In 1972 Lloyd's Life Assurance was set up to underwrite longer-term life business. Its shares are owned only by Lloyd's underwriting syndicates.

Lloyd's, and whenever a new one emerges – like supertankers – the companies may wait for a lead from Lloyd's. But none of this should eclipse the fact that despite the return to profitability of many sections of the market in the early 1970s, Lloyd's has been suffering from weaknesses of which the outside world has been largely unaware.

Lloyd's was born nearly 300 years ago in Edward Lloyd's City coffee house and it still has a whiff of Boodles about it. On the ground floor of a post-war building in Lime Street is the huge Room, capable of holding 3,000 people at once. This is crammed with 'desks', small tables cluttered with atlases and handbooks, and hideously uncomfortable hardbacked pews on which the underwriters sit. Upstairs is a maze of marble corridors and comfortable lounges, and the 'captain's room', a coffee-house relic, all bowls of flowers and genial waiters. Above that are offices used by underwriters and the marine departments of some insurance companies.

Lloyd's is a corporation, run by a committee elected by the members. The committee has very limited regulatory powers, much weaker than those of, say, the Stock Exchange Committee, and probably too weak for the good of Lloyd's itself. The full-time chairman of the committee is elected every year, though he has increasingly tended to serve for several years at a stretch. The last chairman, Sir Henry Mance, took office in 1969; the present chairman, Paul Dixey, in January 1973. The corporation's 2,000 staff run a whole range of back-up services for members, such as the policy signing office and claims settling offices, and carry out some functions which are more logically organized communally.

Apart from the employees of the corporation, there are four types of people connected with Lloyd's: the 'names', who put the money up, organized into syndicates; the underwriters, who assess the risks and sign the policies; the underwriting agents, who manage the syndicates; and the brokers, who place the business. These four groups are enmeshed with each other: everyone at Lloyd's seems to own somebody else.

In late 1973 there were over 7,000 names, grouped into 260

syndicates. The syndicates specialize in one or other market, and a name may subscribe to more than one. About 60 per cent of the names have nothing to do with the running of Lloyd's. These outside names include such well-known figures as Sir Isaac Wolfson and Reginald Maudling, and are elected after what must be the most exclusive means test in the country: British names must be able to show £75,000 of wealth throughout their Lloyd's membership, foreign names £100,000. In return they are eligible for a cut of the syndicate's profits and liable, in theory at least, down to their last silk shirt for its losses.

The other 40 per cent or so of the names work at Lloyd's, as underwriters, as underwriting agents or as brokers. They too have unlimited liability; their wealth qualifications are less demanding than those for outsiders but their underwriting commitments are correspondingly restricted. It is on the second group, the underwriters, that the success or failure of the syndicate ultimately rests. They decide what risks to write at what price. These underwriters may also be names in their own right, or they may just work for a salary and commission from the underwriting agent.

The underwriting agent manages the syndicate. Apart from doing the paperwork and appointing the underwriting staff, the agent is the link between the name and the underwriter. With an outside name he is the only link. Indeed, there is still a species of agent which does not even manage syndicates, but makes a living just by recruiting and negotiating with names.

Finally, the broker: by and large, the only way in which a syndicate can get business is through one of the 260 or so authorized Lloyd's brokers. The main exception is in the motor market, where many provincial brokers have direct access to motor underwriters at Lloyd's. But Lloyd's brokers can place business with the companies: generally more than half the risks they place are with the companies, not with Lloyd's. Feeding business to the underwriters is a broker's main function, but he is also connected in two other ways. As well as being a name in his own right, he may own the underwriting agency.

The agencies were once owned by underwriters, but today

many of them have been sold off. Substantially more than half the underwriting agencies are now owned or partly owned by broking firms or investment houses, and many by the handful of giant brokers which through their agencies control most of the syndicates and thus indirectly employ most of the under-writers. These broker barons are the seven firms of C. T. Bowring (Insurance); Willis, Faber and Dumas; C. E. Heath; Bland, Welch; Bray Gibb Wrightson; Hogg Robinson and Gardner Mountain; and Sedgwick Forbes, probably the biggest of all. No one will agree on whether this relationship affects the distribution of risks. Some Lloyd's men complain that brokers are apt to palm off all the worst risks on the syndicates whose agencies they control, and which would therefore find it embarrassing to refuse. Others grumble that the cream of any broker's business is kept for his agencies' own underwriters. But this is something of a red herring. More worrying is the hold the brokers – through the agents – have on the names.

To watch Lloyd's in operation, you would think the under-writer was the lynchpin. He spends most of his day sitting at his desk in spartan discomfort, waiting like a queen bee in a hive for the broker to feed him. The broker in turn weaves his way through the desks, collecting underwriters' initials on his 'slip'. This is a length of paper with the bare details of the risk typed at the top. Opposite his initials, each underwriter scribbles the proportion of the risk his syndicate will bear.

On any particularly large or difficult risk, the broker will go first to the 'leader'. This would be the syndicate which has built up a reputation as the expert in that particular type of insurance, and which would set the premium rate for the policy. In the non-marine market the system has not been working well, and has helped to aggravate relations between brokers and under-writers. The market is dominated by a few large syndicates, and brokers frequently spend hours queuing for the signature of one of the underwriters before they can take their slips on to the next syndicate. Queuing is inconvenient for the brokers and not always to the underwriters' advantage. The leaders tend to be the big rather than the most competent syndicates, and the system makes the market less flexible. In the marine market underwriters are prepared to follow smaller syndicates provided they have a good track record.

Compared with the insurance companies Lloyd's may look amateurish. But it has two great strengths. First, it is very cheap. Its overheads are incredibly low. They add up to perhaps 2–4 per cent of the net premium. No insurance company with vast premises and highly paid research staff could hope to touch that. And second, if a broker cannot get the risk he wants accepted by one underwriter, he can try the next one. By the end of the day the chances are that he will have found someone who at some rate will take the risk.

This is what gives the market the flexibility which its supporters never tire of praising. Lloyd's has pioneered not only outlandish risks such as insurance against the discovery of the Loch Ness monster, but more serious ones such as supertankers and nuclear power stations, and new types of insurance cover such as excess of loss reinsurance. And when in the summer of 1970 Palestinian guerillas blew up a Pan American jumbo jet in Cairo, it emerged that the only agents prepared to provide war risk cover for the plane had been Lloyd's – and the US government.

Despite its low overheads, and despite its innovatory zeal, Lloyd's in the late 1960s passed through a period of serious difficulties. Like most of the insurance companies it made recurrent and heavy losses, but it also failed to attract new names. Both these immediate problems had disappeared by the early 1970s. But there are still a number of things fundamentally wrong with the structure of Lloyd's. Until these flaws are tackled, the improvement in Lloyd's profit record and ability to attract new names will not have a firm foundation.

Insurance is a cyclical business. Lloyd's accounts are always published three years in arrears, as by then hopefully 90 per cent of the claims against the base year will have been met. When the account for 1965 was closed in 1968, no one expected a golden year. Hurricane Betsy alone had torn a big hole in the results of marine and non-marine markets alike. But Lloyd's losses that year, nearly £38 million, were larger than the profits made in any recorded year to that date. Since then Lloyd's performance has dramatically improved: in 1970 Lloyd's made a record £65 million profit.

The ebb and flow of names in recent years closely follows the rise and fall of profits. Accounts reveal, three years in arrears, a good year. A queue of new applicants for membership builds up. Already, the return to profitability of the world insurance market is encouraging underwriters to compete to hold premiums down. They pare them too finely and a new cycle of lean years begins. Three years later, another bout of losses is revealed. Applications die away. At the time when underwriters are raising premium rates to retrieve the situation, they find that the total premium income they are permitted to write – which is fixed in terms of the deposits of syndicate members – is stagnant or falling. Attractive risks have to be turned down because the underwriter simply does not have the capacity to carry them.

When Lloyd's is making good profits, it tends to forget about this long-term and serious cyclical problem. In bad years, the loss of names worries it considerably. From 1966 the number of new names fell steeply while the number of resignations doubled. In 1968, the year that the disastrous 1965 results were revealed, no less than 148 names resigned and a further 98 died. Both figures were records for the previous ten years. More names resigned in 1968 alone than in the seven years 1959–65.

Lloyd's became alarmed about its future. In 1968 it took the revolutionary step of setting up a working party under Lord Cromer, then head of Barings and later British ambassador to the US, to search its soul for it. The Cromer Committee reported early in 1970. Its criticisms were forthright. Lloyd's has never published the report in full.

The shortened version of the Cromer report that emerged concentrated on the fact that Lloyd's capacity was not growing fast enough to keep pace with the world demand for insurance. It calculated that the appreciation of the deposits of existing Lloyd's members (the amount of insurance a name can write is strictly tied to the size of his deposit) would allow the market's capacity to expand by about 3–4 per cent: this left a further 6 or

7 per cent to be found from new members if no ground was to be lost. An increase of membership on the scale which that implied was, the Cromer Committee pointed out, a 'formidable target'.

In fact Lloyd's has achieved this. First it opened the door to what it elaborately terms 'non-British nationals'. Then women were allowed to become underwriting members. And in 1970 the door was opened to the ultimate intrusion, 'non-British women'. As it turned out, though, it was the return to profitability which had the most striking effect on the number of applicants. In 1972 nearly 1,000 new names joined Lloyd's.

Cromer also proposed that UK companies with a minimum paid up capital of £1 million should be allowed to become members of Lloyd's, a proposal which Lloyd's has rejected, partly because of the difficulty of fitting a company with limited liability into its unlimited liability framework, but more because Lloyd's is freer to insure abroad with its present structure.

To use existing resources better, Cromer recommended higher premium ceilings. Previously, most Lloyd's names could write cover up to six or seven times their deposits. Now they are able to write up to ten times. Together with a relaxation of the barriers between different markets, these measures increased the amount of insurance Lloyd's can carry by about 20 per cent even without new names.

But neither Cromer's published criticisms nor the measures adopted by Lloyd's to meet them touched the more basic difficulties of the corporation. Two stand out: the relationship between underwriting agencies and their names, and Lloyd's dependence on underwriting alone for its profits.

The sole contact between a name and the underwriter is the underwriting agency, which in turn may well be owned by one of the broker barons. The conflict of interest between the broker and the underwriter is blatant. Most Lloyd's men admit that it exists. But at least this conflict has the advantage of being out in the open. The same cannot be said for the way the agencies run the syndicates.

Put bluntly, the agencies (and so indirectly the broker barons who own them) have been taking up to 25 per cent of the syndicates' profits in a good year, while making the names meet all the losses in a bad.

Practice varies from one syndicate to another. Incredibly, there is no prescribed form of agreement between names and agencies. Generally the agency not only receives from each name a 'salary', a fixed fee of £150 to £300 a year, but also gets a cut of the profits of the syndicate. By contrast, the name pays virtually all the expenses of the syndicate and also bears all its losses. Lloyd's view is that the salary goes to cover the agent's expenses: the profits cut, to give him an interest in the syndicate's profitability. But to others it might look like 'heads I win, tails you lose.' There have been other grounds for criticism: agencies have not always made the terms of agreement with their names clear to them, and sometimes have failed to send their names up-to-date accounts of their syndicate. Until recently the committee of Lloyd's was unable to intervene officially between agencies and names even when the names complained to it.

The committee has been aware for some time of the need to curb the power of the agencies, although it has felt that the first remedy lies in the hands of the names themselves. But there has been something of a tug-of-war between the committee and the agencies, backed by their broker owners. By 1972 the committee had won a significant victory. Not only had it drawn up a code of conduct for agencies and required that certain provisions be written into agreements between agencies and names; it had summoned some of the agencies informally before it and reprimanded them; and it had won the important power to approve agencies and to withdraw the name of an offender from the list. Lloyd's claims that these regulations are required for only a small minority of agents and that generally agents and names are on excellent terms.

Lloyd's other major weakness is the extent to which its profits depend on underwriting. Unlike the companies, it has no cushion of investment income to fall back on in lean years. There are two main reasons for this. First, what would serve a company as its capital and reserves is, in the case of Lloyd's, essentially the private wealth of its names. Secondly, most of the funds that Lloyd's does have under its control, its 'float' of premium income, is splintered among 200 underwriting agencies, each of which has to maintain a higher level of liquidity than would be the case if the premium float were pooled.

Lloyd's, unlike the companies, cannot readily carry forward the profits of a good year to set against the losses of a bad. In Lloyd's own eyes, this is a serious defect. Lloyd's has a Special Reserve Fund,* into which underwriters can put sums of money before surtax (though not income tax). The fund can be used only to meet losses and if an underwriter draws from it on resigning from Lloyd's, he must pay surtax. Restrictions have limited the amount put into the fund, and so Lloyd's has tried to go further and establish a catastrophe fund, to help provide a buttress against periodic catastrophes. Lloyd's would like contributions to it to be paid before income tax, but endless debate has failed to win consent from the Inland Revenue.

Does the peculiar structure of Lloyd's and the antiquated and fragmented syndicate system in particular obstruct good underwriting? Certainly the system has drawbacks. How can a Lloyd's man, handling £10 million of risks a day with virtually none of the research backing of an insurance company, underwrite as well as he might do? In the non-marine market particularly there is an almost complete lack of sophisticated data facilities. There are obvious inefficiencies: staff in each syndicate have to record details of risks provided by brokers – details which are being similarly recorded by every other syndicate which has underwritten part of the risk. 'Possibly 80 per cent of the total staff in the Room', according to one underwriter's guess, 'are engaged in simple clerical work, hoarding repetitive information, syndicate by syndicate.'

Having said all this, there are still two outstanding reasons for supporting the syndicate system. One is the relative ease with which a new syndicate can be set up. Young men prepared to take risks – and able to persuade a handful of names to back their judgement – can come to the fore far more quickly and earn

* Lloyd's also has a 'central fund' but the purpose of this is to guarantee policy-holders. See p. 169.

Premium income of the ten largest insurance companies in 1972

Order	Group	Grand total all business	General Total	Order	General Fire and accident	Marine
		£m	£m	Order	£m	£m
1	Commercial Union	668·6	567·2	1	524·3	42·9
2	Royal	559·2	503·5	2	474·9	28·7
3	Prudential	409·2	83·2	7	80·6	2·6
4	Guardian-Royal Exchange	380·6	279·0	4	243·4	35·6
5	General Accident	335·7	288·7	3	279·6	9·2
6	Sun Alliance and London	252·6	218·4	5	187·8	30·6
7	Eagle Star	244·0	125·4	8	111·9	13·5
8	Norwich Union	226·9	105·0	9	96·2	8·7
9	Legal and General	186·0	36·1	11	33·2	2·9
10	Phoenix	173·0	136·7	6	118·7	18·1
	TOTAL	3 435·8	2 343·0		2 150·1	192·7

Source: *Policy Holder Insurance Journal*, 26 October 1973.

much more than they could in the more bureaucratic framework of a company.

The other is that the syndicate system is particularly suited to types of insurance where no two risks are the same, and where there is little experience or precedent to fall back on in rate setting. This is not, unfortunately, the case with the most rapidly growing area of insurance, motor risks, nor with the most profitable, long-term life. It was once the case with marine insurance. It now applies to some industrial business, where rapid technological advance makes rate setting a leap in the dark, and it applies to catastrophe risks, in which Lloyd's leads the world. This kind of business is not necessarily unprofitable. But it is by definition the most risky. Someone has to do it.

(b) The companies

There are about 580 British insurance companies, varying enormously in size. Frequent mergers steadily diminish their numbers. At one end of the scale are a handful of giant composite groups, of which the ten largest underwrite between them some 80 per cent of all non-life company business. (The table lists them in

Ordinary and Industrial life

£m	Order
101·4	7
55·7	11
326·0	1
101·6	6
47·0	13
34·2	19
118·6	4
121·9	8
149·9	2
36·3	18
1 092·6	

order of size.) At the other end are such small and esoteric concerns as the Ecclesiastical, which insures churches and the lives of country parsons to whom it offers, thanks to inspired management, one of the best bonus rates going. Finally, there are the life offices, some of which belong to one of the composites, and some of which are separate.

All of the giant composite groups carry out both life and non-life business. All insure both individuals and companies. But there are differences both in their character and the shape of their business.

Easily the two largest in terms of non-life premium income are Commercial Union and the Royal. Commercial Union has a certain brashness about it. It lives in a tower block in the City with smoked-glass windows and a boardroom whose walls are covered in bottle-green suede. In the late 1960s it unnerved the brokers by cutting them out when it wooed the accounts of Tube Investments and British Leyland away from more conventional houses. It upset them again in the early 1970s by pioneering direct billing, where the client, instead of paying the broker, hands both premium and commission to the insurance company which then pays the broker his commission separately.* Commercial Union is heavily involved in the US.

So is the Royal, a company with a patrician air about it. Indeed the Royal is primarily interested in overseas business: 80 per cent of its premium income comes from abroad and over 50 per cent from the USA alone.

The Prudential acquired its household name in that nineteenth-century brand of door-to-door life assurance, industrial life (described on pp. 156–7). It is in the embarrassing position of being Britain's largest single investor with between £2 million and £3 million of new funds to invest every week. In terms of its life business it is far and away the largest company in the country; in non-life business, it is relatively small. Its railway-Gothic fortress in Holborn conceals a 700–seat theatre on the top floor. Yet there is a distinctly civil service atmosphere in the place. A stock-broker who visited one of the investment staff found him in a temporary office. His own, he said, was being painted. If this one looked a little odd, it was because it was meant for someone in a higher grade. To keep the record straight, they had removed the carpet. . . .

One of the most aggressive of the top ten is Guardian-Royal Exchange, formed in 1968 when Guardian swallowed up its rather Trollopian partner. Today almost all the Royal Exchange men have been eased out. It does a higher proportion of life business than most of the large composites, and has a profitable outlet for motor insurance through a link with the Automobile Association.

General Accident, whose head office is eccentrically located in Perth, is the country's largest motor insurer. Motor insurance brings in 60 per cent of its premium income. A non-tariff company,† it has been left rather exposed by the collapse of the motor tariff. Formerly, it was able to wait to see what rates the tariff companies would set and then quote slightly lower ones.

Sun Alliance is built on three ancient companies, the Alliance (once the most aristocratic of insurers), the Sun and the London.

* See pp. 152–4 for the conflict between brokers and insurers.
† See p. 163 for the motor tariff and its demise.

It regards itself as strong on household insurance, and has extensive connections with building societies through which it probably sells more insurance than any other large company.

Norwich Union has an unusual structure: its Life Society owns the shares of the rest of the group for reasons explained below. The Norwich is also a major fire insurer. In late 1972 it branched out into commercial banking, setting up Norwich General Trust to provide loans to industry through the group's branch network.

Eagle Star is a family company, which has meant that it has been left out of the wave of big insurance mergers. In the late 1960s and early 1970s it went through a bad patch. It does more liability insurance than average; on its fire and accident account it did worse in 1969 and 1970 than any of the other major composites. Its underwriting loss on fire and accident was a staggering 10 per cent of premium in 1969 and 7 per cent in 1970.

Legal and General is, after the Prudential, the country's second largest life assurer; and like the Prudential, its non-life business is rather small. It was one of the pioneers of occupational pension schemes, which still account for a high proportion of its business.

Phoenix is the one large British insurance company with a direct link with an indigenous American insurer, Continental Insurance of New York, with which its American business is pooled. Its overseas business, though substantial, is not as large absolutely or proportionately as that of the Royal or the Commercial Union, and eyebrows were raised in the insurance world when, in 1972, the Phoenix became the first large composite to win the Queen's Award to Industry.

Apart from these ten firms, there are a sizeable number of other general companies, many of them very small. Several foreign insurers have branches in London: the Zürich handles easily the largest amount of general insurance, and Sun Life of Canada is the biggest life office. Then there is a group of specialists such as the British and foreign reinsurance companies of which easily the largest UK company is Mercantile and General.

Finally there are the life offices. There are some 235 insurers writing life business in Britain. Life assurance differs from all other forms of insurance in a number of important ways. First, it is not so much a way of insuring against risk – even the risk of dying – as a form of investment. Second, it is profitable. Because the life offices offer an outlet for savings rather than cover against risks, they suffered none of the massive underwriting losses of the general insurance companies. Third, partly because of strict legal restrictions in other countries on selling life assurance and investing life funds, they do a far smaller proportion of business abroad than non-life insurers. Finally, the life offices provide the main exception to the rule that insurance companies have an ordinary joint-stock capital structure.

The ten largest life funds 1972

	Size of fund	Type of fund
	£m	
Prudential	1 691·4	Proprietary
Legal and General	1 299·0	Proprietary
Standard Life	1 005·3	Mutual
Norwich Union	798·7	Mutual
Commercial Union	710·8	Proprietary
Guardian-Royal Exchange	607·5	Proprietary
Eagle Star	514·3	Proprietary
Sun Life	483·9	Proprietary
Scottish Widows'	477·6	Mutual
Royal	382·2	Proprietary

Source: Life Offices Association.

A number of life offices are mutual. This means that all the capital comes from the policyholders, among whom the profits are shared. This gives a mutual company a built-in edge over a joint-stock or 'proprietary' life company. In theory the proprietary companies are potentially at a perpetual disadvantage, as their profits must also be split with their shareholders.

But mutual organization has its drawbacks. It is extremely hard for a mutual company to expand. It always takes a long time to get a new life fund off the ground and in that time expansion has to be financed from the parent company's capital – which in the case of a mutual belongs to the existing policyholders. The management of mutual companies often seems sleepier than that of proprietary ones, perhaps because there is no chance of a mutual fund being taken over. For thanks to their peculiar structure it is impossible for a mutual fund to be owned by another company: thus the substantial life funds run by many of the big composites are almost all proprietary. The exception is Norwich Union Life, a mutual fund which owns shares in the rest of the Norwich Union group.

Of the largest life offices, most are part of composite groups – such as the Prudential, Legal and General (which has a massive pension business), Norwich Union, Guardian-Royal Exchange, Commercial Union, the Royal and Eagle Star. But there are also some independent life offices. Most are mutual, such as Standard Life and Scottish Widows', but a few, such as Sun Life, are proprietary.

Although the life assurers have not had to suffer the traumas which shook the general underwriters in the 1960s and early 1970s, their industry has been undergoing a revolutionary change. From the early 1960s when the first unit-linked policies* were introduced, life assurance was to become more and more a highly competitive investment business. A rash of new companies sprang up, among them Abbey Life, set up in 1962 by Mark Weinberg which in 1971 was writing more than half the property and equity-linked business. Weinberg left in 1970 to become managing

* There are three main types of life policy: term, whole life and endowment. With a term policy the assurer agrees to pay out a fixed sum if the person assured dies within a fixed period. This is purely insurance against dying: if the person does not die within the fixed period, he gets nothing back. By contrast, with an endowment policy the assurer invests most of the premium, putting only a small portion aside into a term life policy. If the policyholder dies within the period specified in the policy, his dependents receive only a relatively small sum. If he survives, he himself receives a lump sum when the policy matures. Endowment policies vary, depending on the way the premiums are invested. The main variants are 'without profits' policies, where the sum paid back on maturity is fixed; and 'with profits' policies, where in addition the company pays a bonus depending on the capital gains it has made from its investments. With the newer types, unit trust-linked and property bond-linked policies, premiums are invested in shares or a property fund and the sum paid depends on the capital gain on the shares or fund. Endowment policies are by far the most popular type in Britain. Finally, whole life policies are something of a halfway house between term and endowment policies. The insurer pays back a fixed sum when the person insured dies.

director of Hambro Life, set up by the merchant bankers Hambros. Within one year, Hambro Life had a turnover of over £20 million. By 1972, on one rough estimate, unit-linked policies were accounting for 30 per cent of current life premiums.

Unit-linked funds have been followed by property bonds, where the maturing value of the policy is linked to the value of a property portfolio. Property bonds in turn have been followed by managed funds, where the value is linked to an investment fund managed by the life office.

On the whole the old-established life offices have limped along behind this movement. By and large they have been content to concentrate mainly on their traditional with-profits policies, though most now offer a unit trust-linked policy too. But only a few of the older offices have made a feature of these new types of policy and most of this expanding market has been pre-empted by the newcomers.

Among these newer arrivals, there is a feeling that the pure life offices are an anachronism. Mark Weinberg told the Insurance and Actuarial Society of Glasgow in November 1971 that life offices as now known would disappear within fifteen years and be superseded by financial conglomerates offering a full range of savings, loans and life assurance services.

Unit-linked and similar forms of life assurance look like being major growth areas in the later 1970s. In any endowment policy, the proportion of premium going towards providing life cover is extremely small. Typically 90 per cent of net premiums go towards investment, and a mere 10 per cent into life cover. With life assurance increasingly just one more savings outlet and serving a diminishing social function, it is time to question whether tax relief on the whole premium on an endowment policy is still justified on any other grounds than as a means to encourage contractual savings. There is no other logical reason why an investment in a unit trust-linked life fund should be treated any differently from an investment in a unit trust.

The other major growth area for the life companies is likely to be occupational pensions. In 1970 there were already 6,240,000 members of insured pensions schemes. The Conservative White

Paper, envisaging a more important role for occupational pensions, understandably had an enthusiastic welcome from the industry.

MARKETING

The insurance industry's marketing is haphazardly organized. There are three main ways of selling insurance, none entirely satisfactory: through brokers, through part-time agents and directly by the companies themselves. The pattern of marketing varies with the kind of insurance. Lloyd's relies only on brokers, while the companies use all three methods. Brokers sell 90 per cent of all marine business (thanks largely to their connection with Lloyd's), 90 per cent of all UK pension business and 74 per cent of all industrial and commercial insurance. Their hold on the market for personal insurance is weaker: they sell only 30 per cent of personal motor cover, 29 per cent of all ordinary life business and 20 per cent of household insurance.* In these areas agents and direct selling are much more important.

(a) The brokers

Virtually anyone can set himself up as a broker, and in personal insurance just about anyone does. No one has ever counted the number of broking firms in the country, though there are probably some 5,000–6,000 full-time brokers. Apart from the large international broking firms with operations in London, such as the Americans Marsh and McLennan, probably the world's largest, and Johnson and Higgins, the cream of the brokers are the 260 members of Lloyd's Insurance Brokers' Association, led by the seven giants listed on p. 138. Most of the big brokers draw nearly half their income from overseas, the bulk of it from the US. Willis Faber Dumas, for example, probably the third or fourth largest broker in the world, finds about 75 per cent of its business abroad. Most of the giants are geared mainly to wholesale business – industrial, commercial and marine insurance,

* Report by the Economist Intelligence Unit for the Corporation of Insurance Brokers.

though one, Leslie and Godwin, does a considerable amount of pension business.

The structure of broking has been changing rapidly. A series of mergers have taken place. Sedgwick Forbes, probably the largest of all the brokers, was formed by a merger of two broking giants announced in 1972. There has been a growing tendency to diversify into a whole range of other activities. Thus C. T. Bowring draws less than half its profits from traditional insurance-broking business.

Diversifying is the easiest way for a broker to grow big, but the tendency might also suggest a lack of faith in insurance broking as a profitable business in the longer run. Indeed there are good reasons for brokers to doubt whether in ten or fifteen years' time there will be many large firms surviving on broking alone. For the brokers are under attack from both sides. Both their clients and the insurers would like to see their margins whittled down.

The insurers, in the period of heavy underwriting losses, became understandably anxious to snatch all possible profit from the brokers' hands. Brokers, large and small, are paid by commission, a percentage of premium. Some of their profits are generated by investing the premiums they collect in the period between receiving them from the client and passing them on to the underwriter. But the bulk consists of commission income.

Both these sources of broking profits are now threatened. The companies have begun to put pressure on those brokers who spin out the interval between collecting premiums and handing them over. Led by Commercial Union, some are developing direct billing. More important, the commission system has come under attack. It is not easy to defend. It means first that the client in effect pays for the broker's services whether he wants them or not. For unless the client is sophisticated enough to lean on the company or the broker he pays a premium that includes the commission price. Next, the broker gets paid the same, whether he simply arranges a straightforward policy or whether he offers his client valuable advice; and he gets more on a large policy than a small, even if they involve the same amount of work. Finally the commission system means that the broker has a built-in financial interest in getting his client to buy the policy with the highest possible premium, whether it suits him or not.

All brokers strenuously deny that this last point enters their calculations. But they tacitly acknowledge the first two. Thus large companies may get remissions on their premiums from the brokers, while ingenious personal clients can – though less and less – act as their own insurance agents and thus pocket their own commission.

Though commissions are usually on a fixed scale, they tend to be higher at Lloyd's (where in theory, though not in practice, they are all individually negotiated) because a broker for a Lloyd's policy has more work to do than he would for a company.

Many of the difficulties facing the broking profession are the result of the commission system. It has meant first of all that few of the largest brokers find it worth their while to try to make personal insurance pay, although many smaller brokers have succeeded and it is certainly a market with enormous potential. On life insurance policies the commission is particularly profitable. Many smaller brokers are prepared to sell motor and household insurance in the hope of attracting the occasional life policy. Most companies carried out a purge of their small accounts in the early 1960s, and these now tend to be handled either in a separate office outside the City, or by a firm of smaller brokers on their behalf. There are exceptions: some big brokers do subsidize a small amount of personal insurance from their industrial customers in the democratic belief that the small motorist of today may be the ICI chairman of tomorrow. But Norman Frizzell and Partners is the only really large firm with a personal business of any size, made up mainly of motor insurance.

In marked contrast to personal insurance the fastest growing area of broking, reinsurance, involves vast premiums and relatively little work. Commissions are tiny but the sums involved are so large that reinsurance brokers are looked on as an élite. A reinsurance broker, say his lowlier colleagues, is the sort of man who excuses himself from a committee meeting saying he has a dinner appointment in Paris.

Thus the bread and butter of the big brokers is industrial, commercial and marine insurance. Here the unsuitability of the commission system is most evident. The brokers are increasingly finding themselves called on not to sell insurance but to act as consultants; and they are wondering whether they should not be paid on this basis. Once a big company can spend £50,000 a year or so on its insurance bill, it can justify the appointment of a full-time insurance manager. As the insurance bill gets bigger, the company may set up its own insurance department. At this stage the broker can only earn his commission as a specialist adviser. In a few cases brokers have actually set up special consultancy arrangements with large companies which already have their own insurance departments.

The big insurance companies have also been dissatisfied with the commission system. Kenneth Bevins, chief general manager of the Royal, told a brokers' conference:

> Acting on the one hand as 'professional' adviser to your 'client' and on the other as an agent for the insurers . . . is a feat of acrobatics which is obviously perfectly possible, but it does seem to be uncomfortable and to create a number of difficulties. At some time in the future I imagine it will be necessary for you to decide whether you wish to be a profession or whether you wish to be in business, because the two seem to me to be incompatible.*

In May 1969 a panel set up by the British Insurance Association under the chairmanship of Eric Orbell, then a director and general manager of Commercial Union, recommended privately that clients paying more than £1,000 in premiums should be able to choose between buying insurance directly from a company net of premium or paying the broker a negotiated fee for his advice and services. The cries of horror from the brokers which greeted this suggestion induced the BIA to say hastily that the majority of the Orbell committee felt that the recommendations should simply be a basis for discussion.

* Talk to Corporation of Insurance Brokers Conference, 26 April 1969.

(b) The agents

One can understand the reluctance of the brokers to bother with personal insurance when they see their main competitors, the part-time agents, earning almost as much commission for doing little more than arranging introductions. A network of perhaps 70,000 agents* – mainly garages, but also bank managers, estate agents, accountants, solicitors and building societies – act for a number of insurance companies, earning 'perks' every so often by selling their clients and friends insurance. People can even become their own agents to save commission. The agents almost always just introduce the client to the company; they do not pretend to give the sort of advice that a broker should in theory be able to provide, and the chances are that they can only give clients details of the policies of one or two companies.

Part-time agents are dying out. Some companies have already begun to drop those who do not generate enough business and the drive to cut costs may squeeze others out. At the same time the clearing banks are changing the way they sell insurance, and setting up their own insurance servicing organization to replace the private agency of the branch manager.

(c) Direct selling

Direct selling is bounding ahead. As the size of composite companies has grown and competition in insurance marketing has intensified, the insurance companies themselves have been selling more and more insurance direct.

Direct sales techniques are used occasionally in company insurance. In the late 1960s, Commercial Union had a professed policy of encouraging its industrial clients to shortcircuit brokers by buying their insurance directly. Understandably, brokers argue that this practice is not prevalent and indeed Commercial Union subsequently reversed its policy.

Direct selling of personal insurance, on the other hand, has been developing rapidly through branch offices or 'insurance shops', through newspaper and direct mail advertisements, and door-to-door.

* Source: Economist Intelligence Unit report for the CIB.

The large companies, particularly Commercial Union and the Royal, have tried revamping their branches and conducting some imaginative if not entirely successful experiments in selling insurance over the counter in big stores. More profitable (though not strictly speaking a form of direct selling) have been agreements with banks, clubs and associations. Thus Williams and Glyn's Bank offers its Masterguard insurance package in conjunction with the Royal, Phoenix and Eagle Star, and the Automobile Association has a link with Guardian-Royal Exchange and Lloyd's. The companies doubled their spending on advertising – mostly in the newspapers – in the four years to 1970. Their advertisements have also become far more aggressive – witness the transition from Norwich Union's eminently forgettable pictures of British towns – 'A fine city, Norwich' – to Phoenix's despondent man in a mackintosh – 'A man without life assurance must have a pretty low opinion of himself.'

There are two very different worlds of door-to-door selling. There is the Dickensian institution of industrial life, which grew out of the nineteenth-century burial funds. (The 'industrial' refers to the industrious classes, a Victorian euphemism for the working class.) And there is the slick hard sell – geared to the telephone and aimed at the middle class – mainly of unit-linked life policies.

Industrial life assurance is essentially expensive life assurance: as a general rule, its premiums are higher and its bonus rates lower than other forms of life policy. Its only justifications are that it is better than none; and what many people want.

The reason is that industrial life is not only *sold* door-to-door; the premiums are *collected* from each house every week or month. To do this the twenty or so industrial life offices (the biggest by far is the Prudential) employ an army of 46,000 collectors. They call on three out of every four families in Britain, gathering premiums averaging only £8 or so every year. The average sum assured under an industrial policy is only £150 while the average policy in ordinary branch business is nearer £2,000. Yet these offices write rather more than half of the country's life business in terms of premium income written individually – that is, not as part of group schemes – and roughly half of that is collected from the homes of policyholders. The offices claim that industrial life is still expanding at a healthy rate. But it has tended since the war to die out in the US and Australia.

The industrial life offices also sell personal general insurance at the door but their methods could never be described as high-pressure. Despite the arrival of the newer door-to-door salesmen, whom they regard with alarm and contempt, they remain entrenched in their belief that selling life assurance aggressively ultimately leads to high lapse rates.

Unit trust-linked and property-linked life policies, usually sold directly, were the most important development in life assurance in the 1960s. They have survived both the difficulties of Bernie Cornfeld's Investors Overseas Services, whose subsidiary International Life Insurance launched the Dover Plan in England, and the 1969–70 slump in the stock market.

Some industrial life offices have tried to market unit-linked policies but with much less success than the more aggressive companies such as Abbey Life, Hambro Life, Save and Prosper and Sun Life of Canada. These policies have not been sold exclusively door-to-door or over the telephone, but that has been the fastest growing outlet. Roughly 60 per cent of Save and Prosper's new business comes from its direct sales force.

Some companies, especially the foreign-based ones, employ foot-in-the-door tactics and heavy 'front-end' loading. This means that a large part of the early premiums go to salesmen's commission and company management charges. On Dover Plan policies, just over half of the first year's premium was absorbed by the company.

UNDERWRITING PROBLEMS

(a) Inflation

The UK motor market serves to illustrate the problem of inflation. Between 1963 and the end of 1971 the basic rates for motor cover rose by 114 per cent – although for drivers with a full no-claims discount (around two-thirds of all British motorists) the cost of cover rose by only 49 per cent. Meanwhile in the same period the cost of motor repairs rocketed. The cost of garage repairs and servicing (excluding spare parts) rose by 150 per cent, and the price of replacement parts rose faster than the price of new cars. Underwriters had got their sums wrong.

Everyone in the insurance market is now acutely aware of the problem and busy finding ways of living with it. What insurers clearly need is some equivalent of the manufacturing industry's cost-escalation clause. Household insurance policies, such as that offered by Sun Alliance, frequently include an escalator clause which automatically raises the sum insured each year. Industrial insurers in the early 1970s were just beginning to adopt a similar device in some policies, under which the value of the building or equipment insured is deemed to increase daily by a certain percentage. But while such expedients may reduce the threat of inflation with property risks, they are of little help to liability insurers. If a man is run down by a car and breaks his leg, and he and the insurer have to wait three years for a settlement, the chances are that he will get a far larger settlement than the insurer expected when he wrote the driver's policy. One possible solution to this problem might be to assume a high rate of inflation and fix premiums accordingly, refunding part to policyholders on the basis of the inflation that actually occurs.

(b) Technical change

Technical change has thrown up two particular problems. First, insurance rates are set largely on the basis of past experience, but with the advent of supertankers, jumbo jets and nuclear power stations, risks have been created of which the insurers have no experience. Paul Dixey explained the effect of supertankers in a speech in October 1970:

> In all previous developments in shipbuilding, and in under-writing, it has been possible to proceed gradually from one design to another slightly larger, but the demands of the oil industry have been so pressing that ships were being built

without the builders, the classification societies or the underwriters having gained service experience. And it is the underwriter who pays for everybody else's mistakes or inexperience and he has to fix his rates without any records of previous experience of similar types of ship to guide him.

Unfortunately it is not just at the frontiers of technological change that insurers sometimes do not have enough information about the risks they cover. Julius Neave, general manager of the Mercantile and General Reinsurance Corporation, told a conference in December 1970:

> It would, I think, come as some surprise to those in manufacturing industries to discover the extent to which insurance, the handmaid of industry so closely involved in its fortunes, is ignorant of the processes used in the different manufacturing industries which it serves and protects from their special hazards.

More research, perhaps on a pooled basis, will be one answer to this problem.

Secondly, as the type of risk has changed, so has its size. This makes it harder to spread a risk thinly enough for no underwriter to carry a dangerously heavy part of it. To spread the cover on a $24 million jumbo jet, with perhaps another $100 million liability cover for passengers and third parties, or to place a $10 million oil tanker so that the risk does not fall too heavily on a few underwriters needs enormous ingenuity – and a large and healthy reinsurance market.

(c) Negligence

In persuading industry and shipowners to avoid losses in the first place, insurers are faced with the attitude reflected in W. S. Gilbert's description of *The Wreck of the Ballyshannon*:*

> Down went the owners, greedy men, whom hope of gain allured.
> O, dry the starting tear, for they were heavily insured.

* *The Bab Ballads*, 'Etiquette'.

Many companies and shipowners prefer to pay a heavy insurance premium than to pay the even heavier cost of installing adequate fire prevention devices, or making sure that their crews take proper care of their ships. American claims for machinery damage and crew negligence rose between 1968 and 1969 by more than 70 per cent. To borrow from Paul Dixey's October 1970 speech again:

> If a Greek shipowner buys a Norwegian built ship and employs a Chinese engineer, is it likely that the maintenance manual will be understood or followed? And would it really be fair to expect the underwriters to pay claims for the inevitable damage as crew negligence?

Insurers are trying to deal with this problem in two ways. One is to encourage industrialists to carry rather more of their own insurance, on the theory that complete cover simply encourages carelessness. The other solution is to enforce the installation of adequate security measures. Some companies already make loans to firms installing security devices and insist on their installation. This could be backed up with the threat of refusing insurance or charging penal rates of premium. Certainly there is no good reason why insurers should meet claims on readily preventable losses.

(d) International problems

Overseas business accounts for about three-quarters of Lloyd's premium income, and 70 per cent of the companies' non-life premium income. But it is heavily concentrated in one market – North America.

The United States is far and away the largest overseas market, accounting for a quarter of UK insurers' non-life premium income. Indeed for four of the major composites, Commercial Union, the Royal, General Accident and Phoenix, the US market is more important than the UK. British insurers are the only big foreign contingent in the US market. Just how important their operations there are may be gauged from the fact that the assets of UK insurance companies in the US are over a third of all UK investments there, and worth fifty times as much as US insurance investments in Britain.

Unfortunately, throughout the 1960s the United States was a disastrous market. Even US domestic insurers were making considerable underwriting losses. On top of their other troubles insurers had to reckon with the vagaries of the US courts. Liability claims in particular resulted in interminable law suits and generous settlements, with the result that British insurers became most reluctant to undertake liability insurance in the US. Finally, insurers had to work in a tangled regulatory framework of state and federal laws, with premium rates in a large (but thankfully decreasing) number of states actually fixed by law. The main compensation was a generally high level of investment profits in the US.

With the advent of what insurers call 'file and use' in the early 1970s, the US market became more profitable. An insurer who wants to increase his premium rates is now allowed to raise them immediately and then apply for authorization, instead of having to wait first for permission – which might not be granted for months.

A longer-term danger lies in the dependence of British insurers on the American market and in the fact that they are so much the largest foreign contingent in the US insurance market. For Lloyd's and for the large brokers in particular, the US accounts for around half their income. If British insurers fail to establish themselves on a bigger scale in other national markets, they run the risk of finding one day that the American insurance industry wants to reduce the British hold.

The expanded Common Market may perhaps provide them with an opportunity to diversify, though before British membership insurers had little success in Europe. Their main fear is that joining the EEC will mean that the tighter controls on European insurers, particularly on their establishment and on their freedom to invest, will be extended to British firms.

In the developing world, insurers have also had special worries. Their direct overseas interests have been gradually whittled down, as one developing country after another restricts the role of foreign insurers. As Kenneth Bevins, chief general manager of the Royal, says wryly, 'Developing countries looking for funds always look to insurance.' In some countries, insurers have suddenly found themselves confronted with demands that a proportion of their assets be invested locally; in others, a national insurance company takes over all direct local business. It probably reinsures much of it on the world market – but that is small comfort to the insurance companies which have lost the direct business.

Indeed, overseas business is increasingly reinsurance business. Estimating the total amount of reinsurance done in London is next to impossible, though it probably constitutes 50 per cent or more of Lloyd's business and from 25 to 40 per cent of the companies' London portfolios. Does this matter? As the reinsurers – and the reinsurance brokers who feed Lloyd's – are insuring at one remove, they are inevitably making something of an act of faith. In the early and mid-1960s, the market admits, there was too much faith and not enough judgement. Since then reinsurers have begun to keep a closer eye on the underwriter who writes the original policy, on the track record of his company and on the types of business involved. In addition, they are becoming less passive, and trying to improve both their own information and the quality of underwriting in the companies with which they deal.

So though the shift to reinsurance means that London is getting nibbled cake – the first bite has already been taken by the direct insurer – there is plenty of scope in the reinsurance market for London to exercise its traditional skills as an overseas insurer. Besides, nibbled cake is better than none.

(e) The tariff

British insurers throughout the 1960s made life much harder for themselves by clinging to cartel premium rates on motor, household, industrial fire and a few other categories of insurance. By 1972 all these 'tariffs' had been abandoned except that on industrial fire insurance. But the life and death of the motor tariff in particular has been indirectly responsible in the crash of Vehicle and General for the most serious collapse of a British insurance company since the war. The tariff agreements meant that most companies combined to fix minimum premium rates. In the motor market the tariff companies' grip had already begun slipping by the time the tariff was formally abandoned in 1969: they accounted for 50 per cent of all business in 1960 but only 30 per cent by 1969.

The damaging effect of the tariffs was not on the overall level of rates but on their flexibility. Getting agreement among all the companies involved made setting new rates a slow and cumbersome business. In the industrial fire market, where new construction techniques meant drastic changes in fire risks and where the national fire bill approximately doubled between 1960 and 1970, premium rates rose only 30–40 per cent.

In the motor market, 1959–69 was a period of great rate stability. However, this inflexibility of rates encouraged a number of new motor insurers, not all of them run on the most orthodox underwriting principles, to undercut the tariff by offering lower rates on a more selective basis. Several of the newcomers either folded or were closed by the Board of Trade: Brandaris; American Military; Emil Savundra's Fire, Auto and Marine; Craven; Midland, Northern and Scottish, inventors of the Alpha policy with drivers' age the sole criterion of premiums; and Vehicle and General, which crashed in March 1971.

While the motor tariff was in operation the companies that subscribed to it found themselves steadily losing business to the non-tariff companies, stable and unstable alike. In the eight years up to and including 1968, motor underwriting had hardly been profitable: BIA companies' results on motor underwriting had ranged from a loss of 2·8 per cent of premium income to – at best – a profit of 1·4 per cent. But the 1970 figure was a staggering 14·5 per cent loss on premium which was only partly improved to 8·1 per cent the following year. This was largely the result of the orgy of rate cutting that followed the tariff's demise.

The household fire tariff disappeared more painlessly, being finally abandoned at the end of 1970. The abolition of the industrial fire tariff was recommended by the Monopolies Commission in 1972. But the insurance industry wants to keep it. Lloyd's wants the fire insurers to keep it so that it will know what rates to undercut. The fire insurers want to keep it because they are afraid of the confusion and cut-throat competition which they claim would follow its demise. Under the tariff it can take up to two years to get the necessary agreement to change rates. Hardly surprisingly, it has not always been rigidly applied, and the bigger companies have ignored it when it suited them.

INVESTMENT POLICY

For life insurers, investment has always been the core of their business. For non-life insurers, it has become increasingly important as they have come to depend more and more on their investments to make up for their underwriting losses. When in 1969 British insurance companies had their worst year ever for non-life insurance, they attracted a premium income of £1,900 million on their non-life business and made a record £38·4 million loss on it. But it was more than covered by investment profits on non-life business of a happy £135 million.

Insurance companies invest enormous funds. In 1972 these totalled £19,759 million, of which life assurance accounted for 81 per cent. The insurance companies are by far the largest institutional investors on the British capital market. Their new investments in 1972 totalled £1,618 million, with the life funds again providing the lion's share, £1,251 million.

These investments are of considerable economic importance. Each year the insurance companies supply the capital for just under one-fifth of net fixed investment in the UK. Through pension funds the life companies collect a rising proportion of personal disposable income – about 4·6 per cent in 1966–8. This flow, moreover, is steady. People tend to continue paying their life premiums and pension contributions whatever the vicissitudes of the economy and the pressures on their incomes.

Life and non-life insurers require different investment portfolios. A life company can calculate closely the amount of cash it will need to meet maturing policies, so the liquidity of its investments is relatively unimportant. It is not likely to have to sell them unexpectedly. It does, however, have to achieve the highest possible yield as this is usually the base for its bonus payments and bonus payments are the main area of competition between the companies. By contrast, a non-life insurer puts the emphasis on marketability, as it may have to sell investments quite suddenly. The rate of return is less important: it affects the profitability of the company, but does not directly affect its competitive performance against the other companies. These different requirements are reflected in the different composition of life and non-life insurers' portfolios. In 1972 life funds held 29 per cent of their investments in ordinary shares, 14 per cent in real property and the rest in mortgages and fixed interest investments. Non-life, or general funds, held a higher proportion of equity and a lower proportion of property investments – 36 per cent and 8 per cent respectively. Non-life insurers still hardly regard these enormous investments as more than a back-stop. The investment policy of both life and non-life companies has tended to be rather conservative.

There are two steps to improving their investment position that the insurance companies are now beginning to take. One is for them (and indeed all institutional investors) to take a more active interest in the affairs of the companies whose shares they hold rather than simply selling them when things get difficult. The problem is not new. When Keynes was chairman of the National Mutual Life Assurance Society as long ago as 1928, he was urging insurance companies to take responsibility for the mass of individual investors. The companies are only beginning to take Keynes's advice. The Prudential, the biggest investor of all, combined with Hill Samuel and a group of other large investors to induce a change in the management structure of Vickers in spring 1970. The solution which most companies are moving towards is probably pretty close to the one used by Mr Louis Ginsburg who was unbeatably qualified for his job as investment director of Legal and General by being both Jewish and Scottish:

The old theory was that if you felt that the management of a company was bad you just sold your shares, but that's a doubtful tactic. Either you have to sell at a poor price or you cannot sell at all. Anyway, that's a policy of total defeatism. There are other ways of dealing with one's indifferent invest-ments. I'm in favour of the gentle nudge. It has to be done discreetly because as soon as you turn on the searchlight of publicity, then it's self-destructive.*

The other step is to broaden the base of their investments; to realize that they are financial empires and not just vendors of security. So far the companies have been mainly interested in building up their property interests. Legal and General and the Prudential already have very large portfolios, and Commercial Union's bid for MEPC in 1970 was an attempt to acquire one by a short cut.

The 1970s are already seeing more dramatic departures. An insurance fund, for instance, makes an ideal backing for a banking operation. Developments along these lines began in the US, where Continental National bought a unit trust management group and Fireman's Fund linked up with American Express.

What could well happen in Britain is that the insurance com-panies will look for more direct ways of investing in industrial and commercial enterprises. They are already beginning to do so by buying stakes in merchant banks, as for example, the Pruden-tial has done with Keyser Ullmann. Links with finance houses and clearing banks could follow. In June 1971 Guardian-Royal Exchange widened its objects to include 'all normal aspects of the business of banking'. In autumn 1972 Norwich Union set up a subsidiary especially to undertake commercial banking. During the 1970s it would not be surprising to see an insurance company acquire a clearing bank or begin to develop into a major holding company with direct controlling stakes in industrial enterprises.

As the treasurer of a major US insurance company said in April 1968, 'We will invest in a pickle factory if it appears more profitable than insurance.'

* Interview in the *Investors Chronicle* (18 December 1970).

GOVERNMENT CONTROL

Britain's insurance industry has enjoyed 300 years of development with less control by outside authorities than just about anywhere else in the world. Insurers here have almost complete freedom in fixing premium rates, a luxury which insurers in the Republic of Ireland, in many US states and in much of Western Europe do not enjoy.

This freedom is already being eroded. Leaving aside the possibility of stricter requirements following EEC entry, the fire tariff has already been the subject of an inquiry by the Monopolies Commission. But the most urgent calls for more government involvement have been the result of the rash of failures in motor insurance. This area is particularly sensitive: it not only affects half the families in the country but also includes a measure of compulsory cover.

The story of attempts to police the motor insurance industry in recent years is one which does credit neither to the Department of Trade and Industry and its predecessor, the Board of Trade, nor to the British Insurance Association. Each small step by the Department of Trade and Industry has been taken only after some damaging company failure, while the attitude of the BIA has at best been ambivalent.

The first elements of control have existed for a long time, but these were not tightened until 1967 after the collapse of Emil Savundra's Fire, Auto and Marine. The Companies Act passed that year contained a special section giving the Board of Trade substantial new powers. It provided for inspections to investigate the running of companies whose solvency the Board suspected, and for the Board to stop a doubtful company from taking on new business.

The Act may have looked all right on paper. But the Board of Trade lacked the staff, the experience and the statistical information to make the most of its new powers. It has only recently begun to repair these deficiencies. In the summer of 1968 the Board introduced new regulations on the form in which a company's accounts should be published. These regulations, which at least make it possible to examine the provision a company has made to meet future claims, to see the extent of its reinsurance commitments, and to look at its domestic motor account separately, came into force at the beginning of 1969. It is more recently still that the companies section of the Department of Trade and Industry has acquired a staff that is anything like adequate to oversee an industry as vast as insurance.

Despite all these new provisions, spring 1971 saw the worst insurance crash of all. Overnight, with the failure of Vehicle and General, some 800,000 motorists found themselves without insurance. The Department and the BIA had had some idea of the state of Vehicle and General since the previous summer. Yet the Department had failed to gain access to the full Vehicle and General accounts until a month before the collapse became public. The BIA's position was more invidious. Vehicle and General was the first of its members to fail. The BIA had made considerable capital out of earlier crashes by urging the public to place insurance with its members only. After the crash the BIA refused point blank to help the great majority of Vehicle and General policyholders.

It was as a result of this crash that new legislation on insurance was introduced in 1973. But this also deals with some of the problems which have generated among the older life offices an undercurrent of alarm at the mushroom growth of new funds in an area which has been quite inadequately controlled by the government or anyone else. Their alarm was increased by discovering when Vehicle and General collapsed in 1971 that it had been able to borrow £1 million from its subsidiary, Pioneer Life. Herbert Toogood, chairman of the Co-operative Insurance Society, summed up the changes in the regulation of life assurance necessary in the eyes of a growing number of people in the industry:

> Legislation is needed to prohibit the investment of life assurance funds, except with very stringent safeguards, in other organisations under the same control, and also to prevent the 'milking' of life assurance funds by the charging of unreasonable management fees by associated organisations or by the payment of excessive dividends to shareholders out of moneys which should

be retained within the life assurance fund for the benefit of the policy-holders.*

A number of aspects of insurance had clearly called for further control. One suggestion, put forward by Edgar Bowring, chief executive and now chairman of the insurance brokers C. T. Bowring,† was that the industry should set up machinery for policing itself. Lloyd's has long ensured its member's solvency by policing itself, and by running the Central Fund to protect policy-holders to which each member contributes annually.

But there are reasons to suspect that self-policing would not have been the final answer to the industry's problems. Certainly the BIA, since the Vehicle and General débâcle, made it clear that it did not want to be responsible for its members' solvency.

Insurance companies trade on their reputation, a fact of which, where their overseas market is concerned, the insurance companies are well aware. One of the most revealing episodes in the Vehicle and General affair suggested that the companies cared more about the policyholder in Minneapolis than in Manchester. While the British car owners insured by Vehicle and General were left to shoulder their own losses, a fund was set up by Commercial Union and a number of other insurance companies and major brokers to rescue World Auxiliary, Vehicle and General's reinsurance subsidiary, and thus preserve London's good name as a reinsurance centre.

So the government has stepped in. The 1973 Insurance Companies Act enormously increases the powers of the Department of Trade and Industry. It gives the DTI powers to impose and vary minimum solvency standards, and to exclude unsuitable people from positions of authority in insurance companies. Assets of life funds are to be kept separate, and companies are to submit much more frequent and detailed returns. The Department's powers to investigate a company are stronger and more flexible. Finally the Act picked up some of the suggestions made by the Scott Com-

* Annual statement, May 1972.
† Presidential address to the Insurance Institute of London, 4 October 1971.

mittee when it reported in 1973 on equity and unit linked life assurance. The new legislation has introduced controls on advertising and a 'cooling off' period after a direct sale, both covering all life assurance.

Ultimately, the most far-reaching changes in the way the insurance industry is controlled will result not from its immediate underwriting difficulties but rather from the increasing emphasis on the investment side of their business. If the insurance companies are to develop into financial conglomerates, controlling an even more substantial proportion of new industrial investment than at present, inevitably the government will feel the need to scrutinize the ways in which these funds are deployed. That, more than anything else, is going to make the control of the insurance industry the concern of the general public and not merely that of the industry itself.

7

The commodity markets and the Baltic Exchange

WHAT A FUTURES MARKET IS

If you ring up your broker in Atlanta, Georgia, he may very well put you into pork bellies or frozen orange juice rather than General Motors or I.T. & T. But you would look a long time in the City before you came across a private investor who had just bought into greasy wool tops or cleared a small profit in copper wire bars.

The commodity markets do not generally welcome private speculators. This may be one reason why they tend to reach the notice of outsiders only when they are overtaken by some esoteric disaster, such as an epidemic of black pod in the Ghana cocoa crop; or when some firm reveals a massive loss from commodity speculation, such as United California Bank's $40 million lost in the collapse of its Basle subsidiary or Rowntree Mackintosh's £20 million loss in cocoa; or when as in 1973 commodity prices soar to all-time peaks.

When people talk about London as an international commodity centre, they usually mean two different things. They may mean

'merchanting': arranging the buying and selling, insurance ship-
ment and financing of raw materials, usually between third
countries thousands of miles away. Or they may be referring to
the organized commodity markets, the ones where dealing is
organized round a specific meeting place. A few of these are
'physical' markets, on which raw materials are bought and sold;
more are 'futures' markets (in London usually called 'terminal'
markets), whose main function is to provide a mechanism by
which those who trade in raw materials can insure against changes
in their prices.

It is with these organized markets that this chapter is mainly
concerned. These are in two main groups: those in Plantation
the Corn Exchange in Mark Lane dealing in sugar, coffee, cocoa,
wool, tea, rubber, vegetable oils and cotton; and those in the
London Metal Exchange, Whittington Avenue, dealing in copper,
lead, tin, zinc and silver. The chapter ends by looking at the Baltic
Mercantile and Shipping Exchange, which is chiefly a market for
chartering ships (and now aircraft), but which is also the home of
the London grain futures market which suddenly burst into life
with peak prices in 1973; and at the London bullion dealers who
trade in gold and silver.

The bulk of London's physical commodity trade is arranged not
through organized markets but over the telephone or telex. For
most commodities there is no market in a central meeting place,
and where one does exist it may handle only a small part of the
total trade. Usually the goods are shipped between third countries
and never touch the City. In a few exotic commodities, such as
furs and ivories, auctions are still held in London; the goods are
imported, sold and then usually re-exported. Tea is also auctioned
through a market which handles some 60 per cent of the tea
drunk in Britain.

By contrast, all futures trading is carried on in organized
markets. Representatives of the markets' member firms meet daily
on a dealing floor, such as those in Mark Lane or the 'Ring 'of the
London Metal Exchange.

The purpose of a futures market is to provide traders and manufacturers with a way of insuring against a change in the market

price of a commodity. A cocoa trader's job is to buy the quality of cocoa that the manufacturers are likely to want. A chocolate manufacturer's job is to make sure that he is producing the kind of chocolate that the public wants to buy. Both are specialists in judging this sort of risk. But neither wants to carry the additional risk of having to judge how fluctuations in the world market price of cocoa are likely to affect the value of their stocks.

There are two ways in which they can avoid having to take this price risk. Originally in London they used a forward contract. Whenever a trader or manufacturer bought stocks of cocoa which he intended to hold for, say, nine months, he also arranged to sell a similar amount of the same cocoa for delivery at the same time.* If the price of the stocks of cocoa he was holding had dropped by the end of nine months, any loss he made on the first transaction would be offset by the profit on the second. The trouble with a forward contract, though, was that when it matured the trader had actually to find specific goods to deliver to fulfil it.

So a refinement of the forward contract was developed, and became the basis for the present-day futures market. Its most important feature is that, instead of promising to deliver specific goods, it promises to deliver goods of a specific grade. Each futures market has one standard grade (though copper has three) known as the market standard. In this, all contracts are written. So the trader promises to deliver a certain quantity of cocoa of a standard quality – Good Fermented Main Crop Ghana beans – in nine months' time. By the end of the nine months he will have 'closed out' the contract. This means that he buys a similar quantity of the same standard cocoa on the futures market, to cancel his original transaction. A futures market, in other words, deals in promises to deliver and take delivery of a commodity – not in the commodity itself.

If the futures market is working efficiently, the trader can expect the price of the market standard to move roughly in line with the price of the cocoa he actually owns, if only because firms

* All the transactions described in this passage can naturally be made the other way round.

will take advantage of any differential by buying in one market if the price looks low and selling in another if the price looks high. Thus the two prices will keep fairly close together. So usually, when the time comes for him to close out his futures contract, the trader will find that any profit he may have made on it roughly cancels out any loss he has made on the value of his stocks.

If the market is working badly, prices on the futures market may fall by much less than the price of the physical commodity. In that event, the trader may choose not to close out his futures contract and actually fulfil his promise to deliver. A sign of an efficient futures market is one where a very small proportion of contracts run to delivery.

It is not only merchants who find the futures markets useful as a way of insuring against price changes. They are also necessary to producers, exporters and manufacturers of raw materials, to metal scrap refiners and to anyone, in fact, who has to buy or sell stocks of raw or even semi-processed materials. As a commodity passes through the production and manufacturing process, it may be hedged several times on the futures market by several different firms.

A distinction is made on the commodity markets between the terms 'hedging' and 'speculating', even though both are frequently carried on by the same house. Put simply, the firm which enters a futures contract to insure a stock of goods against price fluctuation is hedging; the firm or individual who, say, buys cocoa in the hope that the price will rise is a speculator.

The amount of physical business varies from one futures market to another. On some of the soft commodity markets it may be as low as 1 per cent, while the average is only around 2 per cent. On the London Metal Exchange it tends to be higher, ranging up to 15–20 per cent on the copper market. Some market men, notably on the London Metal Exchange, believe that a high proportion of physical business ensures that the futures price reflects movements in the price of the physical commodity. Accordingly the LME has made strenuous efforts to increase its physical trade. Other market men more logically argue the opposite.

Quite apart from keeping prices of the futures market in line with those of the physical commodity, there is a further important reason why it has to be technically possible for a contract to result in physical delivery: it must, to comply with the Gaming Laws.

THE SOFT COMMODITY MARKETS AND THE LONDON METAL EXCHANGE

In balance of payments' terms, the commodity trade's contribution is quite small. There are no official figures on the contribution that commodity trade makes to the balance of payments. The Committee on Invisible Exports reckons that on 'third country' trade – selling, insuring and shipping goods from one third country to another – earnings are about £20 million a year, while commissions on importing and exporting bring in another £45 million annually. Earnings from the futures markets are apt to be in credit one year, in debit the next.

The largest commodity futures markets in the world are not in London but in Chicago. These deal in everything from live cattle to pork bellies and propane gas, but they trade almost entirely in products produced in the United States for the US markets. They are domestic markets, serving domestic consumers.

The world's main international futures markets are in London and in New York. In some instances, such as cocoa, sugar and coffee, London has the dominant market, while in others, such as silver, New York has the edge. There has also recently been a trend for markets in individual commodities to flourish near the centres of production, such as the Sydney wool futures market, the Penang tin market, the Singapore rubber market and the Colombo and Calcutta tea markets.

Not all London's futures markets are equally successful. For a market to thrive, a whole range of complicated conditions have to be right. The standard and the currency in which the contract is denominated must be the one most suitable for the raw materials which the main customers want to hedge. Prices must not be so dominated either by the existence of large stockpiles of the raw material or by international commodity agreements that manufacturers have no need to hedge their stocks. There must not be a widely used synthetic substitute which manufacturers can easily switch to if the price of the natural material rises sharply. There must be an important group of buyers and sellers of the commodity who want to use the market to protect the value of their stocks. And there must be opportunities for speculators. The experience of the individual London commodity markets shows how vital these conditions can be.

In the course of 1973 the markets in what are known as 'soft' commodities, that is non-metals, moved from Plantation House, a huge and nondescript building in Mincing Lane. They took up residence in the refurbished Corn Exchange in Mark Lane. To make room for the new arrivals the Corn Exchange's beautiful glass dome has been raised and a new floor put in. Unlike Plantation House, Mark Lane has a viewing gallery for the public.

The one large auction market, the tea market, moved in 1972 to new premises in Pudding Lane (where the Fire of London started). To watch a tea auction is to feel almost back in the eighteenth century. The room is full of elderly men who have been in tea broking all their lives, like their fathers and grandfathers before them, partners in firms with ancient names like Thomas Cumberlege and Inskipp, who tell you sadly, 'Britons will drink anything now. They've lost their discrimination.'

The most active soft commodity markets have been cocoa, coffee and sugar. Cocoa is one of the most notoriously volatile of all commodity markets and so a place where a speculator can make the biggest profits or losses. The main reasons for this volatility are that one country, Ghana, dominates the supply; and there is not yet an effective world agreement to stabilize the price. Since the boom of the late 1960s the London cocoa market has taken the lead from New York and is substantially larger than the other two futures markets in Amsterdam and Paris. Cocoa in particular has benefited from a technical advantage which the London markets have over their New York rivals. On many of the New York markets there are strict limits on how far the price can move in a day. On the New York cocoa market trading has to stop for the day once the price has moved 1c. a pound – less than £10 a ton. In London trading has to stop once the price moves £20 a ton – but only for half an hour. For a dealer or speculator who has to operate in a wildly fluctuating market London is more attractive than New York.

Though New York dominates world coffee consumption, London has the only effective futures market. The New York coffee futures market is quieter. There are two other small futures markets, one in Amsterdam and one in Le Havre, which was reopened in 1961 with a splendid party on the liner France and has hardly been heard of since. Swings in coffee prices have been moderated by the International Coffee Organization, which covers over 90 per cent of the world coffee trade. But prices still fluctuate enough to keep the London market reasonably active.

The sugar futures market in London has now overtaken the New York one. In the late 1950s the New York market was larger, but ran into difficulties when Castro came to power because its main standard was based on Cuban shipments. Despite the International Sugar Agreement large fluctuations in sugar prices still take place. Not only does the price of sugar sold under the agreement move within a wide band; a growing volume of sugar is produced by countries outside it altogether, notably the six original EEC members.

Of the remaining five markets, in late 1972 quotations on those in vegetable oils were formally suspended, though there have been attempts to revive them. The futures market in soyabean oil had opened in 1967, and markets in sunflower seed oil and coconut oil had been added later. A main reason for their failure was the fact that the largest users of vegetable oils in Britain – Unilever, Heinz, and Procter and Gamble – were not interested in hedging in them. So in 1973 a dollar soyabean oil market was started.

Another unsuccessful newcomer to London was the raw cotton futures market, set up in May 1969 by the Liverpool Cotton Association. There had previously been, since the late nineteenth century, a lively market in cotton futures in Liverpool, run by the same association that started the London market. It finally closed after a period in the early 1960s when official American policy curbed price fluctuations in the price of cotton, and made hedging virtually unnecessary.

By 1972, quotations on the new London market had been suspended, illustrating the importance not only of having the right standard, but also of denominating it in the right currency. When the market opened in London, it began with a dollar contract, as cotton is traded mainly in US dollars. But the Bank of England refused to allow British residents to speculate on it as sterling was weak at the time. By the time the market authorities introduced a sterling contract, interest in the new market had virtually died.

London's wool futures market, once the world's largest, is now diminutive compared with that in Sydney, Australia. Part of the reason is that wool today is primarily a Pacific commodity, traded between Australia and Japan. The market also had problems with finding a suitable standard. It tried one in the sort of semi-processed wool used by Bradford spinners; found it was being overtaken by Sydney, Australia, and tried also the unprocessed wool standard used there; found it was still falling behind and changed in the late 1960s to a contract in the semi-processed wool used by continental spinners. Wool, like cotton, faces the long-term challenge of synthetic substitutes. Though prices have recovered dramatically since 1971 there is nothing any market man can do about the challenge of synthetics.

The rubber market has also lost its former supremacy. The world's largest rubber market has long been in Singapore, next door to Malaysia, the world's largest rubber producer. Both London and Singapore have been severely hit by the development of synthetics. Unlike all the markets described so far, the London market is essentially a physical one. Its trading system differs from the open outcry system used in the futures markets and described below: indeed, it hardly functions as an organized market at all. Trading is by private treaty. That means, as one of the market's officials put it, 'brokers sidling up to dealers and whispering in their ears'. This eccentricity, fiercely defended by the older members of the market, is driving more and more business to the telephone.

Finally there are a handful of auctions. There are occasional auctions in ivory and bristles; and more frequent and lively auctions in tea. The London tea market's once pre-eminent position is now challenged by other markets in Pakistan, India and Ceylon, while turnover at both the Colombo and Calcutta auctions is now higher than that on the London market.

There are a number of commodities in which the Mark Lane firms deal, though not through organized markets. Auctions were once held in shellac, which was originally used to put the shine on top hats and which enjoyed a boom when it was used for '78' gramophone records. Auctions in jute have also stopped, though trade goes on, as does trade in sisal and that other well-known hemp, *cannabis sativa*, now dealt in Mincing Lane under a Dangerous Drugs licence.* There are trade associations for firms dealing in mica, almonds, Indian carpets and 'general produce' which includes such exotica as essential oils (aniseed, camphor, eucalyptus), gums, spices and beeswax.

The other main group of futures markets in London are the five metal markets of the London Metal Exchange. These markets are much more closely linked than those in soft commodities: they are all run by the same bodies, the board of the LME and a management committee; and each metal is traded in the same ring by the same firms one after the other. While the various soft commodity markets have separate memberships (though the same firm may belong to several) a member of the LME can deal in any metal dealt on the LME. The markets have a different ambiance. While dealers on the floors of the soft commodity markets are usually fairly junior, senior members of LME firms come to ring sessions.

Of the five metals – copper, tin, lead, zinc and silver – it is the fortunes of copper which dominate the exchange. The rise of the copper market dates from the mid-1960s, when copper

* Graham L. Rees, *Britain's Commodity Markets* (London, Elek Books, 1972), p. 291.

producers outside the United States had tried and failed to control world prices. Today US producers still try to fix copper prices in the US – but their prices tend to follow the LME price.

Despite the influential position of the LME copper market, its turnover is still smaller than New York's, where there is more speculation. However the New York lead and zinc markets have died. The US price of both these metals is fixed by American producers, but elsewhere the price of lead and to a lesser extent of zinc is strongly influenced by the LME. In tin the New York market is also very small. There is a larger market in Penang, in Malaysia, but it is a purely physical market, without hedging facilities.

Finally the silver market, the newest on the LME, opened in February 1968 in response to demands, mainly from abroad, for a new market in London that would offer the same sort of trading facilities for silver as were available for other non-ferrous metals on the exchange. The market has two rivals: the London bullion market, described below, and the New York market, which probably has more influence on the world price than either of the London markets, and certainly has a far larger turnover.

On the LME, unlike the soft commodity markets, a relatively large proportion of physical business is carried out. This is actively encouraged by the exchange which is very proud of the fact that its contracts contain no *force majeure* clause (as do those of most metal producers) to provide an escape in case of strike or other obstacles to delivery. A purchase made on the LME is guaranteed to be delivered on the due date whatever happens. In the 1960s the LME took two steps to increase the volume of physical business. It opened a number of overseas delivery points, warehouses on the Continent. These allow someone in Hamburg who sells copper on the LME to deliver it straight to the LME warehouse in Hamburg, instead of going all the way to London first. Secondly, the exchange replaced the old copper contract, which was so broad that buyers could never be sure what grade of copper they would get. Instead, two separate contracts are now used, in copper wire bars and in cathodes.

The LME's influence on the prices of the metals it trades in shows how successful its efforts to encourage physical transactions have been. Although at most only 5 per cent of world trade in the metals it handles passes through the LME, its prices reflect changes in supply and demand at the margin. When there is the threat of a surplus, LME prices fall, but producers and manufacturers can always find a market through the LME. When there is a shortage, prices on the LME will rise, and attract sellers – and buyers who cannot find supplies at any price anywhere else. Prices on the LME have become the basis for contracts between producers and manufacturers all over the world.

Useful though this volume of physical trade makes the LME as a barometer of supply and demand for metals, it has caused serious difficulties for the exchange itself. As already argued, an efficient futures market is one where very few contracts run to delivery. In the LME copper market, delivery can represent a fifth of turnover. The result has been endless problems in finding a suitable standard, especially for copper. A standard general enough to be useful to hedging is too vague for a buyer hoping to take physical delivery: in a futures market it does not matter if several different grades of a metal can be delivered to fulfil a contract, but for a manufacturer who wants a certain quality of metal, it matters very much. Dealers on the LME cope with this problem through an informal arrangement whereby if one firm finds the copper it has bought on the exchange is of the wrong quality or will be delivered at an inconvenient point, it rings up another firm and arranges to swap that copper for a more appropriate brand, if necessary paying a premium on the deal. In other words a second, informal copper market has had to evolve to solve the problems which the mix of physical and futures business on the exchange creates. Moreover to work properly a futures market needs speculators, and the high proportion of contracts running to delivery on the LME has tended to discourage them. Sooner or later the LME will clearly have to make up its mind, and find a way of separating its futures from its physical market.

It may also have to introduce a longer contract. While on the soft commodity markets it is generally possible to buy and sell for up to eighteen months ahead, on the LME, for all markets except silver, contracts only run for three months. There is a suspicion among those who find this inconvenient that the reason for it is the extra commission an LME firm collects each time a contract has to be renewed to extend the length of a hedge. But another substantial reason is that metals, unlike soft commodities, are not subject to seasonal price fluctuations.

RUNNING THE MARKETS

Some 100 firms belong to the eight futures markets in soft commodities and to the LME. Though nearly two-thirds of these belong only to one market, many deal in several.* A firm that has a seat on the LME may also be a member of some of the soft commodity markets: thus Rudolf Wolff, as well as dealing in all metals on the LME, is also a full member of the coffee, cocoa, sugar, rubber and the suspended vegetable oil markets. Generally, though, firms tend to stick either to soft commodities or to metals, while tea and rubber are mainly handled by firms which do little else.

Firms carry out a great range of activities, which fall basically into three groups: there are merchants, who trade in a physical commodity, hedging it in the futures market and carrying stocks of it themselves; there are brokers, who offer much the same service, but do not carry physical stocks; and there are commission houses, which generally transact no physical commodity trade, but deal in futures markets on behalf of clients. The large commission houses in London, like Bache and Co. or Merrill Lynch, are Americans, but there is one large British commission house, G. W. Joynson, now owned by the Inchcape group.

Each kind of firm may specialize in one commodity, or in several. A firm may be brokers in one commodity, and merchants in another. Firms in recent years have tended to become bigger, either by amalgamation or by linking up with some other City institution, for merchanting, in particular, requires substantial capital resources. Some firms have moved into the

* See Rees, op. cit., p. 425.

production and processing of raw materials, as well as buying and selling: thus Czarnikow, probably the world's largest sugar broker with a staff of some 170 and a capital of about £6 million, also has a cattle-food broking business in Liverpool, a spice grinding and distributing company, and it brokes in rubber and in the Malaysian oil pool. Czarnikow has a stake in the stockbrokers Sandelson, and other firms have also begun to diversify out of commodities. Thus Vavasseur has entered unit trusts and money broking and Guinness Peat, insurance and merchant banking.

All futures markets try to restrict their membership to some extent. Membership of the soft commodity markets is usually divided into two main categories: floor members and associate members. The floor members are the commodity houses; the associate members, generally manufacturers, shippers and so on. Anyone who wants to deal on the market must do so through a floor member. The associate member also deals through a full member – but at a reduced commission.

To become a member of one of the soft commodity markets, a firm usually has to buy its seat from an existing member. In most markets some firms own more than one seat, which they may be persuaded to part with often for a five-figure fee. The number of seats on all the markets is strictly limited and the market association tries to keep the number of floor members down. The sugar market association, for instance, actually reduced the number of available seats in 1971. The number was previously over sixty-five but the association managed to keep this embarrassing fact quiet, and less than half the seats were in fact filled. Accordingly, the number of seats available was reduced to correspond more closely with the current membership.

The London Metal Exchange is even more exclusive than the soft commodity markets. New members have to be admitted by the board and the committee of the LME. Older members joined after showing a capital of £50,000 and bank guarantees of £20,000. But in 1970, after two years in which no new member had been admitted, Vavasseur-Kirk applied for membership. The LME insisted that it show capital of £250,000 and bank guarantees of £300,000. A subsequent arrival, Triland, backed by the Japanese Mitsubishi group, was asked to show even larger guarantees. Not surprisingly, in autumn 1973 only thirty out of the LME's forty seats were filled. The LME's justification for this is that it wants to make sure recent arrivals are financially sound. It is also trying to persuade existing members to show more resources.

Foreign firms are excluded from floor membership. This does not stop the American broker Merrill Lynch from buying cocoa for its clients, nor the vast German Metalgesellschaft from actually having a seat on the Metal Exchange, but both act through a British subsidiary whose board must have a certain proportion of British members. Most xenophobic of all is the sugar market, on which no foreign firms are formally permitted to be floor members. This regulation dates from the First World War, when the sugar market lost all its German members. As they then dominated it, the sugar market nearly disappeared.

The alleged reason for limiting floor membership of both the LME and the soft commodity markets is that an open outcry market with too many members is chaos to run. On all the markets except the London rubber market trading is by 'open outcry'. Everyone shouts their bids at the tops of their voices across the floor and the noise is a rough indication of turnover. They are sometimes described as 'call' markets, because at specific times of day, representatives of all the floor members or broking firms sit round in a ring making their bids, while (in the case of soft commodity markets) a chairman conducts business. While most dealing is done at other times, it is at these sessions that official prices are fixed.

The trouble with this argument for limiting membership is that a similar system of trading is used on most of the world's smaller stock exchanges, exchanges which have a much greater volume of business and number of members than the London futures markets. Besides, if the reason for keeping membership down were really the limitations of the open outcry system, and not the fear of new competition, then the sensible solution would be to change the system. All the commodity markets already have telephone arbitrage dealings with other commodity centres while in the livelier markets 'late kerb trading' is also conducted over the telephone after the market is closed. This could well be the way that the commodity markets develop. The foreign exchange and money markets of the City have proved that it is perfectly possible to run a market with a world-wide membership efficiently over the phone.

The market rules are laid down by the association which runs them. These set commission rates, and occasionally expel members who try to undercut them. They determine who is allowed to deal in what capacity, the number of seats in the market and the market's standard. The associations themselves are made up of representatives of the various commodity houses, and sometimes of producers and shippers as well. The five markets of the London Metal Exchange are governed by the LME management committee. Separate associations cover physical trade and there are a few associations, such as the Tea Brokers' Association, the Timber Trade Federation and the Federation of Edible Nuts Association, for commodities which have no futures markets.

There are a number of people who specialize in running these associations. Association secretaries may be responsible for running more than one market, and occasionally may launch a new one.

Contracts made on the soft commodity futures markets are registered and cleared through the London Produce Clearing House (though the rubber market, ever eccentric, has its own Rubber Settlement House). The LPCH is a wholly owned subsidiary of the finance company, United Dominions Trust, though nobody at UDT ever seems quite certain how it came to be mixed up in sugar and vegetable oils. Besides registering contracts, the LPCH guarantees that they will be carried out, thus protecting each party to a contract against default by the other. No such central clearing house exists on the London Metal Exchange.

It is the LPCH, too, which polices the deposit system on the soft commodity markets. Whenever a floor member's client takes a speculative position in a market, the member must put up a deposit. The size of these deposits varies from one market to another, and is fixed in terms of the lot, or normal trading unit. Thus in cocoa it is £40 per 5-ton lot, and in sugar £100 per 50-ton lot. As a proportion of the value of a deal this is very small. If the price moves against the speculator, his liabilities increase: so the floor member must put up additional 'margin' to maintain the deposit. The LPCH collects the deposit and margin from the broking house which handles the transaction. It is up to the broking house to decide what part of the margin it asks the client to pay himself, and how far it is prepared to carry the deposit lodged with the LPCH itself.

Because the LME has no central clearing house, it has no central body to guarantee the fulfilment of contracts – or to enforce the taking of margins. Indeed, the margin system exists only in the silver market, and without a central clearing house there is no ready way to make sure that all firms observe it. This is another reason why contracts on the LME run for a much shorter period than those in soft commodities. The longer a contract runs, the bigger the chance of price fluctuations and the risk that a client will not be able to cover them.

THE FUTURE OF THE MARKETS

The experience with new futures markets in London in the 1960s and early 1970s was not encouraging. A fishmeal market, launched in 1967, died in less than a year. The Liverpool cotton market, reopened in London, began sluggishly and has since petered out. The vegetable oils markets have never really got off the ground. The LME silver market went off to a disappointing start. This is in marked contrast to the US experience. Of the States' ten major commodity markets in 1970, six – including live cattle, pork bellies and silver – did not exist in 1960.

London's relative lack of success in launching new commodity markets inevitably raises the question of London's future as a commodity centre. There are a number of reasons for expecting it to be difficult. There is the growth of synthetic substitutes, which reduces both the market for raw materials and the fluctuations in their price. There are international agreements to stabilize commodity prices, and national stockpiles of raw materials, both part of deliberate government attempts to curb price movements. To the extent that these attempts succeed, hedging facilities become less necessary. Then there is the concentration of buyers and sellers into larger groups, increasingly trading directly with each other and controlling bigger shares of the market. A manufacturer buying raw materials directly from a national marketing board and controlling a large part of the market may feel strong enough not to hedge.

But as long as supply and demand fluctuate, prices fluctuate too. It is this risk which brings futures markets their business. There is still a fair range of commodities which could take advantage of hedging facilities. Futures markets in fertilizer and tea were being seriously considered at the end of 1973, and with the demise of the Egg Marketing Board two years before, there were suggestions of a futures market in eggs. EEC membership and the winding-up of Britain's guaranteed farm price system could provide opportunities for futures markets in a number of farm products. Amsterdam has a potato futures market. On the LME, two subcommittees have been looking at the possibility of markets in aluminium and nickel, while in summer 1972 ICI announced that it was looking at the idea of a futures market in benzene and a number of other chemicals. Finally, it is not only tangible goods that need hedging facilities. In 1972 the Chicago Mercantile Exchange launched a futures market in foreign exchange.

One reason for London's lack of success in starting new markets may be its attitude to speculation. Private commodity speculation especially is small in the UK compared with the United States. Those firms which are anxious to encourage private speculation on the commodity markets blame this difference on the refusal of the Stock Exchange Council to allow the same firm to carry on stockbroking and commodity broking. In America almost all the big firms do both.

Without speculation there is always the danger of too volatile a market with, say, everyone hedging against a rise in prices and nobody betting on a fall. But the attitude of many commodity men is ambivalent towards speculation and particularly hostile to private speculation. Any of the livelier markets sound like the bookies' ring at a racecourse. A commodity man will quote a price on anything.* But officially, the markets have always tried to avoid any whiff of the gambling den.

Where private clients are involved, houses are worried both by the cost of handling their business and by the possibility of bad debts. That this possibility is a real one is largely the result of the way the deposit system operates. The reason for the deposit system is that the basic unit in which most commodities change hands tends to be far more expensive than most shares or bonds. But it means that for a comparatively small initial deposit, the speculator risks a massive loss, which he may not be able to stand. Thus the system in turn exposes the broker to considerable losses if his client cannot pay. The risks are even greater on the London Metal Exchange where no formal system of deposits and margins exists. The house on the LME that tries to persuade a client to pay a deposit risks losing him to a more adventurous (or less scrupulous) firm. This was particularly apparent in the boom of 1973.

As long as the commodity markets feel that they do not want to encourage the private speculator they can argue that the current mixture of trust and small deposits is a sufficient protection against bad debts; and that the world of the commodity trader is still sufficiently close-knit for gossip to be the market's best defence. But for the markets to flourish, they may find they need the private client and his money. If they do, they will have to consider introducing much larger deposits for private customers. In this respect London is a lot less strict than either New York or Chicago.

One possible way of involving more private speculators in the markets would be through commodity funds. These are rather like unit trusts. They trade directly in commodities, taking positions in futures markets and in physical commodities, with dealing decisions taken by a central management. Because of DTI regulations commodity funds can only be sold privately in Britain, but they are becoming popular in the US.

---

* At the 1970 General Election they were buying Labour's majority at 30 and selling at 35. Ask a commodity man to guess your age and he may well reply, 'Buy at 26, sell at 29.'

THE BALTIC MERCANTILE AND SHIPPING EXCHANGE

The Baltic operates from a lofty Edwardian hall,* lined with marble pillars, and almost as big as the floor of the Stock Exchange – though far more sparsely populated. At one end of the floor is the 'ring' – a sort of circular wooden fence – around which members gather to trade in grain futures. Elsewhere, there is a market in secondhand ships. But the Baltic's main activity is providing a market for the chartering of tramp ship cargoes.

The bulk of the world's shipbroking still may go through London. But since the last war, the Baltic and its brokers have been finding life harder. First, less and less ship chartering is actually done on the floor of the Baltic. While before the war brokers would frequently spend the whole day on the exchange, today they tend to use it increasingly simply as a place to swap market gossip. Some members, who turn up only to eat at the Baltic, are nicknamed 'lunch members'. More and more broking is done by telex and telephone. Indeed many members involved in the Baltic's newest market, in air chartering, rarely turn up at the exchange at all, preferring to conduct their business on the phone.

While modern communications are taking business from the floor of the exchange, changes in the organization of world shipping are altering the work of a Baltic broker. The exchange has suffered from the fact that the fastest growth in shipping has not been in tramp shipping but in containers, which are run by shipping lines, and in bulk carriers and tankers which are usually chartered by their owners directly, often before they are built, for many years ahead rather than for specific voyages. Shipowners indeed can go directly to shipbrokers in the US or other centres for a cargo, or can find it directly without using a broker at all.

As a result, few brokers now depend entirely on competitive chartering of tramp shipping for a living. Commission rates in that field have been pared to $1\frac{1}{4}$ per cent. Most brokers rely for

* Though it has plans for a 500,000-square-foot development.

their bread and butter on monopoly charters, arranging all the shipping used by a large industrial firm processing raw materials. On such charters, commissions may range up to around a more rewarding 3 per cent. Brokers have also tended to diversify into other activities. Almost all the Baltic's brokers today are either subsidiaries of shipowning firms, or have shipowning subsidiaries themselves.

As the Baltic is having to fight harder for its living, old restrictions on the membership of foreign firms have been partly relaxed.* The Baltic's long-term future as an organized market in shipbroking is uncertain. An attempt to set up a similar exchange in New York died quickly, as brokers found they could do business more quickly and efficiently over the phone. The Baltic's shipbroking members claim it still has three uses. First, it gives the market a central meeting place, where brokers can meet and discuss. Second, membership gives a broking firm a sort of seal of approval, useful for a company that deals on an international market and has to handle substantial sums of other people's money. And finally, some of the brokers who specialize in larger ships claim that it is easier to deal on the floor of the Baltic than over the phone. None of these arguments is sufficient to suggest that the London shipbroking market will not become, in a few years' time, largely a telephone market.

THE GOLD AND SILVER BULLION MARKETS

The London gold market has always managed to shroud itself in a carefully cultivated aura of glamorous mystery. The result has been an attractive myth about the way it works, which runs something like this. The price of gold is decided twice daily at the 'fixing' by the five gold bullion dealing firms. Men from Samuel Montagu, Johnson Matthey, Mocatta and Goldsmid and Sharps Pixley meet in the elegant offices of N. M. Rothschild. They sit with telephones beside them and little flags in front of them, which they raise to stop the price being fixed during tense conferences with their offices. Their decisions are flashed round

* Though the Baltic remains the last all-male bastion in the City.

the world, and gold prices from Bombay to Manila follow their lead.

Sadly, much of this is now charming fiction. London was indeed until 1968 the world's largest gold market. It owed its pre-eminence to two things. First, it was through the London markets that the Bank of England, on behalf of the world's main central banks, operated the 'gold pool'. Through it, the market price of gold was kept within narrow limits on either side of $35 an ounce. Second, until 1968 London was the market on which South Africa, which produces 80 per cent of the non-communist world's gold, sold its stocks. Since then, although neither centre produces turnover figures, Zürich has certainly overtaken London. With the Washington Agreement of 1968 establishing a free and an official price, the gold pool was disbanded and South Africa decided to sell most (possibly all) of her gold through Zürich. This may have been because she wanted to be sure that the size of her sales would not be retailed to the US Treasury by the Bank of England. Moreover, after the gold market was split, the Swiss banks continued to build up large stockpiles of gold (naturally bought through Zürich) in the hope that the official price would ultimately be raised, while the London bullion dealers were more cautious. As a result, the Swiss banks certainly lost a lot of money (the official price was not raised from $35 to $38 an ounce until 1971) but the London dealers lost South African custom.

The gold fixings themselves are an overrated activity. True, they are the only moments in the day when demand and supply from the world's two main gold markets are matched up; for the three big Swiss banks which run the Zürich markets are constantly on the line. But of the five London firms at the fixing only two are continuously active in the gold market: Johnson Matthey, which has a large industrial demand, and Samuel Montagu, which has easily the biggest share of the London markets. And most gold is bought and sold outside the fixing, on the telephone and telex, at prices which change constantly during the day.

As British citizens are not allowed to own gold bullion, the bulk of London's business is with international clients. Gold is bought only for immediate delivery though London is watching with interest the progress of the world's only gold futures market, opened in Winnipeg in autumn 1972.

Three of the firms that make up the gold market, Mocatta, Sharps Pixley and Montagu, also form the silver bullion market. Silver, unlike gold, can be bought forward as well as spot. The bullion market has been put on its mettle since the LME started dealing in silver, although it claims that the LME has taken little business from it. When the LME silver market was under discussion, the bullion firms improved their contract and halved their commission rates. From the buyer's point of view the main difference is that with the LME he has – in theory – either to put up 10 per cent of the purchase price as margin or deposit one-tenth of his purchase with the dealing firm. The bullion market by contrast has no deposit requirement. Beneficial though this relaxed attitude may be to their clients, it sometimes proves expensive. In 1970 Johnson Matthey lost a staggering £7 million on an unnamed client. But then on commodity markets, losing money is an occupational hazard.

8
The Bank of England

THE PARADOXICAL OLD LADY

The Bank of England is the link between the City and the government. There is an inherent contradiction in its situation: it is the government's arm in the City, and the City's representative in the government – the gamekeeper and the poacher, the foreman and the shop steward. Understanding this paradox is crucial to understanding how the Bank works.

It began life as a private bank, backed by a group of City merchants and wealthy landowners, but with the special distinction that it was set up to raise money for the government. The first loan, of £1·2 million, was to finance William III's wars against France. Gradually the Bank accepted responsibility for the smooth working of the country's financial system and of the City's banking community. In 1946 its changed position was finally recognized when it was nationalized. Since then, it has continued to become more the servant of the government, less a part of the City.

The Bank's links with the City are emphasized by its location. The 'Old Lady of Threadneedle Street' stands right at the centre of the Square Mile, at the City's main crossroads. Cornhill,

Lombard Street, Poultry and Threadneedle Street, all lined with clearing banks, merchant banks, discount houses and foreign banks, radiate from it. Outside, the Bank's tall windowless walls, built by Sir John Soane in 1828, give it the look of an elegant fortress. Inside, mosaic floored corridors run round a square of laboriously cultivated grass. The doors are guarded by pink-coated footmen. Near one side door, where it can be entered discreetly, is the discount office. It is through this office, as explained later, that the Bank has its most regular contacts with the City. The office is designed rather like the stage set for a French farce, full of small rooms each with two or more doors. One banker can be shown out quietly as a second arrives, without any embarrassing meetings.

The Bank's contact with Whitehall is at many levels, mainly with the Treasury, but also regularly with other government departments. It is from the Treasury, as the Bank of England Act of 1946 made clear, that the Bank's powers ultimately derive. The Treasury owns the Bank's shares and has formal authority over it. In any dispute between the Bank and the Treasury, the Chancellor of the Exchequer has the last word. Or as Montagu Norman, the Bank's best-known Governor, put it back in 1926: 'I look upon the Bank as having the unique right to offer advice and to press such advice even to the point of "nagging"; but always of course subject to the supreme authority of the Government.'* This is important, for the Bank is often blamed for implementing government decisions. While the Bank must be held responsible for the technical expertise with which it performs any operation, the broad outlines of its public policy are determined by the Chancellor of the Exchequer.

The Bank carries out an enormous range of functions. First of all it is a bank. It is the government's banker, holding the accounts of the government departments. More important, it manages the government's finances, handling the note issue and raising government loans. And it gives the government advice on economic and monetary policy, which it also helps to put into

* Answer to Question 14,597, Minutes of Evidence, Royal Commission on Indian Currency and Finance, 1926.

force. It is the bankers' bank, holding accounts for the clearing banks, the discount houses and the accepting houses.

Next, it operates on behalf of the government in three financial markets. It controls the foreign-exchange market (and also administers exchange control); and it operates in the bill market and gilt-edged market, two markets in government debt.

Finally it controls the level of credit and it takes responsibility for the good order of the City. Most other central banks perform this under a legal banking code. The Bank of England is unique in that to a large extent it lays down the code itself.

Some of these roles clash or overlap with others. Thus the Bank's responsibility for raising funds for the government may make it difficult for the Bank also to enforce the monetary policy which the government wants it to pursue. In controlling the banks, it may find it difficult to perform another function: that of channelling their views back to Whitehall. And in maintaining good order in the City, it may find it difficult to promote competition energetically among City institutions.

HOW THE BANK IS RUN

The Bank is not a branch of the Civil Service. It is a nationalized industry but with a number of special peculiarities. While the boards of other nationalized industries are appointed by a minister, that of the Bank, called the Court, is technically appointed by the Crown. In reality directors are chosen by the Prime Minister with the advice of the Chancellor of the Exchequer. While in other nationalized industries, directors' salaries are laid down by the minister, the directors of the Bank have the pleasant duty of deciding how much should be paid to the Bank's six full-time or 'executive' directors (including the Governor and the Deputy Governor). Perhaps it is not surprising the then Governor, Sir Leslie O'Brien,* received a disclosed £30,000 in 1971, more than any other head of a nationalized industry. Four of the part-time directors sit, together with the Governor, Deputy Governor and one of the full-time directors, on the Committee of Treasury

* Sir Leslie (now Lord) O'Brien was succeeded by Gordon Richardson in June 1973.

which meets the day before the Court and helps to prepare the ground for it.

The Court is made up of the Governor, the Deputy Governor and sixteen directors. It meets once a week, on Thursday mornings. Today it is still made up predominantly of bankers, but industrialists and the odd trade unionist also serve on it. Only four of the directors, apart from the Governor and his deputy, work full-time. These six are the men who really run the Bank. The part-time directors are vaguely justified as 'contributing outside expertise'. They do attend Court meetings and sit on internal committees of the Bank. But they cannot take policy decisions as these are made by the Governor with or without consultation with the Chancellor of the Exchequer. If the part-time directors are in the confidence of the full-time directors, they have to perform strenuous mental gymnastics to separate their private interests from their official duties. If they are not in the confidence of the full-time directors, they cannot comment effectively on the work of the Bank. In fact they are generally left in the dark. When Cecil King resigned his part-time directorship in May 1968 he described them as 'dignified old gentlemen who turn up every Thursday and do what they are asked'.* The small body of full-time advisers employed by the Bank have far more influence. So do the heads of the more important departments of the Bank. Unlike the part-time directors, they have full access to the Bank's confidential information and in practice play a large part in formulating the Bank's policy.

The Bank is divided into ten departments. A glance at what they do gives some idea of the wide range of work the Bank performs. Easily the most important is that of the chief cashier – Sir Leslie O'Brien himself once held this post. Besides having his signature on the country's banknotes, the chief cashier is also the Bank's chief executive officer. His department's two main responsibilities are the Bank's banking operations, and its activities in the various financial markets. The discount office, the Bank's window on the City, also comes under his control.

The accountant's department, which employs about a quarter

* Interview with Nicholas Tomalin, *Sunday Times* (12 May 1968).

of all the Bank's City staff, handles the Bank's work as registrar. The Bank keeps the register of the holders of all quoted government securities, and for the stocks of nationalized industries, some Commonwealth governments and several local authorities. A separate department operates exchange control.

Through the economic intelligence department and the overseas department, the Bank collects information on the economies of Britain and other countries, information which forms the basis of policy advice to the Governor and to Whitehall. The internal administration of the Bank is in the hands of the establishment, secretary's and audit departments and – since the Bank called in the services of the American management consultants, McKinsey's – the management services department. The largest department of all is the printing works in Debden, Essex, which employs 1,900 of the Bank's 7,000 full-time staff in producing all new Bank of England notes and destroying old ones.

THE BANK AS A BANK

The Bank of England is banker to three types of customer. It has a few private accounts, some commercial accounts left over from before nationalization and some acquired since. Others are held by the Bank's own staff who enjoy splendid cheque books but no overdrafts. Private accounts are kept on mainly because the Bank wants to give its staff experience in the techniques of commercial banking. Infinitely more important are the Bank's institutional customers, the government and the banks.

It was as the government's banker that the Bank of England began life. As the government's banker, the Bank handles the main accounts of all government departments. It considers this one of the essential roles of a central bank. However, handling these accounts is, from the Bank's point of view, neither a particularly profitable business nor an expanding one. The Bank has relatively few branches outside London and does not attempt to do the business of all government departments. It simply operates the government's central accounts.

Out of this role as the government's banker arises the Bank's task of advising the government on monetary policy, for the Bank tends to see this in terms of a banker advising his client. If it is the Treasury which usually decides the policy which the Bank implements, the Bank still has views of its own, as the Governor's speeches often reveal. Indeed, there are grounds for arguing that the Bank does not press its views upon the government often enough. Obviously the elected government should not be subject to the conservative dictates of the central bank. But central banks invariably tend to see themselves as custodians of the purchasing power of their currency and as restraints on a spendthrift government. It is not hard to think of occasions since the war when the Bank of England could have acted as a counterweight to an electioneering government pursuing inflationary policies.

Above all, besides handling the government's accounts, the Bank also balances the government's books by borrowing for it. Spending which the government cannot cover from tax revenue has to be met by borrowing: and it is the Bank which handles the National Debt.

A small part of the debt is covered by the note issue, though today this is determined not by the government's needs but by public demand. The British public dislikes handling used notes, and the 1,800 million new notes which the Bank issues each year is a high figure by international standards. Besides printing the notes, the Bank distributes them through its branches to the commercial banks, withdraws and destroys old ones, and looks after over 100,000 applications a year to have mutilated notes replaced.

The vast bulk of the National Debt is held by the banks or by the public in Treasury bills or gilt-edged stock. Managing it is a formidable task. For Britain's National Debt is bigger, compared with national income, than that of any other major industrial country: in early 1973 it stood at £36,526 million nominal value. Just under 10 per cent of this debt is in the form of irredeemable stock, with the $3\frac{1}{2}$ per cent War Loan (launched originally at 5 per cent amidst a welter of jingoism in 1917) the largest single issue, accounting for $5\frac{1}{2}$ per cent of the total debt.

Since it would be unacceptable to issue irredeemable debt again the Bank has the never-ending task of paying off dated stock as it falls due – by issuing more debt which in turn will have to be paid off over periods up to forty years ahead. If it were just a question of rolling over existing stock, it would be a massive task. But in most years the Bank has also to get rid of a staggering amount of new debt. The central government usually spends more than it raises in tax because it has to help finance the investment programmes of local authorities and nationalized industries. Not surprisingly the Bank is constantly haunted by the fear that some day, perhaps because of a sudden collapse of confidence in the gilt-edged market, the public will refuse to hold long-term government debt. To ensure that in such an eventuality it would still be able to raise money for the government, the Bank has as its line of last resort the Treasury bill market. It has given the discount houses their special privileges on the condition that they invariably take up any Treasury bills not bought by other banks at the weekly tender each Friday.*

The Bank of England holds the accounts of some 100 foreign central banks, many of which keep large sterling balances in London; and it also acts as banker to around ninety commercial banks, including the accepting houses, some of the overseas banks in London and the discount houses. The most important of the commercial accounts are those of the clearing banks, held with the Bank for two practical reasons. First, under the old system for controlling bank lending – explained shortly – the clearing banks were required to hold part of their deposits in cash or their accounts with the Bank. Under the new regulations, the banks – and all other banks covered by them – can choose to hold deposits at the Bank as part of their reserve requirement. The Bank now has an agreement with the clearing banks that they will still keep a certain level of deposits with it. There is a second reason for the clearers to continue to keep a part of their cash on deposit at the Bank. After the cheque clearing, their residual balances are settled by adjusting their accounts at the bank and they are not allowed overdrafts.

* See chapter 4 for an explanation of the work of the discount houses.

Of the other banks' accounts, those of the eighteen accepting houses are today little used. But the discount houses use their accounts regularly, as they alone among the Bank's customers are allowed overdrafts. This is a part of their special privileges. As explained below,* on days when the discount houses are short of funds, they can borrow from the Bank.

From the Bank's point of view these banking accounts have one final use: they give it a useful threat to hold over the head of a mutinous banker. For a bank to have its account at the Bank closed down would not only be an inconvenience; it would be the ultimate gesture of no confidence.

THE BANK AND THE MARKETS

The Bank of England is the government's arm in three key financial markets, the bill market, the gilt-edged market and the foreign exchange market. In the foreign exchange market the Bank's role is relatively straightforward: to control the exchange rate of the pound as it is bound by international convention to do.

In the bill and gilt-edged markets – the two markets in government debt – the Bank's role is more complicated. Its operations in these markets are one of the two ways in which the government operates its monetary policy. The other way, described shortly, is through direct controls on the banks. Monetary policy in simple language means controlling the amount of money in the country. This is not as simple a job as it might sound, for it means more than controlling the level of notes and coin in circulation. Definitions vary, but 'money supply' is usually taken to mean both notes and coin – and bank deposits, on the grounds that most people use a bank account just as if it were cash in their pocket. One of the main determinants of the level of bank deposits is the amount banks lend, because a loan from one bank usually ends up as a deposit with another. So if the Bank wants to control bank deposits it has to control the level of bank lending.

The other main determinant of the money supply is the way in which the government borrows. If the government borrows by

* See also chapter 4, pp. 80–1.

printing banknotes it is obviously increasing the money supply. If, however, it borrows by issuing long-term debt to the general public, then it is not. So the essence of market operations is to reduce the money supply by selling debt to the public (taking in money in exchange); or to increase it by buying debt from the public (paying for it with money). But by buying or selling debt in the market, the government also influences its price and hence the return on it.* As the government is competing with other borrowers for funds, the rate at which it borrows affects all other interest rates.

The bill or discount market is the market in Treasury and commercial bills – three-month debt. What happens in it affects short-term interest rates including rates in the parallel sterling money markets described in chapter 4 and indirectly bank over-draft rates. The Bank influences the bill market in two ways. First it varies the amount of Treasury bills it issues to the market, through the 'tender' every Friday. Secondly, it varies the con-ditions under which it 'helps' the discount market. Usually it helps by the 'back door', buying bills from the houses through the so-called 'special buyer' Hugh Seccombe, the chairman of Seccombe, Marshall and Campion, set up by Montagu Nor-man specially for this purpose. But if it wants to push rates up sharply, it forces the houses 'into the Bank'. This means that it helps by lending straight to the houses at a penal rate. (Until October 1972 the lowest rate this could be was called Bank rate and was decided by the Bank, with the Treasury. Since October 1972 the rate has been calculated on the basis of the Treasury bill rate and has been renamed minimum lending rate.)

What happens in the gilt-edged market influences long-term interest rates, such as the rate on industrial debentures. The government controls the supply of stock to the market through a private broker, the stockbrokers Mullens and Co. Their senior partner, Thomas Gore Browne, is known as the government broker. For his services his firm charges the Bank a low (or in

* Since the interest rate on debt is fixed, if its price rises, the return on it falls. Take £100 of government stock offering interest of 5 per cent: if its price drops to £80, the return on it will rise to 6¼ per cent (or £5 per £80).

many cases no) commission. This varies from year to year but because of the size of the business involved could typically add up to about £500,000.

When a new government stock is issued, it is promptly announced to be fully subscribed. In fact, any stock not taken up by the public on the market is immediately bought for government departments. The issue then becomes a 'tap' stock. This means that it is sold off by the broker over subsequent weeks as there is a demand for it. The Bank usually tries to have at least two 'tap' stocks, one long-dated and one shorter-dated. The price at which the government broker is prepared to sell is generally known in the market, and it influences the whole structure of longer-term rates. Besides selling off new stocks, the government broker also buys in any issue which is approaching maturity so that by the time its redemption date arrives, the bulk should already have been bought back. This process of spreading the selling off and buying back of stocks over weeks or months helps to smooth the trend of gilt-edged prices.

There are a number of constraints on the Bank in its market operations. Thus in the bill market it also has to act as lender of last resort; though it can vary the amount of Treasury bills it supplies to the market it must either buy bills from the discount houses if they present them – or lend against them. It can however make it expensive. The Bank also faces handicaps in the gilt market. It wants first to smooth out any violent fluctuations in the price of gilt-edged and thus to make it easier for the Bank to float new issues and redeem existing ones; and secondly, as mentioned, it wants to influence the level of the country's money supply. Until the late 1960s, the first aim was the dominant one. Then came Britain's slow recovery from the 1967 devaluation, a recovery which in the eyes of the visiting International Monetary Fund mission and of some Treasury officials was hindered by the rapid growth of the money supply. The Bank came under attack for being too ready to buy securities in the gilt-edged market to support sagging prices at a time when the public was generally unwilling to hold government debt. Its policy, however necessary to cope with rising government borrowing, was behind the expansion in the money supply. These criticisms ultimately struck home, for in 1971 the Bank announced that in future it would not necessarily support the longer-term gilt market.

In the early 1970s, this clash of interests temporarily faded into the background with the return of public willingness to hold government debt. But it did not disappear completely. As the Governor of the Bank told the Select Committee on Nationalized Industries in 1969 (Question 735), 'We have found recently and I think will continue to find in the future that it is often difficult to reconcile the pedestrian day-to-day desire for an orderly gilt-edged market and the overall policy desire to let us restrain the money supply.' In 1972–3, this problem re-emerged. With a massive government deficit and political pressure to keep interest rates down, the Bank lost control of the money supply.

This underlines the problem that the Bank faces in all its market operations: it cannot simultaneously control both the amount of debt it sells and the price at which it sells it; nor both the money supply and the level of interest rates at the same time.

In the foreign exchange market, unlike the other two markets, the Bank operates through its own team of foreign exchange dealers. Technically it is managing the 'Exchange Equalization Account', in which the country's gold and foreign currency reserves are held. This involves the Bank in buying and selling sterling for foreign currencies (and usually for dollars, the world's key currency), in order to stabilize the sterling exchange rate. Since the Second World War, the limits within which sterling can move have generally been fixed by international agreement. This in a sense has made the Bank's task more straightforward than in the other two financial markets. For in them, it has constantly to choose between the price at which it sells and the amount it wants to sell. In the foreign exchange market its priority is clear: to maintain a chosen exchange rate – the price of sterling in foreign currencies. The amount of foreign currency it buys or sells is generally determined by the need to maintain the exchange rate. There may however come a point when sterling is at its 'ceiling' and the government is unwilling to let the Bank hold more foreign currency, or where sterling is at its 'floor' and the authorities have no more foreign currency to sell and cannot borrow more from other central banks or from the International Monetary Fund. In the first case, the government's obvious course is to revalue: in the second, to devalue. It has either to announce a new fixed rate, or to let the pound float.

For four months in 1971, again from 1972, and for several years during the 1930s, sterling was allowed to float. From the Bank's point of view any move towards floating rates has the effect of giving it more freedom to choose between selling foreign currency to make sterling appreciate, or between buying foreign currency to make the pound depreciate. It should also be easier for the authorities to avoid repeating some of the more disastrous mistakes in their foreign exchange operations in the recent past.

For a considerable period in the mid-1960s when sterling was under heavy pressure, the Bank intervened not only in the spot market but also on the forward market, buying pounds for delivery in one, three and six months' time. This support for the forward exchange rates was designed to bolster confidence in the pound; but it also gave businessmen cheap insurance against the sterling devaluation which was generally expected. When devaluation duly took place in 1967, the Bank sustained disclosed losses of the equivalent of £356 million in foreign exchange when these contracts fell due. After devaluation, the authorities made the further mistake of abandoning their policy of supporting the pound in the forward market – thus giving the impression that they had no faith in the new parity. Who was to blame for these policies has never been clearly established. Ultimate responsibility for major decisions in the foreign exchange market rests in theory with the Chancellor of the Exchequer; actually operations in the forward market at this period were closely followed by the Prime Minister, Harold Wilson, and his special adviser Professor (now Lord) Balogh. But the Bank could certainly have taken a stronger line to oppose the policy than it did.

For the weakness of sterling had revealed that the Bank, in its international operations, had considerable prestige – and potential independence. The Bank organized the complicated network of swap agreements with other central banks which propped up the sterling exchange rate in the years before devaluation. These swaps provided the government with its only access to loans of foreign exchange apart from the International Monetary Fund. Through the swaps, the Bank lent sterling to other central banks in exchange for foreign currencies which it then sold on the foreign exchange market to support the pound. Just after the Labour government came to power in 1964, Lord Cromer, then Governor of the Bank, raised $3,000 million to stave off the foreign exchange crisis which threatened to force a devaluation. Charles Coombs, then vice-president of the New York Federal Reserve Bank, has said of this operation* 'Each central bank's decision to lend was squarely based on the character and integrity of the Bank of England and its Governor.' It is the Bank's international reputation that is the foundation for such independence as it has.

Soon the Bank may find that it has to extend its operations into another market. During the 1960s London became the home of the eurodollar market and the Bank gradually assumed a vague custodianship of the London banks' eurodollar activities. For example these banks have to report regularly to the Bank on their liquidity positions in foreign currencies. But though the Bank has steadfastly refused to intervene directly in the market as a dealer, or to impose formal controls, other central banks feel that the time is coming when the Bank should start to step into the market. This may prove its next task.

The Bank's involvement in these financial markets has a profound effect on its attitudes towards government policy. It is the fact that the Bank has to sell public debt that makes it so concerned with the level of government spending; the fact that it has to try to keep the gilts market happy that made it so nervous about the Treasury's brief flirtation with the doctrines of the Chicago monetary economist Milton Friedman after devaluation. And it is the fact that the Bank has the job of defending sterling in the foreign exchange market that makes it so anxious about UK rates of inflation compared with those of Britain's industrial

* *The Banker*, November 1966.

competitors. Like all central banks the Bank of England sees itself as custodian of the value of the country's currency. But it is noticeably more worried about inflation when sterling is weak than when it is strong.

THE BANK AS POLICEMAN

(a) Controlling credit

The Bank of England polices large parts of the City, and in particular the banking community. Long before nationalization in 1946 the Bank's dominant position and its emergence as lender of last resort had led it gradually to assume responsibility for seeing that the other banks ran their affairs in a safe and stable way.

As the government came to pursue a more active part in managing the economy, so the Bank's job altered. Today it still maintains its role as guardian of good order in the City. But it has also acquired the task of inducing the banks to follow government policy, policy which often conflicts with their commercial interests. Thus the Bank controls bank lending for the government and enforces its policy of exchange control.

Not only has the Bank's work changed; the basis of its power has altered. The Bank's responsibility for the City's good order had its origins in the City's long tradition of self-policing. With nationalization the Bank's authority acquired a semi-legal basis. But this has not substantially changed the way in which its authority is exercised. Britain, unlike most other countries, still has no detailed code of banking law to tell the banks what they can and cannot do. Instead the Bank is given vague and general powers under the Nationalization Act, enforceable with vague and general sanctions. The Bank still uses its powers flexibly, relying heavily on personal contact to cajole and persuade the banks into doing what it wants.

Only in administering and enforcing exchange control does the Bank's job come close to that of a government department. What banks can and cannot do is laid down by the Treasury under the powers in the 1947 Exchange Control Act. The Bank of

England administers control through a network of 213 'authorized banks' which are allowed to deal in foreign exchange. (The Bank tends to grant permission fairly automatically to any large, reputable and well-established banking business, but more arbitrarily to others.) From time to time individual exchange control cases have to be referred back to the Treasury. But the Bank operates as flexibly as is possible within the rigid framework of the rules. It does not really like exchange control and this dislike probably helps it to operate it in a way that makes it tolerable for the banking community.

Adjusting the level of bank lending is one part of the mechanism by which the Bank controls the money supply, the other part being its management of the National Debt. In 1971 the system of credit control was completely overhauled. But in order to understand the present system (and to see where the old one went wrong) it is better to start with the pre-1971 system of bank control.

In theory the old system worked like this. The clearing banks had to maintain two ratios linking their assets to certain types of debt controlled by the Bank. For every £100 they took over the counter they had to hold £8 either in cash or in their non-interest bearing accounts with the Bank of England. This 8 per cent ratio was called the cash ratio. The next £20 they had to hold as liquid assets: assets they could turn into cash within a day or so. The three most important of these were money with the discount houses, Treasury bills and eligible bank bills.* This 28 per cent ratio (i.e. £8 plus £20) was called the liquidity ratio. The rest of the bank's deposits (i.e. £72) were in theory available to be lent to customers, but in practice banks held £15 to £20 of them in the form of investments, mostly short-dated gilts. Thus only about £50 to £55 out of each £100 taken in by the banks were in fact re-lent.

The liquidity ratio was the Bank's principal instrument of control. It occasionally reinforced it by calling for special deposits. This meant that it required the clearing banks to hold a proportion of their deposits in balances at the Bank, earning on

* See chapter 4 for a description of these types of assets.

them an interest rate – the average market rate on Treasury bills – very much lower than they could have made by lending the money elsewhere. In the 1960s the Bank tended to use its power to call for special deposits not so much as an integral part of its controls over the banking system as to back up calls for restraint in lending, and even as a punishment when the banks were recalcitrant.

So this was what the old mechanism looked like. In some countries, the central bank varies the amount of lending by the banks by changing the size of their ratios. The Bank of England could have done so by using special deposits more flexibly. Instead it preferred to vary not the size of the banks' ratios, but the supply of assets the banks could include in them. What it did was to change the amount of Treasury bills it issued, so tending to squeeze the bank's lending through their liquidity ratios.

That, at any rate, was what happened in theory. As the famous report of the Radcliffe Committee on the Working of the Monetary System described it, the Bank squeezed the supply of Treasury bills, and that squeezed bank lending and so reduced the money supply.

But Radcliffe was over-optimistic. The links in the system it described were in practice more elastic than the committee realized. First, reducing the supply of Treasury bills did not necessarily squeeze the banks' liquidity ratio if they could replace them by buying eligible bank bills, and the early 1960s saw a great boom in these bills. Secondly, even if the supply of assets which counted towards its liquidity ratio was squeezed, a bank could still increase its lending by selling off its investments. Radcliffe had argued that the banks would not sell their investments if they had to take a loss on them; in practice the banks preferred to sell their investments at a loss rather than cut back on their more profitable overdraft lending. Thirdly, the liquidity controls only affected clearing-bank lending. Radcliffe did not realize how fast the parallel market banks – merchant, foreign, overseas, and ultimately the clearing banks' own subsidiaries – would increase their lending and take up the slack.

But there was an even more fundamental flaw in the way the system was intended to work. It was that the only way that the Bank could cut down the supply of Treasury bills, if the demands of government finance were unchanged, was to issue more long-term debt. To issue more long-term debt might be to risk a steep drop in its price. And for much of the 1960s, the Bank's fear was that a sudden drop in the price might leave the gilt-edged market too shaken to buy securities, and the Bank unable to service the National Debt. Treasury and academic economists might argue that there was bound always to be a price, however low, at which the public would buy government debt; the Bank's view was that this price might turn out to be so low as to be politically unacceptable to the government and utterly demoralizing to the markets. Accordingly its ability to organize a credit squeeze depended on the government. If the government needed money it could not organize a squeeze; if the government did not, it could. In the late 1960s government spending went through the roof just at the moment when it hoped to restrict the money supply. As a result the Bank had to resort to the crudest system of controlling the amount the banks could lend: simply telling them.

Ceilings on the rate of growth of bank lending were first introduced in May 1965 and lasted, apart from a few months in the middle of 1967, right up to the introduction of the new system of control in September 1971. What ceilings did to the various aspects of the City's business is described elsewhere in this book. They certainly stultified competition among the main banks. But paradoxically they were also a force for innovation, as the rest of the City devoted much energy to finding ways round them. They did strain the relationship between the Bank of England and the clearing banks. But by and large they succeeded in doing what they were intended to do: keeping bank lending down. Whether they could have continued to do so much longer is more doubtful.

Is the new system of control introduced in September 1971 proving any more effective? At first glance, it looks remarkably similar to the old. Like the old, it is based partly on a ratio and partly on special deposits. But there are differences. The ratio under the new system, called the reserve ratio, is much lower than the old liquidity ratio: the banks must keep only £12·50 of every £100 in approved assets (now called reserve assets). The range of these approved assets is a little wider than it was under the old ratios: it includes not only cash held on account with the Bank of England (but not in bank tills), call money with the discount market, Treasury bills and eligible bank bills, but also short-term gilts. More important, the new system applies not just to the clearing banks but to all banks.

The new system is certainly an improvement on the old. Of the four major flaws in the old system, two have disappeared. First, all banks are now covered. And secondly, as the amount of eligible bank bills which the banks can count towards their reserve ratio is limited to 2 per cent of deposits, they can no longer buy them *ad lib* to replace scarce Treasury bills.

But the two other flaws in the old system remain. The clearing banks can still sell investments to increase their lending. Second – and potentially more dangerous – is the fact that if ever the Bank had to raise large sums by issuing Treasury bills, it might 'fill up' the reserve ratios of the banks, which would then be able to increase their lending.

In theory neither of these situations should ever arise. If the banks sell their investments, the Bank of England can mop up this lending power with special deposits. If the authorities are serious about withdrawing support from the gilt-edged market, they will never have to raise large amounts by issuing Treasury bills. In the past, when gilt-edged prices fell, the government broker bought gilts and the weight of government borrowing was switched to the Treasury bill market. Now, if the Bank holds firm, it can refuse to buy gilts even when the gilt-edged market is weak.

The crucial question hanging over the new controls is, how far are the authorities prepared to let interest rates move? The most important single difference between the old system and the new lies in the fact that the authorities now claim to be willing to allow interest rates to fluctuate. Under the old system, the government broker's intervention in the gilt-edged market determined the trend of gilt prices, while direct government controls on the banks determined who borrowed from them and how much they lent. Now, in theory at any rate credit is rationed not by government fiat or bank preferences but by price.

In 1973, the new system was put to severe test. The Bank was faced with an impossible combination of a massive government deficit, accelerating inflation, and growing political pressure to halt the rise in interest rates. In September 1973, the authorities took one step back from the spirit of Competition and Credit Control by imposing a ceiling on personal bank deposit rates in an effort to protect the building societies from high interest. In November, they took another, raising Minimum Lending Rate by fiat instead of using market operations to push it up. In 1972–3, the Bank called several times for Special Deposits, but showed no sign of using them as a flexible policy instrument. It remains to be seen whether the Bank will salvage its new policy.

(b) Controlling the City

The Bank's control over the banking community goes beyond determining the level of bank advances. It has a wider and vaguer responsibility for the good order of the banking system. This is exercised through constant contact with the banking community at many levels. This contact allows the Bank both to tell the banks what it wants them to do, and to discover what the banks are thinking and what is going on elsewhere in the financial community.

Most banks and all discount houses are in frequent touch with the Bank. Almost every week, for instance, the principal of the discount office, Jim Keogh, or one of his officials visits each of the twelve discount houses, and both discount houses and clearing banks talk every day on the phone to the office. Then the discount office deals with other, less routine business. Bankers drop in to sound out the Bank's views on anything from plans for opening a new branch to what the latest trade figures mean. If one City house wants to link up with another in a different area of business it may ask the discount office to act as marriage broker and find it a suitable partner. The special buyer in the discount market and the government broker in the gilt-edged also keep the discount houses, banks and stock market in touch with the Bank's views.

The heads of the clearing banks have a formal meeting with the Governor twice a year. Until recently there was also a highly confidential one every month, when the chief cashier told the banks how he saw the economy and the availability of funds moving, and the banks in return described the demand for loans and the supply of deposits which they saw developing. But the Governor still sees the clearing banks at half of the twelve annual meetings of the Committee of London Clearing Banks, of which he is an *ex officio* member. These meetings the clearing banks find less useful, partly because they have become steadily less consultative and more platforms for the Governor to lecture the banks; and more recently, because the increase in competition among the banks puts a restraint on joint discussions. Agendas tend to be non-controversial when the Governor is there; more controversial when he is absent.

The Bank likes and encourages the formation of City groups like the CLCB. It means one forum where it can put its views, one spokesman to deal with and fewer letters to write. The merchant banks talk to the Bank formally through the Accepting Houses Committee, whose chairman has access to the Governor whenever he wants. The American banks' organization, the American Bankers in London Association, was set up at the behest of the Bank of England to give the Bank a body to talk to. But the heads of all London banks can – and do – easily call on the Governor to discuss any major policy issue. 'The great thing about the Governor', in the words of one of the older and more establishment merchant bankers, 'is that he is infinitely available.'

Why do the banks go to see the Bank? Usually it is either to find out whether what the bank wants to do is acceptable to the Bank, or to tell the Bank of some new move. A bank doing a large operation in foreign exchange or corporate finance for a client might ring the Bank and ask, without mentioning names, what the Bank's reaction to such an operation would be. A bank moving its headquarters would tell the Bank in advance, largely as a matter of courtesy. A foreign bank setting up a branch in London would come to the Bank for initial permission, which would be granted on condition that it employed at least one person from the Bank's list of experienced and often elderly London bankers to show it the ropes.

When an established bank wants to embark on an entirely new venture, moving into a new line of business or linking with another bank, communication is more delicate. A clearing or top merchant bank might feel strong enough to chance telling the Bank at the last moment; but only if it judged that the Bank would not regard this as too serious an act of defiance. An American bank, conscious – and from time to time reminded by the Bank – of its dependence on the Bank's goodwill for its place in the City, would be more cautious. Before the First National City Bank introduced dollar certificates of deposit in London, it discussed the proposition with the Bank; and when it wanted to go on to introduce sterling CDs, it went along with the Bank's view that a British bank should do so first.

If the banks do not ask the Bank what they can do in advance, the Bank sooner or later tells them. This is how it has in the past controlled bank lending. It keeps a tight hand on mergers and takeovers. It is widely believed to have dropped a clear hint to the discount house Gerrard and Reid that it would like to see it take over the failing business of the National Discount Company; and it gave a firm warning to Sir Kenneth Keith, head of the merchant bankers Hill Samuel, that it would not like to see him link up with a clearing bank.

The Bank's power, then, is exercised in what is arguably a highly arbitrary way. The City is made aware of its general prejudices, and understands that a nod from the Bank is as good as an order. If a bank is recalcitrant, the Bank's policy is first to talk to it. But the Bank's hints and suggestions are in the last resort backed by considerable sanctions. The discount houses are dependent on the Bank for their livelihood. The banks are all vulnerable. The Bank can advise the Treasury to withdraw their authorized status. In the case of the major banks, whose acceptance makes commercial bills eligible, the Bank could simply remove their name from its list of banks whose paper is eligible.

The system, then, has two essential aspects: good communications between the Bank and the banks, and the existence of these sanctions which are in practice never applied. Almost invariably, after a bank has been 'talked to' by the Bank, it does as it is told. The system also has considerable dangers. For a start, the informality of communications results in misunderstandings. The most remarkable example of this was over the Bank's policy on clearing-bank mergers. After the report of the Colwyn Committee in 1918 discouraged clearing-bank mergers, an informal agreement was reached that no more would occur without the agreement of the Treasury. Not till 1968 did any merger among the Big Five take place. This followed a hint dropped in the 1967 Prices and Incomes Board report on bank charges, indicating that the authorities would look favourably on further mergers. Immediately there was a scramble to merge, a scramble which was ultimately stopped by the Monopolies Commission. Not only had the Bank and the clearing banks managed to misunderstand each other. The informality of the Bank's controls on mergers allowed it to avoid thinking through what its real policy should be. As a result it suffered the indignity of seeing such policy as it had reversed by the Monopolies Commission.

A somewhat similar confusion existed over the Bank's 'rules' on links between the accepting houses and the clearing or foreign banks. What these rules were was never made clear until the Bank announced, in autumn 1972, that they were being changed. With the announcement, it was apparent that the rules had been honoured in the breach as well as the observance. UK clearing banks, the Bank proclaimed, would henceforth be allowed (in cases where the Bank approved) to take more than a 25 per cent stake in accepting houses. EEC banks, though not other foreign banks, would be allowed to buy more than 15 per cent of a merchant or overseas bank. Yet already Midland Bank had its 35 per cent stake in Montagu Trust, and First National City Bank owned 40 per cent of National and Grindlays.

This confusion is serious enough. But more worrying is the

fact that the informal system of control discourages initiative among the banks. There have been occasions when the banks have hesitated to introduce new services because of a fear – real or pretended – that the Bank would not like them to do so. For example they hesitated to reintroduce personal loans in 1970 only to find that they were beaten to it by National Giro.

Although the system of control may look arbitrary, even damaging, the banks claim to like it. The alternative, they argue, is the American situation where a detailed code, like British company law, covers what banks can and cannot do, and a bank that wants to embark on any new venture has first to consult a team of lawyers. In London the banks – particularly the Americans – would prefer to stroll round to see Jim Keogh.

They may well be right. Despite its imperfections the system does probably work better than the obvious alternatives. The dilemma is a familiar one in the City. An infinite variety of complex situations have to be controlled. Each requires a rapid ruling, and many involve vast amounts of money. The ideal form of regulation is that exercised by a body acting on the basis of the broadest possible, publicly stated guidelines, and one capable of delivering instant and authoritative interpretations of them. If the guidelines are vague, it will be far harder to find loopholes in them. If the interpretations are delivered rapidly, it will be easier to act quickly. If the judgement is authoritative, there will be no danger of finding it rescinded after it has been acted on and large sums have been committed.

At present, the main problem with the Bank's method of control is that its guidelines are too vague. Indeed, a tête-à-tête with the Governor or chief cashier may be the nearest a banker gets to finding out what they are. This means that lazy banks can tell themselves that the Bank stands in the way of innovation, and that changes in Bank thinking may take too long to filter through to the City. What are really needed are more specific guidelines stating what banks can and cannot do. They could be policed in the flexible manner that the Bank uses to implement exchange controls. And when the Bank changes its mind, it could publicly alter the guidelines.

But the more explicit the Bank's regulations become the more explicit will become the conflict between its role as policeman in the City and its role as spokesman. In the late 1950s there was a tendency, especially among the clearing banks but also among other parts of the banking community, to regard the Bank as the City's ally against Whitehall. But in the course of the 1960s the clearing banks in particular found that they had to move into new areas of business – hire purchase, money market activities and merchant banking – in order to expand. The Bank did not whole-heartedly approve. At the same time, the Bank was persuading the banks, and again particularly the clearers, to accept increasing restrictions on their lending. Relations between the Bank and the banks became more distant.

Now there are signs that the City would like a more inde-pendent representative. The clearing banks have joined the CBI and there have been calls for a City 'little Neddy'. The Bank's status is inexorably shifting: it is becoming the east end of White-hall. This matters to the Bank. One senior clearing banker mis-chievously suggests that Bank officials live in constant fear of having their substantial City-based salaries pared down to meagre Civil Service levels. Certainly if the Bank lost its function as the City's representative its standing in Whitehall would be diminished.

It may be possible for the Bank to preserve its dual role for a few years yet. Attitudes long engrained in the City do not dis-appear overnight. But they are changing. Discussions with the Bank used to be cosy chats over tea. Now the monthly heart-to-heart with the chief cashier has been dropped.

When John Thompson, then chairman of Barclays, was asked in an interview in the *Economist* in 1965* what he would do if he wanted to see the Chancellor of the Exchequer, he said, 'I would ask the Governor and he would probably go with me.'

By contrast, when the new credit controls were being dis-cussed the (very brief) meetings between the Governor and the clearing banks were like negotiations between two foreign powers. At one tense point Sir Archibald Forbes, chairman of

* 4 September 1965.

Midland, who presented the case for the clearing banks, said, 'Mr Governor, I shall have to go and see the Chancellor.'

'All right,' said Sir Leslie O'Brien. 'You can.'

When Sir Archibald finally saw the Chancellor of the Exchequer it was at the IMF meeting in Washington after the regulations had been announced in September 1971 . . . and in the company of the Governor of the Bank of England.

9

Where the City goes now

A large number of people in Britain see the City of London as a parasitical growth on the economy. It is inhabited by rich, arrogant young men and cigar-smoking tycoons, interested only in making money for themselves. They have no sense of responsibility for the national good, no ideals and no morals. They make vast fortunes from share speculation, property speculation and commodity speculation, activities which are no more than legalized gambling and require neither intelligence nor effort. They loathe the working classes and the welfare state, and they engineered the fall of the Labour government of 1964–70.

Now to the City this sort of criticism looks ludicrous. The City, its defenders argue, has been reborn as the leading international financial centre despite years of stagnation in the British economy and of weakness of the pound. It not only helps to keep the balance of payments out of the red; it provides the best banking system and capital market in the world.

Yet there is a great deal of truth in the standard left-wing criticism of the City. The truth is usually lost in the emphasis on the City's morality – often questionable, but probably no more so than that of many other sectors of British industry. The severest criticism of the City is that its extraordinary renaissance as the world's major international financial centre has been coupled with a failure to serve its British customers as well as it has served its overseas clients.

Personal customers in Britain probably enjoy better financial services than in other countries, yet in the international banking capital of the world, banks are not open when ordinary people want to use them. In the international insurance capital of the world 800,000 private motorists suddenly lost their insurance cover through the collapse of a member of the British Insurance Association. On the world's leading international stock exchange, the small private client finds stockbrokers less and less interested in his custom.

Industry is worse served. In general, communications between the City and industry are worse and the City provides industry with less guidance and discipline than do the financial institutions in most other developed countries. London's clearing banks may be the giants of Europe, but they have still failed to teach British industry that the overdraft is not the only way to raise money. London's merchant banks may provide the brains behind the eurodollar market, but one still managed to lead the City blindly into the Rolls-Royce crash. Even though British firms have a highly efficient capital market on their doorstep, the City has done little to persuade them to take advantage of it.

The lack of interest the City shows in its dealings with British industry compared with the importance it attaches to its international performance is striking. It goes back many years: the City has a long history as a centre for raising international finance and government funds, but an extremely short one as a centre for raising domestic industrial capital.

One reason for this lack of interest is that the very qualities which have made the City successful internationally are those which least fit it to serve British industry. The City's particular skills are those of taking risks – as in jobbing on the Stock Exchange or underwriting at Lloyd's; and in broking – as on the money markets. It is less successful at giving a company general financial advice and at analysing its industrial prospects, or the viability of a project of advanced technology.

This is part of the answer. There is something more, altogether harder to pin down, but something that anyone who has worked in the City will recognize. It is a quality that is anti-intellectual, that is clubby; a combination of considerable dealing skills with a casual, even cavalier attitude to risk and a pride in amateurishness. Everything is a gamble, for finance is such a boring pursuit that the only way to make it bearable is to treat it as a game.

Now this ethos, so alien to the puritanism of the Left, wins the City international business. If it has to put together a eurocurrency loan for Olivetti, reinsure a fleet of jumbo jets for Pan Am or mastermind an international merger, the City does it dazzlingly well. In each case someone else has done the dull solid work of running the day-to-day financial business of the companies involved. But the City finds it next to impossible to take an active interest in what goes on in the research laboratory or on the shop floor of a medium-sized Midlands factory. That, as almost anyone in the City will tell you, is the job of the clearing banks. Everyone recognizes that the clearing banks do it inadequately. No one is anxious to take it over.

But now the City is changing faster than at any previous time in its history. This chapter looks first at the changing structure of the City's institutions; then at the shifting pattern of its international business; and finally at its role within Britain. Could it be that the City's international dominance will now begin to decline, and that it will begin at last to serve Britain as well as it has served the rest of the world?

THE CITY'S STRUCTURE

In the later 1960s and early 1970s many of the demarcation lines in the City have become blurred. This has come about partly through mergers, takeovers and the setting up of subsidiaries; partly through the erosion of cartels and restrictions, self-imposed and government-inflicted, which previously divided the City's institutions into fairly watertight compartments, firmly labelled according to their function. New markets have developed and old ones have declined. An obvious example has been the development of the parallel banking system, encouraged by the clearing banks' cartel and the ceilings on bank lending. Specialist firms have branched out into livelier activities. Thus the merchanting and commodity dealing firm of Vavasseurs has moved into unit trusts and money broking; the insurance brokers C. T. Bowring into merchant banking.

Many mergers have been touched off by the search either for more capital or for better outlets for investment. The search for more capital has decimated the numbers of firms in many sectors of the City. Mergers among jobbers on the London Stock Exchange cut their numbers from eighty-three to twenty between 1962 and late 1973. The number of insurance brokers has dwindled, while insurance company mergers may soon cut the number of big composites to half a dozen.

Some City firms have sought new capital not among other firms doing the same job but among different institutions handling vast funds and short of investment outlets, notably the insurance companies. One dramatic example is the relatively small merchant bank of Keyser Ullmann. Within a matter of months in 1972 the Prudential took a 20 per cent stake in Keyser Ullmann, which in turn took over the property company of Central and District, and merged with the 'fringe' merchant bank, Dalton Barton. Another was the merger between the accepting house, Guinness Mahon, and the commodity merchanting house, Lewis and Peat.

Institutional investors, particularly insurance companies and pension funds with huge portfolios of funds to manage and the relatively restricted field of the Stock Exchange to place them in, have tried to buy property companies, as did Commercial Union with MEPC in 1970; have succeeded in buying merchant banks; and have taken stakes in finance houses or jobbers, as did Triumph Investment Trust in Smith Brothers. The Bank of England's policy change in autumn 1972 opened the way for new links between the clearing banks and the merchant banks. Thus Midland took full control of Samuel Montagu in 1973.

This whole process may be further encouraged as a result of the study of the City completed in November 1972 for Lord Rothschild's Central Policy Review Staff – the cabinet 'think tank' – by the Inter-Bank Research Organization. The report called for the setting up of a high level City study group to work with Whitehall in formulating policy on just such matters as mergers between different types of financial institution.

It is not only through mergers and the setting up of subsidiaries that City institutions have begun to move into fields which they once regarded as the exclusive territory of others. Firms have begun to experiment in offering services which they were once content to leave to those whom they regarded as the specialists in that particular field. Increasingly, if they have access to the market for a certain type of service, City institutions will consider selling it. Thus the clearing banks with their massive networks of retail branches have begun to broke in insurance. They no longer just sell unit trusts; they run unit trusts of their own. The industrial life assurance companies, which once sold just that, now sell a whole range of personal insurance policies. The largest hire purchase company, United Dominions Trust, now offers a basic banking service. The change has taken place fastest in the marketing of consumer services, but there are signs of it at the wholesale level too. The merchant banks, which once used to offer mainly financial advice, now endeavour to provide a full banking service as well. The clearing banks, which once used to offer only cash, are now trying – with limited success – to provide companies with financial advice.

While demarcation lines have been fading, cartels and government quantitative controls have been disappearing. Neither have ever worked very well in the City. In most City activities, skills have been a more important ingredient for success than capital. This has helped outsiders to set up new markets, which compete with those where entry is artificially restricted, turnover restrained or charges inflated. In the case of banking the parallel markets developed outside the restraints, and when these markets were in turn controlled, companies began to evade the new restrictions by lending directly to each other through City brokers. In the case of the Stock Exchange, inflated commission charges and jobbers' turns are driving the accepting houses to set up a stock trading system of their own.

The breaking down of City boundaries is entirely to the advantage of the City's customers. It means both greater competition and greater choice, and it should help to keep the price of City services down. But it also carries with it a number of problems, of which the most serious is that of regulating the City, to ensure both that its institutions are stable and that they give due priority to their customers' interests.

Compared with other financial centres, the City has an enviable record for stability. In living memory there has been no major banking crash, and very few serious collapses of broking houses. There have, however, been a number of disastrous insurance failures, of which the most serious was that of Vehicle and General in 1971. That the City should have this record of stability must be attributed to the peculiar combination of official regulation and self-policing by which the City is governed. But the City's self-policing is, for two reasons, inevitably going to be increasingly replaced by government restrictions.

First, an essential element in the City's self-policing is the village atmosphere of London. When every banker knows every other banker by his first name and has lunch with him once a month, the chances are that if any member of the community oversteps the line, his colleagues will be the first people to know and are well placed to put pressure on him. As soon as cartels disappear and restrictions on new entrants are eroded, the force of this village policing is weakened. Inevitably it becomes harder both to spot a bad firm and to exclude it.

But more important, the public has been made aware that self-policing may still mean that the City is prepared to put loyalty to its own members before responsibility to the public. The Vehicle and General crash demonstrated the willingness of the City to close ranks. A considerable number of people in the insurance world, elsewhere in the City and in the financial press knew that Vehicle and General was not a sound company long before its collapse was made known and while it was still recruiting some of the 800,000 or so motorists who were left without insurance cover. Yet nothing was done to check the company.

In the case of the insurance industry, the British Insurance Association is not a body with policing powers. But in the case of the Stock Exchange, the self-policing body (the Takeover Panel) has shown itself unable to take a really strong line with its colleagues in the City who put their own interests before those of the general public. The names of the five men accused by the panel of insider dealing in 1971 were kept discreetly anonymous and their punishment was merely an order to hand over their takings to charity. It is hardly surprising that the government has had to step in in both these areas.

THE CITY OVERSEAS

As far as its international business is concerned the City has entered the 1970s in a confident mood. And why not? During the 1960s despite what seemed serious obstacles – the weakness of sterling, exchange controls, government curbs on capital movements – it clearly re-established itself as the world's international financial capital. By the end of the decade London had replaced New York as the centre of international banking. It housed the world's largest international insurance market, the stock exchange where the largest number of international shares were quoted, the largest international shipping and air freight markets, the largest foreign exchange market and arguably the largest metal futures and international commodities markets.

There are good reasons for the City to maintain its confidence throughout the 1970s. The market for its international services seems bound to grow. London is still well placed to provide them. Right on the City's doorstep there is what may well become the largest single financing enterprise ever undertaken, the development of the North Sea oil fields. And there are the still unexploited opportunities of the Common Market. But despite these exciting prospects, a closer look at the way the City's overseas business has been developing suggests that the City may find the going much harder in the later 1970s than it has done in the past.

The most dramatic single change of the 1960s in the City's overseas business was indubitably the rise of the eurodollar market. Quite apart from giving the merchant banks a new lease of life and cramming Moorgate with American banks, it taught the City how to manage without sterling. (The lesson has still not been wholly absorbed. City elders continue to propound the need for a strong pound to preserve the financial stature of Britain.)

But in the long run what may be more important is that the City's rise as an international banking centre has been something of a fluke. It has been the result less of the City's own efforts or of any intrinsic advantages London possesses than of the arrival of the American banks. That the eurodollar market came to Britain in the first place was in part the result of accidents of British and American monetary policy. That it stayed and developed in London is very largely the result of the influx of American banks, with American techniques and American talent. Daniel Davison, then head of the London end of the New York bank, Morgan Guaranty, puts this point forcibly.

The American banks have brought the necessary money, customers, capital and skills which have established London in its present pre-eminence. . . . We have brought the money because the dollar is our natural medium – and the dollar has been the staff of international commerce. Dollars are owned in their thousands of millions by non-Americans and deposited in vast amounts in non-American banks. But it is a fact of life that banks, to be credible, must have a lender of last resort. . . . Only the American banks have a dollar lender of last resort. The Federal Reserve Bank of the United States can, and does, create dollars when necessary. Without the Americans the big dollar deals cannot be put together. Without them London would not be credible as an international financial centre.*

* Daniel P. Davison, 'The crucial impact', *Morris Wigram Rosenthal Ltd. Newsletter* (April 1972).

Of course, as Mr Davison is the first to acknowledge, it was because of London's financial infrastructure, its money markets and so on, that the Americans chose it rather than, say, Frankfurt to base their operations. More than this, the early entry of the British overseas and merchant banks into the eurodollar business – for they really invented the market – made sure that no other centre was ever a starter as the home of eurocurrency banking. Banks which have tried to base their international banking operations elsewhere have either run into trouble or at least shown slower growth than those in London.

Nevertheless, although there has been no substantial shift of international banking business away from London yet, other financial centres are starting to catch up. The share of the market nominally on the books of London banks is falling slightly. In Europe foreign banks are now opening new offices in Frankfurt as fast as in London. In the Far East Singapore has a much publicized Asian dollar market. While this is still tiny compared with London, it shows that there is no necessary reason why other centres should not carry out for themselves the business of putting together international loans. In Toronto, too, there is an established eurocurrency market. Tokyo is at last pulling down its restrictions on foreign banks and is widely expected to emerge as a major financial centre. London money brokers are reacting to the development of these local money markets by setting up offices in Europe, Toronto and the Far East. New York is now dealing in eurodollars, using Bahamas subsidiaries. Once a really broadly based market exists outside London, there will be a strong incentive for business to move away.

What may well happen is that only those international credits that are either particularly specialist, difficult or big will be put together in London, while more run-of-the-mill loans are handled at the local centre closest to the borrower. Or perhaps, with improving communications and changes in banking regulations, the business may go back to the head offices of the organizing banks. Some will stay in London, but much will be handled by New York, Tokyo or Frankfurt. Perhaps there may even be a decline in the size of the international capital market, with more companies borrowing funds on their own local capital markets. In short it is perfectly possible that in the later 1970s the focus of growth in international banking will begin to move away from London, and the City will find itself more and more handling only specialist business.

As with international banking, so with much of the City's other overseas business. In the later 1960s and early 1970s, most of the international financial markets centred in London faced growing competition from other newer overseas centres. There are reasons peculiar to each market for this competition, but there are also a number of factors common to much of the City's overseas business.

In the case of insurance, still by far the largest earner of foreign exchange in the City, London has become largely a reinsurance market, and reinsurance is growing rapidly. It is also the main market for highly specialized risks which other centres are either too small or too inflexible to handle. But life is likely to become harder for the City's international insurers. London has seen a gradual but steady decline in the proportion of world business it is underwriting. All overseas insurance business is becoming increasingly sensitive. Developing countries are striving to become self-sufficient in insurance industries of their own. National restrictions make life assurance, the largest growth area of profitable insurance, mainly a domestic business and since the débâcle of IOS it is likely to remain so.

In the case of the commodity markets the challenge has come mainly from markets nearer the major producers, or sometimes consumers, of the raw materials involved. Thus wool, a commodity traded very largely between Australia and Japan, now has its main futures market not in London but in Sydney. The London gold market by the early 1970s was no longer the world's largest: since the disappearance in 1968 of the gold pool, through which the Bank of England channelled gold from world reserves onto the London market, South Africa has sold its gold through Zürich.

There are also a number of more general reasons why London may have a tougher fight to remain the leading international financial centre in the later 1970s. First, in a number of markets – the Baltic, the commodity and metal markets, the Stock Exchange – some of London's pull has been due to the fact that dealers meet at a specific place. While to deal on the London foreign exchange market a bank abroad need only have a telephone connection with London, to deal on the London commodity futures markets needs some kind of physical representation there. In the next couple of decades all London's open markets will probably dwindle and be replaced by telephone networks. In the case of the Baltic, the newest market, in air charter, operates largely on the telephone rather than on the floor of the exchange, while a growing volume of ship-chartering is arranged directly by shipowners. In the case of the London Stock Exchange the prospect of a computerized dealing mechanism, Ariel, could make it possible for companies all over the world to bypass both brokers and jobbers.

Another factor which may increasingly drive international business from the City is the sheer cost of operating in London. The fact that London is not just a financial centre but also Britain's commercial centre, seat of government, the focus of the tourist trade and the middle of the third largest population agglomeration in the world is both a strength and a weakness. It is bound to mean increasing pressure on communications with London – particularly by air and by telephone. It is bound, too, to mean a relentless upwards pressure on office rents. Without devastating the Square Mile still further there is probably now not much space for more extensive office development in the City, and City firms have been extraordinarily feeble about moving their clerical and computer operations out of the centre. Yet office rents in the City are already higher than anywhere in the world except Tokyo. Sooner or later, there is bound to come a point where the financial costs of operating from London exceed the intangible benefits of having an office in the City's centre.

The City's international financial success has up till the early 1970s rested largely on its ability to provide a greater collection of skills than any other centre. These may be dealing skills, or an ability to assess a risk quickly and accurately, or a wide knowledge of a highly specialized market. That they should be found together in London is largely a historical accident: London has been a centre for a particularly wide variety of financial services for a very long time. But skills can be bought and can be exported. Headhunting is an internationally organized activity.

Already the pressure to find vital skills has broken down many barriers. Women have become top money brokers. Men with state-school educations underwrite for Lloyd's syndicates. And in general only the more sluggish City firms can still afford the luxury of nepotism.

Its concentration of skills should ensure that the City remains a specialist financial centre. But if it is to retain its hold on the bulk of its international business it may well have to mobilize capital on a far larger scale. In a number of sections of the City there have been signs that the structure has not changed quickly enough to attract a sufficient volume of capital. Lloyd's is a good example: the cumbersome way in which syndicates raise cash has helped to create serious bottlenecks of capacity. Jobbers find that their capital resources have lagged far behind the vast blocks of shares in which the Exchange increasingly deals. The merchant banks are a third instance: without direct access to savings, they have found it quite impossible to compete with the giant American banks in carrying shares of the vast eurocurrency loans.

The international development of the City may well be directed in the later 1970s into far greater specialization: competition from other financial centres may syphon off much of the City's bread-and-butter business. To fill the gap, the City could well find itself driven to concentrate harder on serving its own domestic hinterland.

THE CITY IN BRITAIN

The 1960s reminded the City – if it had ever forgotten – that the weakness of the British economy and the pound sterling had very little to do with its international prosperity. By the same token it confirmed the view of a large part of the City that domestic business did not matter. City houses have found it possible to be

highly successful in banking or insurance and yet remain pro-
foundly uninterested in the way British industry is run or personal
customers in the UK are served. Now this is altering. The sort
of changes that seem likely to take place in the course of the
1970s in the way the City deals with its domestic market could
mean both that the personal client is better served by the City
and that British industry begins to get from the City the sort of
attention it needs.

In a number of ways the City looks like being forced to interest
itself more directly in the affairs of British industry. To start with,
it faces increasing competition for what was once a captive market.
The clearing and merchant banks are finding themselves fighting
a serious challenge from a variety of competitors: American
banks, building societies, finance houses. Foreign insurance companies, or more accurately foreign-owned UK insurance companies, have shown substantially faster growth in Britain than
UK-owned ones. Elsewhere competition has emerged from
small British organizations outside the traditional groupings of
financial institutions: small merchant banks and insurance companies, money brokers, the computerized stock trading system,
separate unit trust companies and so on. And finally competition
has sprung up from within industry itself. The insurance companies have found an increasing number of industrial and commercial firms carrying much of their own insurance, leaving only
the worst risks to the London market. The banks have found
companies increasingly becoming their own bankers, lending to
each other in the intercompany market.

Increasing competition for domestic financial services is one
important force shaping the City's attitude to British business.
There is another. There are strong indications that the City's
institutions, far from just competing to provide services, will
involve themselves more directly in industry's fortunes.

At the moment, the City channels money into industry on the
American, as opposed to the continental or Japanese, pattern.
British banks rarely take equity interests in firms. Instead they
lend to them, mainly on overdraft. Industry has access to personal savings on a long-term basis mainly through the Stock

Exchange into which funds are increasingly funnelled through institutional investors: life assurance companies, pension funds, unit trusts and so on. Endless debate rages round whether this British and US system is better than that in Europe and in Japan, where long-term lending to companies is done mainly by the banks and where banks actually own substantial chunks of industry. The crucial questions are whether a bank or an institutional investor is better able to judge the allocation of resources; which of the two can collect funds more efficiently; and which provides the more stable system. The only conclusion one can draw with any confidence is that in times of financial instability a stock exchange-based system is more likely to survive than a bank-based one. If people put their money in a bank, they expect it to be absolutely safe: if they put it on the Stock Exchange, they realize they are taking a risk. Whatever criticisms one makes of the City's involvement in the Rolls-Royce collapse, it at least demonstrated the stability of the British financial system. If a similar situation had occurred in Germany, a bank might find that not only would its loans to the company itself have to be written off; the bank would also lose its equity interest in the company and quite possibly other loans it had made to other industrial groups on the security of these other groups' shareholdings in the original company.

The trouble with the British system is not that the stock market provides too high a proportion of finance. Rather it is that the institutions that provide the funds – the institutional investors as well as the banks – do not take a sufficiently active part in industrial management. The only real sanction the City has against ineffective management in a firm is to persuade another firm to take it over. This is relatively easy and profitable. Even more profitable is asset stripping. Sometimes a takeover may be the best solution to a company's problems, and even asset stripping may be justifiable on grounds of industrial logic. But that the City has nothing short of capital punishment to ginger up poor management is a serious shortcoming.

The answer must be more day-to-day involvement in industry. This is widely recognized in the City, and changes are taking place both in the way industry is financed and in the attitude of institutional investors. During the last ten years there has undoubtedly been a move towards bank financing. After years when banks lent to industry almost exclusively on overdraft, there has gradually been a shift towards medium- and long-term lending. As long as they were lending to industry on rolled-over overdrafts, banks were able to pretend to themselves that their involvement in their debtors' affairs was a temporary matter. With the increase of term lending, they are beginning to drop the pretence.

With an equity interest in a company, it is harder to ignore the competence of its management than with a loan. Institutional investors in Britain are gradually showing signs of taking a more direct interest in what industry does. In 1970 the institutional investors in the engineering firm of Vickers, led by the Prudential and the merchant bank Kleinwort Benson, got together to replace its top management. And in 1973 major insurance companies and merchant banks brought pressure on Distillers to improve its compensation to the thalidomide children.

Generally, however, institutional investors hate acting as industry's nursemaids or indeed its conscience. They claim they lack the management time to examine thoroughly how well a company is being run, and they prefer to sell off their holdings and invest in something with a better record. But in practice this option is less and less open to them. As the size of their holdings grows, they become locked in situations. Once you have 10 per cent of a company, to sell your holding is as likely to knock the share price as to shout 'stinking fish'. A working party was set up in May 1972, on the initiative of the Governor of the Bank of England, to try to find a way round this dilemma. Its brief was to look at the feasibility of setting up a central organization through which institutional investors might, as the Bank discreetly phrased it, 'stimulate action to improve efficiency in industrial and commercial companies where this is judged necessary'. Unfortunately what actually emerged was a weaker body than Sir Leslie O'Brien had intended. Two of the six organizations on the working party, the Institutional Shareholders' Committee, the Accepting Houses Committee and the Issuing Houses Association, have refused to join the ginger group; and it will be little more than a formalization of existing co-operation arrangements for investment protection among the Association of Investment Trust Companies, the Association of Unit Trust Managers, the National Association of Pension Funds, and the British Insurance Association.

Yet whether they like it or not both the banks and the institutional investors will find themselves becoming more involved with the way commercial and industrial companies are run. This means that both will have to buy skills that they do not at present possess. But it also means that the City's institutions may make a more positive contribution to the efficiency of British industry than they have done in the past.

Personal customers have also been affected by changes in the City. For them the change that has been taking place in the last few years is rather a different one. It has been the replacement of choice by the package deal. Most City institutions discovered, in the course of the 1960s, that personally tailored services – be they stockbroking, insurance, accounting or banking – could only be provided at a cost beyond most personal customers.

Indeed the only reason why small customers had been able to go on enjoying such a range of services for so long was because of the City's antique methods of costing. The commission system, which bases the charge on the value of the service bought rather than on the cost of the time taken to provide it, has allowed the private client to afford his own stockbroker and insurance broker. But this has been possible only because the stockbroker has been subsidized by his larger clients, and the insurance broker by the life assurance policies he has sold. Very gradually, kicking and screaming, the City is being dragged away from the commission system and the ridiculous fees involved for large deals – a welcome and much needed development but one which will make it increasingly expensive for the small man to afford personally tailored service.

Personal customers of the City will increasingly have to buy their services in mass-produced, bulk packages. Instead of having a stockbroker they will have to invest in unit trusts. Instead of buying separate insurance for their car, house and so on through a broker they will find it cheaper to buy a single policy direct from the company. Instead of getting an overdraft from their bank, based on an assessment of their individual creditworthiness by their bank manager, they will have to settle for a personal loan based on their income and outgoings. Anyone who wants anything 'custom-built' will find it increasingly expensive.

This change will not necessarily mean that the City's service to the individual will be any worse. As long as it remains possible for the personal customer to choose – at a price – between 'bespoke' and 'off the peg' financial services, consumer choice will be expanded rather than diminished. And the development of high-quality mass-produced financial services should ultimately put the services of the City within the reach of a great many people who once could never have afforded them, as Marks and Spencers or Sainsbury's have done with consumer goods. Anyone who doubts it should consider the number of outlets available for the savings of the ordinary person today, compared with the range of alternatives at the beginning of the 1950s.

In the course of the 1970s the City may well come to devote as much attention to serving British industry and the British public as it has given in the recent past to serving the international financial community. For anyone living in Britain this will be more welcome than all the City's much publicized contribution to Britain's invisible earnings.

Index